PORTRAIT OF LEICESTERSHIRE

Portrait of
LEICESTERSHIRE

by

BRIAN J. BAILEY

ROBERT HALE · LONDON

© *Brian J. Bailey 1977*

First published in Great Britain 1977

ISBN 0 7091 6005 4

Robert Hale Limited
Clerkenwell House
Clerkenwell Green
London EC1

PHOTOSET AND BOUND BY WEATHERBY WOOLNOUGH,
WELLINGBOROUGH, NORTHANTS,
AND PRINTED IN GREAT BRITAIN BY
LOWE & BRYDONE LTD., THETFORD,
NORFOLK

CONTENTS

To

RALPH BROOKE

– a token
of gratitude
long overdue

ILLUSTRATIONS

Between pages 32 and 33

Between pages 64 and 65

PICTURE CREDITS

The copyright photographs listed above were
supplied as follows:

The author, 1, 17, 35; Cambridge University Collection, 2; Corah Ltd, 36; Tony Craddock, 6, 8, 9, 25, 28,
30, 31; *Leicester Mercury*, 15, 23, 24, 37; Newarke
Houses Museum, 5,7; Kenneth Scowen, 3, 4, 10, 11,
12, 13, 14, 16, 18, 19, 20, 21, 22, 26, 27, 29, 32, 33, 34

ACKNOWLEDGMENTS

A list of all the individuals and organizations who have been kind enough to answer my questions during the writing of this book would be very long indeed. Some of them are mentioned in the text, but I am equally grateful to those who are not, and I ask all of them to accept my heartiest thanks for their help.

Although all the main printed sources on which I have drawn are listed at the end of the book, I feel bound to make special mention here of the work of Professor W. G. Hoskins, to whom every modern writer on Leicestershire must be heavily indebted.

My particular thanks are due to Jonathan Inglesant, former Secretary of the Quorn Hunt, who gave me much helpful advice on Chapter VII, although he knew that my views on the sport differ from his. I am especially grateful also to Mr J. A. Daniell of the Newarke Houses Museum, Leicester, and to the staff of the City of Leicester Reference Library, who were unfailingly helpful during my researches.

My friends Kenneth Scowen and Tony Craddock readily took up the challenge I have made on page 68, and responded to my suggestions with characteristic enthusiasm and artistry. Whatever the drawbacks of my text, everyone will agree that the book gains enormously from the work of these two very fine photographers.

Marilyn Prejac performed an admirable feat of accurate typing from my labyrinthine draft, making it possible for not only my publisher and his printer to read the thing, but also my friend Van Phillips, who was thus able to make a number of valuable suggestions towards its improvement.

Finally, I must record my enormous debt to my wife, who has been a model of patience, encouragement and practical help. Without her support, the book would have been both slower in completion and poorer than it doubtless is.

INTRODUCTION

The first writer who declared that Leicestershire is not a tourist county has a lot to answer for. His confident assertion has been faithfully echoed by every author who has written on the county ever since, and it now wears the uniform of an established fact. As Bernard Shaw observed, if you say a thing often enough, people will eventually come to believe it, and everyone living outside Leicestershire must be convinced by now that the county possesses nothing worth seeing.

It is, one must admit, hardly likely to go down as a sensation to a camera-clicking American globetrotter 'seeing Britain' in five days. It does not intimidate the traveller with extremes like the bleakness of Dartmoor or the blackness of the Rhondda, nor hypnotize him with the showbiz salesmanship of Woburn Abbey or Stratford-on-Avon. Its most attractive features are shy, and have to be sought out, but they amply reward the keen explorer, and it is a pity they are not better known.

An Englishman may have travelled in every country of the world, and seen the Champs Elysées and Skid Row, the Taj Mahal and the Pyramids of Egypt. But if he has never walked through Swithland Wood at bluebell time, nor heard the bells of Loughborough Carillon, nor seen the Easter Monday festivities at Hallaton, his experience is sadly incomplete. Every schoolboy can describe events at the Battle of Bosworth Field, and every fox-hunting man has heard of Billesdon Coplow, but who knows Robin-a-Tiptoe, or Cradock's Ashes, or Rundle Beck, or Bloody Oaks, or Buttermilk Hill?

The publishers could hardly have chosen a better time to celebrate this unknown county, after the arranged marriage between Leicestershire and Rutland. The engagement was a long and stormy one, broken off at one stage because the fiancée wanted to remain single, but the union being finally accomplished, no wedding in England ever saw a more beautiful bride.

11

This is not a book about churches, nor about fox-hunting. There are plenty of those already, and Leicestershire has other things to offer which have been sadly neglected. I have, of course, mentioned all the churches worth seeing, but those readers with a passion for ecclesiastical architecture will know where to look for more comprehensive information. The matter of fox-hunting is a little more difficult. How much space should one devote to a sport which is, on the one hand, among the few things the county is famous for, but which, on the other, is confined to a 'privileged' minority? Books have been written about Leicestershire which give the impression that the entire population dons scarlet coats in November and spends the winter on horseback. I have given the subject a chapter to itself, so that those who have not the least interest in it can read the rest of the book without hindrance.

Finally, this is a book about the living as well as the dead; a portrait of Leicestershire as it is, not merely as it once was. I only need to add that I am no flatterer. Nostalgia is an unreliable portraitist. Unable to absorb the shock of disillusion when the subject is examined afresh at close quarters, it recalls how beautiful the model once seemed, and leaves out the bags under the eyes.

I

THE NATURE OF LEICESTERSHIRE

WHEN writing about any area in isolation, we necessarily falsify it: among the early notes I made for this book is one which says: "Do not write about Leicestershire as if it were an island." The character of a place, no less than of a person, is formed by its environment as well as its hereditary characteristics, and Leicestershire is a small part of Midland England, formed millions of years ago, and distinguished from its neighbours only for administrative convenience in relatively recent times.

That primeval emergence from chaos which formed the earth and the stars already contained the seed of what we now call Leicestershire. The land mass we recognize as Britain issued from the womb of Nature after stupendous labour, and some of its oldest and hardest rock was thrown up by volcanic eruption like vomit from the guts of the earth. Those terrestrial upheavals laid the foundations upon which Leicestershire's personality is built.

The area of Charnwood Forest, in the north-western part of the county, is noted by geologists for its exposed Pre-Cambrian rock, Charnwood being one of the few places in Britain where it is found at surface level. Its age is uncertain, but two thousand million years is not considered unlikely. Further west, Carbon-iferous rock – a mere three hundred million years old – compressed rotting vegetation into coal measures 1,200 feet thick, whilst to the east granite and slate were formed. For countless ages these rocks were covered by younger layers of rock of the Triassic Period, when the first dinosaurs roamed the land.

It has been suggested that Charnwood may once have been a mountain range higher than any other in England. The effects of compression and shattering during the ice ages, when an ice-sheet nearly 800 feet thick probably covered the whole county, reduced its height drastically, and gradual erosion reduced it still more, leaving the Pre-Cambrian rocks exposed and surrounded by other igneous rock and the sedimentary Red Sandstone and debris which once covered it.

Little wonder that occasional shifts occur in an area where events of such colossal dimensions have taken place. Of the more fully documented earthquakes of recent times in Britain, five are thought to have been related to a deep-lying fault on the north-east side of Charnwood Forest. Woodhouse Eaves was the epicentre of a tremor in 1839 which loosened mortar in the roof of the village church. Then in 1893, on the evening of 4 August, the same village was the focal point of the first impulse in a so-called 'twin earthquake'. The second and slighter tremor was felt two seconds later in a wide area around Burton Overy, and witnesses compared the accompanying sounds to thunder and explosions.

At 3.30 in the morning of 21 June 1904, a slight quiver was felt in the villages of Groby and Markfield, and two hours later Burton Overy, again, was the epicentre of a double shock, separated by a few moments. Witnesses spoke of the sound of "passing waggons" and "rushing wind".

I well remember the Midland earthquake of 1956 sending a shiver of apprehension through the building in Leicester where I was working. This had its epicentre at Diseworth, near Derby, and dislodged chimneys in Loughborough. Geologists are cautious in attributing this disturbance to any known fault, but it is remarkable that Diseworth is on a direct line drawn through Burton Overy and Woodhouse Eaves. The extreme north of the county also has thunderstorms more frequently than anywhere else in the British Isles, and the high ground of Charnwood Forest naturally has the county's highest rainfall.

It was predetermined, in an age before Man first appeared on Earth, that mining and quarrying should become the industrial preoccupations of this part of Leicestershire, and that the eastern half of the county, characterized by limestone of the more recent Jurassic period, which eventually produced the undulating slopes and lush pasture-land of the Wolds, should be occupied almost entirely with agriculture.

The low plateau of the south-western area was more open to the accidents or designs of civilization, and it is remarkable that the county's industrial areas should be separated so neatly from its agricultural parts by the course of the River Soar, which rises just over the county boundary in Warwickshire, south of

Sharnford, and flows roughly northwards for forty miles to join the Trent as soon as it crosses the county boundary again. Leicestershire is truly the heart of England, being both central and vaguely heart-shaped, and its chief river is one of a number of vital arteries that pulse through it. The majority of the county was covered by swamp and forest even as late as the Roman occupation. Nowadays it has a fairly low proportion of woodland, and most of it is deciduous, the clay soil particularly favouring oak and ash.

There is evidence of early human penetration of the inhospitable Charnwood area, where the varied rock no doubt provided workable material for the primitive weapons with which Neolithic man hunted the horse and the mammoth for his meat. There are also Iron Age hill forts at Breedon Hill and Beacon Hill, and at Burrough Hill in the east.

This whole region, stretching to the west as far as Shropshire, was the stronghold of the Coritani tribe when the Romans came. To the east were the Iceni, whose queen was Boadicea; to the north the Brigantes; to the south the Catuvellauni. It seems likely that the Coritani in the Leicestershire region, like the Brigantes, came to terms early with the Roman invaders, though the more westerly branches of the tribe appear to have resisted. Ratae, the Roman military camp which was the origin of Leicester, was transformed into a native capital, and apart from the roads, there is little evidence of Roman activity in the county except at Ratae and Great Casterton – a sure sign that the legions were not constantly engaged in suppressing native rebellions. Besides, it is fairly certain that the region was only sparsely populated at that time, because the heavy clay soil did not encourage agricultural settlement by the early Britons.

Of the Roman roads that cross the county, the chief ones were Ermine Street – now the A1 trunk road – and Watling Street and the Fosse Way, intersecting at right angles at High Cross, which the Romans called Venonae, and which they calculated to be the centre of England. (Modern geographers say they were fourteen miles out, for what it is worth.)

During the fifth century, raids by the Germanic Angles and Saxons, by way of the Wash, penetrated Leicestershire, and the eventual invasion by those peoples established their ascendancy over the former territory of the Coritani, in what became the kingdom of Mercia. When Augustine, the first Archbishop of

Canterbury, arrived in Kent on his mission from Pope Gregory I to convert the natives of Britain to Christianity, the king of Mercia was Penda, who was a pagan and resisted the progress of the new religion, but his son was baptized, and by the time Offa came to the throne, Mercia had become a powerful Christian kingdom.

It was then the turn of the Vikings to make their mark on the shape of Leicestershire-to-be. The Scandinavian invaders of the ninth and tenth centuries were, like the Saxons, undeterred by the clay soil of the region, because they had heavy ploughs with which to turn it. Hence they found the eastern parts of the county more hospitable than the western. Clearing of the forests and cultivation of the soil, begun by the Saxons, was continued by the Danes, and communities of settlers grew up and established the hundreds of villages which are among the chief characteristics of the county.

The names of the Leicestershire villages are in themselves an enlightening introduction to the pattern of development in the area. The name endings '-by' and '-thorpe' – evidence of Scandinavian foundation – occur throughout the former county of Leicestershire, but are much more frequent east of the Soar, whilst in the former county of Rutland, where a belt of harder rock made the land more resistant to agricultural development, they hardly occur at all.

The '-ton' ending, of Anglo-Saxon origin, is predominant in the Rutland area. A notable feature of the western villages of Leicestershire is the large number of places ending in the Anglo-Saxon '-stone'. Of the following, only two lie east of the Soar, and they are now in Leicester itself, which stands astride the river: Aylestone, Barlestone, Bilstone, Braunstone, Congerstone, Humberstone, Nailstone, Odstone, Ravenstone, Shackerstone, Snarestone, Swepstone, Thringstone, Whetstone. There are other names which may originally have had '-stone' endings, although, by the same token, some of the names listed may once have had '-ton' endings. The corruption itself remains significant, however. Most of these villages lie on the Leicestershire coalfield. Throw in Stoneygate and Stoney Stanton for good measure, and you have as hard evidence for Saxon foundations as you could hope to find anywhere.

It is of interest, therefore, that some experts consider the dialect of this area of the Midlands to be the purest Anglo-Saxon form of the language which has come down to us, and that modern English speech is based on it. Written down exactly as it sounds, the speech of typical local schoolchildren *looks* like a primitive language: "Yo i'nt arf gorra run if ya gooin catch that buzz." This is more an example of careless accent than of genuine local dialect, but it gives the right flavour. The sounds of many of the village names – Willoughby Waterleys, Enderby, Frisby-on-the-Wreake, Burton Overy – are (regardless of their derivation) expressive of the Midland language, being usually less hard than northern names like Heckmondwyke or Cleckheaton, but not as lyrical as southern ones like Glyndebourne and Haslemere.

For the moment let us return to the Viking invaders. During the ninth century they were constantly at war with Alfred the Great, King of Wessex, who eventually came to an agreement with them to establish the Danelaw, the region occupied by the Danes in the Midlands and north of England, and roughly divided from Alfred's kingdom by the Roman Watling Street. Leicestershire was thus a frontier territory for a time. But part of the deal was that the Danes should be baptized, and as their object in coming here was to settle and farm the land, and not to conquer the island and extend their power, they agreed to Alfred's bargain and were left in peace. It was then that the Danes divided their region into the 'shires' that remain with us today, and of which Leicestershire was one. The spread of Christianity, which was bringing new learning to the islands (though it was largely confined to the growing number of monasteries), then merged gradually with the administrative ability and enterprise of the Danes to set England on a level of civilization it had not experienced since the Roman occupation.

A study of the distribution of blood groups, by Doctor Ada Kopeć, throws an interesting light on the ancient history and population movement and development in the county. People of Celtic origin are characterized by a high incidence of blood group O, and in Leicestershire a remarkable pattern shows a very *low* incidence of this group in a tongue projecting through Rutland and the central part of the county around Leicester – the route of the invaders. Higher levels of O group surround this tongue, as if pushed outwards by the concentration and inter-marriage of successive invading peoples, and there remains a particularly high proportion of group O blood in the Hinckley area, which was on the frontier of the Danelaw.

After the Norman Conquest, many of the villages which had been established by the Anglo-Saxons and the Danes were depopulated, and in some cases disappeared completely. There were several causes. The growth of manufacturing led to declining rural population, and this trend was escalated by the increasing use of arable land for grazing, which required less manpower for its management. The economic consequences of the dissolution of the monasteries were also important factors. Then there was the Black Death. Henry Knighton, a canon of Leicester Abbey, described the devastation caused by the dreaded disease in Leicestershire: "At Leicester, in the small parish of St Leonard, more than three hundred and eighty people died; in the parish of Holy Cross more than four hundred; in the parish of St Margaret more than seven hundred; and so on in every parish." And again: "In this same year a great number of sheep died throughout the whole county, so much so that in one field alone more than five thousand sheep were slain. Their bodies were so corrupted by the plague that neither beast nor bird would touch them."

There is reason to believe that the canon's figures are exaggerations, but in Leicestershire, as in the rest of the country, the Black Death brought terror, chaos and loss of life on a scale never experienced before or since. It is believed that the population was reduced by at least a third in the space of a few years, and the plague undoubtedly accounted for the desertion of many villages. Because of the resulting scarcity of manpower, the wages of farm labourers doubled, and this led to further conversion of arable land to pasture.

Few of the depopulated villages disappeared permanently. One that did, however, was Ambion, near Stoke Golding. It is not to be found now on any map, but once it was there, recorded in Domesday Book. It is only because the village had also lent its name to the neighbouring hill where, over a century later, the armies of Richard III and Henry Tudor gathered before the Battle of Bosworth, that we ever have cause to think of it today.

As many as seventy or more villages established in Leicestershire and Rutland by the thirteenth century are known to have been totally deserted or destroyed by the fifteenth. I shall have occasion to mention a few of them in later chapters, but it may be said here that there are some Leicestershire village names in Domesday Book, such as Legham and Lilinge, the locations of which are still a total mystery. The layouts of some of these lost villages are seen more easily in aerial photographs than at ground level. The fields where buildings once stood cannot be ploughed, because the ground is too uneven and solid foundations lie close to the surface. Leicestershire is still very much a county of villages, nevertheless, and the opportunity to follow their development further will arise as we tour the area with more detailed observation in subsequent chapters.

Meanwhile, the county's growth in agricultural importance naturally followed from its possession of rich pasture land in the east. Early in the eighteenth century Daniel Defoe passed through Leicestershire during his tour through "the whole island of Great Britain", and remarked:

> The sheep bred in this county and Lincolnshire, which joins to it, are, without comparison, the largest, and bear not only the greatest weight of flesh on their bones but also the greatest fleeces of wool on their backs of any sheep of England: nor is the fineness of the wool abated for the quantity; but as 'tis the longest staple, (so the clothiers call it) so 'tis the finest wool in the whole island, some few places excepted, where the quantity is small and insignificant, compared to this part of the country. These are the funds of sheep which furnish the city of London with their large mutton in so incredible a quantity.

> The horses produced here, or rather fed here, are the largest in England, being generally the great black coach horses and dray horses, of which so great a number are continually brought up to London, that one would think so little a spot as this of Leicestershire could not be able to supply them.

The next major changes in the landscape were made by the Enclosure Acts and the Industrial Revolution. The Enclosure Acts changed the medieval 'open field' system of farming into the present familiar closed system, in which fields are separated by hedges and trees. In Leicestershire, the hedges are of hawthorn and the trees commonly ash. The trees are sparsely distributed – a fact that becomes all too evident on a hot summer day when one is driving along looking for a shady spot to park. Elm is relatively scarce in the county, so Leicestershire has escaped disfigurement by the recent epidemics of Dutch Elm Disease which have affected so many English counties. Sutton-in-the-Elms gives us the hint that such elm as there is may be found in the southern extremity of the county.

The landscape today is an unspectacular but very friendly and 'human' one. The fields in May, bright with carpets of buttercup and cowslip, bordered by cascades of hawthorn blossom, and alive with the hum of insects, are something to be treasured as a local contribution to human happiness. The young shoots of the hawthorn used to be called 'bread and cheese', for some unfathomable reason, and were often picked off the twigs by children and eaten. I can remember doing this myself, but doubt if the local children do it now, when all their entertainment is electronic, and they have no need to explore the fields and lanes, casting round – bright, observant and innocent – for a satisfying activity.

In July, the hawthorn gives way to elder, and the hedgerows sport honeysuckle and wild roses. Because of the relative scarcity of trees, in both number and variety, Leicestershire is not a colourful county in autumn, and autumn always seems short. In winter, the sight of gulls following the tractor-drawn plough is less delightful than when horses were used in the fields, but is still something to stand and watch, and the flocks of lapwing, rising into the air as one when you clap your hands, seem a part of that balanced co-operation between man and nature which the more extreme forms of landscape do not have. In the Highlands, nature dominates man; in South Wales, man dominates nature. In Leicestershire, men fishing on the canal banks, needle spires piercing the sky beyond the fields, cows standing in the shade of oak or ash, lambs gambolling in the meadows, seem to me to deny domination, and assert that respectful interdependence which ecology rightly holds to be of paramount importance for our survival.

The growth of industry, of course, has had effects more far-reaching than any other changes we may notice, but the most obvious result of development since Victorian times is the even sharper contrast between the eastern and western halves of the county than existed before. Industry has been confined, as Nature decided for us millions of years ago, to the west of the Soar, and the towns and villages there tend to be drab affairs of red brick uniformity, while the east retains the rural village character it has had for centuries.

The city of Leicester stands at the centre of the county, and there are four towns spread round it as at the corners of a square – one falling into each quarter. The two in the eastern half,

Melton Mowbray and Market Harborough, still have the
character of market towns and have grown only slowly in
comparison with the western towns, Loughborough and
Hinckley, which are frankly industrial and expansive. Oakham
in the east (the former county town of Rutland) and Coalville
in the west reinforce the distinction.

Public-house names can often serve as guides to the nature of a
place, if one ignores the universal Red Lion or Bull's Head.
Forest Gate and Forester's Arms occur in the Charnwood area of
Leicestershire, with Miner's Arms or Coalminer's Arms further
west. The sheep-farming east of the county has its Golden Fleece
and Shoulder of Mutton, while Hinckley has a Weaver's Arms
and the Belvoir area has The Marquis of Granby or The Peacock.
Naturally, Fox Inn, Fox and Hounds and Foxhunter can be
found all over the county, whilst The Navigation and The
Wharf occur along the canal routes. There are more obscure
names, however, like the Man Within the Compass, at
Whitwick, the Drum and Monkey at Packington, and The
Burmese Cat at Melton Mowbray.

It would take an astute observer to notice any real difference
in the pace of living between the two halves of the county, but it
does exist, and is more evident in the villages. Those in the west
are as dependent on industry as the larger towns, and are run to
factory time-tables, with the consequent pace-setters of working
wives getting children off to school, 'rushhour' spells on the
public transport, and evenings devoted to washing, ironing,
cooking and housework.

It is still possible in the east of the county to drive along the
country roads for an hour and pass no other vehicle except
perhaps a tractor pulling a haycart. One may be held up by a
herd of cattle coming down the road to a fresh field, but as one is
in no hurry, that is something of a rare pleasure rather than a
hindrance.

The country roads often have very wide verges – the hedges
planted when the fields were enclosed having been set well back
to allow the passage of coaches in bad weather, when the old
unsurfaced roads were likely to present obstacles such as deep ruts
full of water. The dead grass on the verges in winter was called
'fog' locally.

If you enter Leicestershire from the London direction, it is
instructive to watch the gradual change through Bedfordshire

and Northamptonshire from village churches with towers to those with eight-sided spires. They are usually of mellow iron-stone in this corner of the county, and pierce the sky above the trees and gently undulating hills where farmland stretches on either side of you as far as the eye can see.

How can one describe the people of Leicestershire, except in vague generalizations? We can tell the stories of the rich and influential families, whose money built the churches and the great houses; of the industrial pioneers whose enterprise laid the foundations of the county's prosperity; of the ministers of religion whose sermons denounced the iniquities of their times. But what of the ordinary people whose lives give them no claims to the immortality of the history books? The farm-labourers, the factory-workers, the clerks and the builders, the housewives and parlour-maids, are anonymously covered by a convenient collective noun, 'the people'. But the people have included, for instance, a man named Charles Leader, who was paid fifteen shillings by the Constable of Sapcote in 1749 for catching moles. What manner of man was he? Did he teach his dog tricks (he *must* have had a dog), and get free ale for entertaining the customers at the local inn? What of Ann Chawner, whose first child died in 1789, while she was pregnant with her second, which also died, to be followed to the grave by two more infants within five years? Or of Mrs Frith, who did public penance for brawling in church at Stoke Golding? What sort of man was John Phipps, who lived to be a hundred and nineteen, and lies in the churchyard of St Margaret's, Leicester, with a headstone of Swithland slate above him complaining that "Life is but a fleeting shadow"? Alas, they are merely names on gravestones or in account books, and if they were typical Leicestershire folk, we shall never know it. We must perforce fall back on general-izations.

The people of Leicestershire are different in character, in many respects, from those of both the north and south of England. They are less reserved, and very much less self-centred, than people in the south, but at the same time they are rather more cautious in giving of themselves than people in the north. Guarded extroverts, one might say. They are far from being unfriendly, but they are fiercely independent, and this makes them a little suspicious at first. They do not readily give away information about themselves. Watch women in the shops –

particularly the older women – lean forward confidentially when asking the assistants for their requirements. It makes no difference whether they are asking for a diamond ring or an Oxo cube; they are as little inclined to show off as to reveal their poor financial circumstances.

If you want to confide in a Leicestershire woman when you have a problem, you will find her a good and sympathetic listener. She will not, like the southerner, merely pretend to be listening whilst really thinking about her own affairs. But when you have finished telling your story, she will not necessarily respond by telling you her own, as women in the north are more likely to do.

They are wary of doctors, too. 'Do-it-yourself' remedies for all manner of ailments – such as gargling with vinegar and sage for a sore throat – are passed down from generation to generation, and it is only something relatively serious (when she describes herself as feeling "really badly") that will send a Leicestershire woman to her doctor, and then reluctantly. A disinclination to reveal herself to a stranger, either physically or psychologically, is combined here with a slight distrust of scientific interference with natural processes. I knew a man in Leicester who showed similar tendencies by firmly refusing to speak to anyone when he was in the 'Gents'. A sociable enough fellow on other occasions, saying "Good morning" to him there was like talking to the wall. He was like a sinner at confession – sublimely oblivious of all but the release of his burden.

Leicestershire men are generally practical and hard-working, with a strong sense of duty, especially towards their families. It is still common for large families, of which all the members are grown up and married with children of their own, to live within a radius of a few miles, if not in the same village. The father still dominates the family unit and when times are bad, the mother will make considerable sacrifices of her own comforts to ensure that her children go to school well fed and well clothed. What the neighbours might think carries much weight with the women of Leicestershire.

Not that such attention to the material wellbeing of their offspring is equalled by a parallel approach to the more psychological aspects of parental responsibility. The ordinary people tend to be unimaginative. Once when I was standing in a bus queue in Leicester on a Saturday night, groups of boys with greasy hair and pointed shoes stood in noisy groups with giggling girls in high heels and hemlines. An elderly couple stood behind me, glancing round anxiously at the youngsters and asking each other what the younger generation was coming to, whilst all around them infants with pale faces and tired eyes drooped over their fathers' shoulders, breathing in tobacco smoke and the smells of alcohol and cheap cosmetics, and listening to the coarse language of their elders. In the towns, at least, men consume vast quantities of beer, and the public house with the 'room-at-the-back-for-children' is too often the school where youngsters learn what their lives are destined to be all about. 'Soft' methods of child-rearing are derided as strongly as refined tastes. The men do not drink wine much in Leicestershire.

I am dedicated to the proposition that all men are created unequal. They grow out of the soil in the same sense that buildings do – nature determines how they are built. And as Leicestershire became a red-brick county because the local stone was granite which could not be worked, so the same unyielding land made the people work hard to get a living from it; made them discipline their children to prepare them for a hard working life; made them despise illness and find their own remedies rather than take time off; made them practical and independent. They have no coastline to make them wonder about distant horizons; no mountains to challenge their spirit of adventure; no natural spectacle to make them reflective and imaginative.

The familiar form of address in common usage among working people in the county is 'duck'. Between woman and woman, adult and child, husband and wife, even man to man, the term is as universal as 'luv' in Lancashire and 'darling' in the theatre.

'Mardy' is another colloquialism commonly heard. It is a corruption of 'marred' and is usually applied to a spoilt child, but can just as readily be used of an adult. A child who sulks because he cannot have his own way whilst playing with friends in the streets or 'jitties' (alleys between buildings or gardens) is liable to be greeted with a derisive chorus:

> Mardy bum,
> Play the drum,
> Tell yer muther
> The cat's come 'um!

Leicestershire people do not 'mend' dying fires or 'brew' tea, as is done further north. Here, fires are 'made up' and tea is 'mashed'.

If you ask a Leicestershire woman to do something when she is busy, she may say: "Oo, a can't awhile, duck." And if you speak to her of someone she dislikes, she may say: "Oo, a can't abear that woman!"

There is no great literature of the Leicestershire dialect – nothing to match D. H. Lawrence's Nottinghamshire or George Eliot's Warwickshire. There are words and phrases in the works of both authors which would be familiar to Leicestershire folk, but although Lawrence uses 'mardy' and 'ducky', 'yo' for you, and 'allers' for always, Morel in *Sons and Lovers* could never be mistaken for a Leicestershire man. His speech is closer to Yorkshire – broader and more earthy than that of his neighbours to the south.

George Eliot, who was born at Nuneaton, just across the Watling Street from Hinckley, perhaps gets closer to the commonly heard speech of Leicestershire. She uses 'feyther' for father, and 'gells' for girls, and when Tulliver in *The Mill on the Floss* remarks that ". . . there's folks as things 'ull allays go awk'ard with", a Leicestershire man might well reply: "Ar, yo can allus foind somebody wuss off than yersen."

Although I have never heard it myself (as far as I can remember), it once used to be quite common for Leicestershire people to convert a singular word to its plural by the device of the Saxon ending, as the modern German language does. So, one place, pronounced 'pleace', would become not several 'pleaces', but 'pleacen'.

Dr A. B. Evans, a headmaster of Bosworth Grammar School, published a collection of Leicestershire words and phrases in which he included a nice story of a dour farm labourer who was known as 'Fun'. Someone innocently asked his employer why they called him that. "Whoy," the farmer replied, "a wur ca'd 'Fun' coz a wur fun under a 'edge!"

It is true to say, of course, that all such regional characteristics are slowly losing ground in the face of increasing communications and the willingness of younger generations to move away from the areas where they were born and brought up. But local language, tradition and folklore do survive here to some extent, as elsewhere, and we shall notice particular instances as we visit their places of currency.

One example worth considering at this stage, however, is the fact that the county used to be known – from the outside – as 'bean-belly Leicestershire', on account of the crops of beans which formed part of its staple diet in more poverty-stricken times. "Shake a Leicestershire yeoman by the collar," it was said, "and you will hear the beans rattle in his belly." The village of Barton-in-the-Beans survives as a reminder of those long-gone days. Bean-fields were not exclusive to Leicestershire, of course, but it was said that the beans grown here were sweeter and more tender than elsewhere, and that consequently they were considered fit food for men, whereas in other counties they were fed only to swine.

A local riddle – often asked me by my grandfather – related to beans. If a child was airing his knowledge to a grown-up, he would be challenged with: "Ah, but yo dunno 'ow many beans mek foive." The answer was: "One bean, two beans, a bean and a half and a half a bean."

A 'cob' in Leicestershire is a small round crusty loaf of bread. An interesting line of demarcation is formed in this usage by Watling Street, for a 'cob' in Leicestershire becomes a 'bap' in Warwickshire. In the south, the same object is absurdly described as a 'roll', but when you have patiently explained that you want a round roll, not a long one, and a crusty one, not a soft one, you still do not get a cob as good as the bakers of Leicestershire make them.

The most important historian of Leicestershire, until publication of the Victoria County History began in 1907 (it is still incomplete), was John Nichols. His *History and Antiquities of the County of Leicester* was published in eight massive volumes between 1795 and 1815, ran to five million words, and was dedicated to the king, George III.

Nichols was a jolly-looking Londoner, an author, printer and publisher, and his only qualifying connection with Leicestershire seems to have been that he found his second wife there, Martha Green of Hinckley. He did not write the entire work himself, but master-minded it, collecting and editing contributions from various authors, and printing and publishing the resulting manuscripts. He said afterwards that he had worn out his eyes in the service of the county and I, for one, can well believe it! Nichols' monumental history is often unreliable, but remains a fascinating and indispensable work, to which all writers on the county must turn and acknowledge their debt.

Having thus drawn the outline and painted in the background of this portrait of Leicestershire, let us now examine and delineate its features in greater detail. We have a patient model who will sit still and maintain the pose, not only until we finish the picture, but whilst observers consider the likeness, for according to its motto, the city of Leicester, where we will start, is 'Always the Same'.

II

THE MAKING OF A BOOM TOWN

LEGEND has it that Leicester was founded by King Lear; and as we shall scarcely come across poetry again in our look at the city, let us not dismiss the idea too hastily.

The earliest record of the legend we have is by Geoffrey of Monmouth, a twelfth-century Benedictine monk and as unreliable a witness as we could ever hope to find. His *History of the Kings of Britain* was based, he claimed, on ancient British texts, which have never come to light. According to him, however, Lear nobly governed his country for sixty years, and "built upon the river Sore a city, called in the British tongue Kaerleir, in the Saxon, Leircestre". Moreover, when the king died, his daughter Cordeilla "buried her father in a certain vault which she ordered to be made for him under the river Sore in Leicester and which had been built originally under the ground to the honour of the god Janus. And here all the workmen of the city, upon the anniversary solemnity of that festival, used to begin their yearly labours".

Modern scholars scoff at this unproven story, and assure us that the name of Leicester is derived, not from King Lear, but from the old British name for the River Soar – Leir. (Ler or Llyr was the name of a Celtic sea-god. There is also a small village called Leire not far from the source of the river.) All the same, we are entitled to believe that the legend possibly has slightly more truth in it than the sceptics will allow, as a divided kingdom has been proposed as an explanation for the disappearance of the tribal name of the Coritani, who inhabited the Midlands at the time of the Roman invasions. Perhaps Shakespeare had the wild and rugged country of Charnwood in mind when he had Lear bid the "all-shaking thunder ... crack nature's moulds".

What is certain is that the advancing Roman legions under Aulus Plautius established a military camp here on the east bank

28

of the river, probably on the site of a native settlement. They called it Ratae, and it was one of a chain of bases which they connected to the legionary headquarters at Lincoln by means of the Fosse Way. There is no evidence that the Coritani tribe put up any fierce resistance to the Roman progress. Indeed, the legions were soon moved from this line of garrisons to advance against the northern Brigantes, and Ratae became the chief town of the Romanized Coritani of the region, and was then called Ratae Coritanorum. Building probably took place under Roman supervision but with Coritani labour.

Chief among the city's Roman remains is the so-called Jewry Wall – a massive piece of masonry, the purpose of which, and the origin of its popular appellation, are still disputed. At one time it was thought that the wall must be either part of the enclosing wall of a Jewish ghetto, or a wailing wall. But a delightful piece of irony threw some light on the mystery in the thirties of this century. The city planned to build itself some public swimming baths, and the site chosen was the area of land in front of the Jewry Wall, where all that was required was the demolition of some derelict buildings. Local archaeologists, however, conscious of the possibility that the Jewry Wall might be a signpost to other Roman remains in the vicinity, persuaded the City Council to proceed with caution, and allow the site to be excavated scientifically. Dr Kathleen Kenyon took charge of these proceedings, and within three years she and her team had uncovered the foundations of the largest Roman baths in England!

Dr Kenyon then regarded the Jewry Wall as the west side of a basilica, through which one entered the baths, these having replaced a forum on the site. This interpretation has been challenged, and an air of uncertainty still surrounds the remains. But it is accepted that the baths were built early in the second century AD, at about the same time as Hadrian's Wall. The Jewry Wall itself, at any rate, is an impressive reminder of Leicester's Roman beginnings. It is built of alternate courses of local stone and Roman brick, and includes granite from Mountsorrel, seven miles away.

Many other Roman remains have been found, including various fragments of pavements. As a schoolboy I was taken with a party to see a mosaic *in situ* in the cellar beneath a corset shop. Thus far had the foundations of the Roman Empire been overcome by those of the women of Leicester.

Dominating the Jewry Wall as if to assert the power of Christianity over paganism is the church of St Nicholas, the oldest in Leicester. This was originally a Saxon church, built partly of debris from the Roman ruins. It has been much altered by Norman and subsequent builders, but a good deal of its Saxon masonry can still be seen.

For nearly five hundred years, from the departure of the Romans to the arrival of the Danes, Leicester's history is cloaked in obscurity. Angles and Saxons were well established here by the sixth century, but whether they came as raiders to conquer the town, or merely infiltrated the existing British elements, is an open question.

When the Danish invaders established their frontier along the line of the Roman Watling Street, Leicester became one of the important boroughs of the Danelaw, with Nottingham, Derby, Stamford and Lincoln, and until the Norman Conquest its fortunes no doubt fluctuated with the changing circumstances of the former kingdom of Mercia. It is thought that the population of Leicester may have been about two thousand at this time, and most of the people were occupied in cultivating the open fields which surrounded the town.

The first Norman overlord of Leicester, granted the town when William divided up the spoils of his conquest, was Hugh de Grantmesnil, who built a castle of timber on a mound beside the river. His son sold his rights in Leicester as his father's successor to Robert de Meulan, the first overlord of the Beaumont family, the fortunes of which were to be linked with those of Leicestershire from that time forward. He replaced the timber castle with one of stone, and built close by in about 1107 the second of Leicester's surviving historic churches, St Mary de Castro. This has been much enlarged, altered, added to and restored in the centuries since its foundation, but it is still one of Leicester's most fascinating churches, and its needle-like spire perhaps the best known. Much of the original Norman work remains, particularly the chancel, where beautiful Norman decoration can be seen in the capitals and arches of the sedilia. Many grotesque heads surround its exterior walls.

The second Beaumont overlord, Robert le Bossu, was styled Earl of Leicester, and he ruled the town for fifty years. From this period dates the Great Hall of the Castle, since used as the assize court, and claimed to be the oldest surviving aisled and bay-divided hall in Europe. During Robert le Bossu's earldom, Henry II introduced the innovation of trial by jury. This replaced the Norman practice of trial by battle, which had itself taken the place of the barbarous ritual of trial by ordeal. The aldermen of the borough were called 'jurats', and it is possible that a corruption of this word accounts for the name 'Jewry Wall', if they held court near it.

Leicester Abbey, which has now disappeared, was also founded by Robert le Bossu. It was one of England's largest monastic houses for Augustinian canons, consecrated as the Abbey of St Mary de Pratis (St Mary of the Meadows) in 1143. It was built on the west bank of the Soar, half a mile north of the town, and an account written in the Tudor period describes its situation by the river, which contained fish of all kinds, and was surrounded by "meadows and large open common fields of arable land, yearly sown with corn".

The second earl, Robert Blanchesmains, supported the rebellion against Henry II instigated by Queen Eleanor, and brought upon Leicester in 1173 the vengeance of the king, who placed the town under siege for three weeks and finally reduced it to ruins, massacring the population. The attack was so devastating that it was a quarter of a century before the ruined town began to recover and rebuild its houses. It may be that Leicester's reputation for radicalism began to gain currency at this period.

The entrance of Simon de Montfort on the stage of English history was an event that Leicester takes particular pride in, without much justification. But since the town, despite its long history and its growth in importance since Roman times, has a noticeable dearth of great men, we will allow it a special interest in Simon de Montfort.

He was born in France and inherited the earldom in 1231, after a good deal of wrangling, from his father of the same name. His grandfather had married the sister of the last Beaumont earl, Robert Fitz Parnel. With the earldom, Simon de Montfort also acquired the stewardship of England, suzerainty of the borough of Leicester, and a considerable amount of land in various parts of England, including (in Leicestershire) Hinckley, Earl Shilton and Desford.

In January 1238, he was secretly married to the youngest sister of the king, Henry III. Eleanor had been married before, when she was nine, but she was a widow by the time she was sixteen; wealthy and childless. The clerics were shocked at her re-marriage, saying she had broken her vow of chastity. The king later accused de Montfort of seducing her, leaving him no choice but to give the royal assent to the marriage, to avoid an unpleasant scandal. The accusation was probably justified. Simon de Montfort was an ambitious, ruthless and arrogant man. The marriage certainly produced a son very soon, and added much to the earl's wealth and possessions, including Kenilworth Castle in Warwickshire, where the earl and countess usually lived when they were in England. For many years Simon was one of the king's most favoured servants, carrying out important missions in France and gradually improving his own and his family's fortunes.

Growing rumblings of discontent among the English populace were reinforced in 1257 and the following year by bad harvests and winter floods. Many people and livestock were drowned, and famine threatened the country. The barons, taking exception to the weak and vacillating king's misrule, extravagance, and the flow of money to his foreign friends, drew up the Provisions of Oxford, which appointed a council of fifteen nobles to superintend the king's activities and safeguard the rights in the Magna Carta.

The growing opposition of baronial and royalist interests gradually escalated a purely political rivalry into a military one, and at this point Simon de Montfort assumed the leadership of the barons' revolt. Louis IX of France and the Pope announced their support of Henry against the Provisions of Oxford, and the Earl of Leicester was excommunicated.

During the sporadic outbreaks of fighting that were taking place, the army of the barons was accused of plundering churches and slaughtering Jews. De Montfort had in fact crushed a supposed rebellion of Jews in London, killing four hundred and seizing their riches, and he expelled the Jews from Leicester at about the same time and no doubt for the same reason.

The climax of the revolt came at the battle of Lewes, when the barons won a decisive victory over the king. It was the turning point in their campaign. Simon de Montfort virtually ruled the country, and the parliament of 1265, called by him and including representatives of various boroughs, was the seed from

Rock outcrops at
Beacon Hill

The lost village of
Ingarsby

Landscape near Scalford, on the Wolds

Jewry Wall and St Nicholas church, Leicester

Inside the Guildhall, Leicester

Leicester's Clock
Tower at the
turn of the
century

The Clock
Tower today

Town Hall Square, Leicester

The Market Place, Leicester, with statue of the fifth Duke of Rutland and staircase of the Corn Exchange

The Foxton 'staircase'

Hallaton – the village green

Market Harborough, the church and old grammar school

Charming Jacobean brickwork – Quenby Hall

Bizarre Norman stonework – Tilton-on-the-Hill church

which the future House of Commons was to be germinated.

De Montfort's ascendancy did not last long, however. Dissension among the barons focused on the earl's autocracy, and in further battle, Simon de Montfort was killed amid thunder and lightning, his head and limbs being cut off and his mutilated body carried away by monks to be buried in the Abbey church at Evesham. These events led to comparison of his end with that of Christ, and rumours of miracles began to spread. It was said that sick people were cured, and that Simon's hands, sewn up in a cloth, clasped themselves in prayer. It is difficult to take stories of de Montfort's piety – alive or dead – very seriously, but the absurd rumours do show the extent to which he was venerated by the common people as their champion.

A long period of peace and prosperity followed the death of Simon de Montfort. His lands and title were given by the king to his son Edmund, and the succession of Lancastrian earls of Leicester, unlike de Montfort himself, resided in Leicester for considerable periods, bringing valuable trade to the town. Leicester sent its first burgesses to Parliament, and people from the county were allowed to bring their produce into the town for sale at the markets on Wednesdays and Saturdays. Various guilds grew up to protect trade and ensure fair dealing, and the county's lush pastures ensured its capital's rapidly growing importance as a centre of the wool trade.

Chief among the guilds was Corpus Christi Guild, which became associated with the eminent people of the town, and for which the surviving Guildhall was built, about 1350. This was altered considerably in Tudor times, when it came into use as the town hall of Leicester. It remains as one of Leicester's finest historic buildings, where – among other things – a collection of chamberlains' maces is kept, and the petrified jawbone of a boar can be seen in the medieval hearth.

For many years the people of Leicester had been permitted to gather dead wood from Leicester Forest, which was "so great, thick and full, that it was scarcely possible to go by the paths . . . on account of the quantity of dead wood and of boughs blown down by the wind". As much as a man could carry was allowed him each week for a farthing, a horse-load for a half penny, and six cartloads for a penny. The wood was brought into the town via the Wood Gate. The medieval town extended from this point, near the grounds of the Abbey, to South Gate, near the

Castle, and from the banks of the Soar to Gallowtree Gate and Church Gate.

Henry of Grosmont, who succeeded to the earldom in 1322, planned and began the 'New Work' which has since become known as the Newarke. It was originally a walled close, the main entrance to which was from South Gate, via the Magazine Gateway, which has so far survived threats to demolish it, and so called because of its later use as an armoury. The Newarke was also connected to the Castle by the Turret Gateway. Inside the close the earl founded a hospital for fifty old men, which later became Trinity Hospital. This was rebuilt in 1901, but its character was retained, and the sundial on the gable over the main doorway is still one of the Newarke's interesting features. The earl's son founded a Collegiate Church there, which has since disappeared, but at one time it rivalled St Mary de Castro in importance, and was said to be "not very great" but "exceeding fair".

The Black Death struck Leicester in 1348 and 1361. Its effects were disastrous here as elsewhere. It reduced the population by a third, and took a particularly high toll of the learned men of the town, these being chiefly the monks and priests, who faced almost certain death by visiting the sick. Its economic effects were such that the building of churches stopped, and a long trade depression set in. The scarcity of labour led to a rapid rise in wages, and the catastrophe brought about far-reaching changes in the relations between peasants and landowners.

One of the victims of the second epidemic was the Earl of Leicester, Henry, Duke of Lancaster. He was succeeded by the last of the Lancastrian earls of Leicester, John of Gaunt, brother of the Black Prince and father of Henry IV. John was generally unpopular, but not so in Leicester, where he spent a good deal of his time at the Castle. He entertained Richard II there, and was the friend and patron of John Wycliffe. It was John of Gaunt who made Wycliffe, Rector of Lutterworth.

Chaucer was a friend of John of Gaunt and there is a tradition that he might have married his wife Philippa at Leicester. She was the sister of Dame Catherine Swinford, who was more or less in permanent residence at Leicester Castle, and bore the earl several children before he got round to marrying her. If Chaucer knew Leicester well, he would certainly have known the

Franciscan and Dominican monks in the town, the only traces of whose establishments today are the streets known as Grey Friars and Black Friars respectively. Eleven Franciscan friars were executed in Leicester in 1402 for opposing Bolingbroke's displacement of Richard II.

After the death of John of Gaunt, the earldom of Leicester passed into the titles of the Crown. In the year following tme accession of Henry V, Parliament met at Leicester, in the Hall of the Grey Friars, and twice again during the reign of his son, Henry VI, who as a boy of five was knighted there after keeping his vigil in the Church of St Mary de Castro. Leicester was thus in the royal favour, and profited from the granting of a fair and some tax concessions.

The last scenes of medieval Leicester were enacted at the Blue Boar Inn, which – until its demolition in 1835 – stood at the corner of High Street (now High Cross Street) and Blue Boar Lane (opposite Freeschool Lane) near what was then the centre of the town, High Cross. At this inn on the night of Friday, 19 August 1485, Richard III arrived with his retinue from Nottingham Castle. Five armies besides his own were converging on the county that day.

Some mystery surrounds this event. Why the King of England spent two nights at the Blue Boar Inn, and not at Leicester Castle, is a matter for speculation. The Castle was owned by the Crown, and had housed Henry VI not so many years before, so it seems unlikely that it had fallen into such a state of disrepair that it was unable to accommodate the king.

Whatever the truth of the matter may be, romance was not slow to add more colour to the story. It was said that the bedstead on which Richard slept had been brought with him from Nottingham, and that it contained treasure hidden in its oak structure. This was supposed to have been discovered nearly a century later by the owner of the inn, a Mr Clarke, who thus became a wealthy citizen and a mayor of the town. After his death, his widow was murdered for her money by two men named Harrison and Bradshaw who had been staying at the inn. They were subsequently arrested and executed.

Fact and fancy are difficult to separate after the passing of centuries. However, on the morning of Sunday, 21 August 1485, Richard formed up his army to the sound of trumpets and left Leicester, crossing the two arms of the Soar by the West Bridge and Bow Bridge, on his way to Bosworth. And legend enters with one more tale. It was said that an old woman foretold that where the king's spur struck, there should his head be broken. Richard's spur struck the parapet as his horse crossed Bow Bridge, and we shall return to this point later.

The Tudor period was one of great enterprise and prosperity for England as a nation, but for Leicester, as for many other towns, it was a time of stagnation. There was little new building, no expansion to speak of, and much destruction and deprivation to face. Labourers – though now freemen and not serfs – still worked long days in the town's open fields, known as St Margaret's Field, St Mary's Field and West Field. The poor continued to gather their fuel from Leicester Forest until it was enclosed by Charles I. They drew their water from wells situated in various parts of the town. One of these was known as 'the Cank', on the site of the present Cank Street. 'Cank' was a local colloquialism for gossip, and we do not need much imagination to visualize the women of the town gossiping as they gathered round the well to draw their water.

Idle gossip could be a risky business in those days. A woman who let her tongue run away with her at another person's expense might find herself a victim of Leicester's 'cucking stool'. She would be exhibited round the town in the 'scolding cart' and then ducked in the river by the West Bridge – a humiliation which doubtless taught a woman to hold her tongue in future.

A popular local festival of the time was the 'Riding of the George', an annual pageant in which representations of St George and the dragon paraded through the town. The Borough accounts for 1536–41 include "Itm paid for dryssyng the dragon – 4s". This custom disappeared with the dissolution of the monasteries, but one that lasted longer was the May Day tradition of children scattering flowers at the doors of the houses.

One of Leicester's benefactors was William Wyggeston, an enormously wealthy wool merchant of the town, who twice became its mayor, and founded a Chantry chapel in the Newarke, and a hospital for twelve men and twelve women. The hospital was moved to new premises in the nineteenth century, and the Wyggeston Boys' School built on the site with funds from the greatly increased value of the Tudor merchant's original endowment, which provided a separate girls' school at the same time.

Even ordinary tradesmen were apt to leave sums of money or useful articles in their wills to one or more of the religious guilds or monastic houses, no doubt with the thought of securing safe passage of their souls to heaven. Thus in 1521, one Hugh Yerland left five pounds "to the three orders of ffreres in Leicester for fifteen masses", and John Rygmadyn, in 1530, bequeathed twelve pence to the Grey Friars of Leicester and desired that a priest should sing for his soul and all Christian souls for half a year.

To the Augustinian monks of Leicester Abbey, death soon brought a more weighty legacy. The once rich and mighty Cardinal Wolsey, deprived of health and wealth, was arrested for treason at York and ordered to London to answer the charge. On 26 November, travelling from Nottingham to Leicester, he was so ill that he almost fell from his mule, and that night he came to the doorway of the Abbey, where the Abbot and all his convent met him with lighted torches. "Father Abbot," he said, "I am come to lay my bones among you."

He lingered for three days, dying at eight o'clock in the morning of 29 November. The Mayor of Leicester was called to witness the body, and it was buried next day in the Lady Chapel after solemn mass had been sung by the Abbot.

Shakespeare transformed into poetry the contemporary accounts of the Cardinal's end:

> At last, with easy roads, he came to Leicester,
> Lodged in the abbey; where the reverend abbot,
> With all his convent, honourably received him;
> To whom he gave these words, "O, father abbot,
> An old man, broken with the storms of state,
> Is come to lay his weary bones among ye;
> Give him a little earth for charity!"
> So went to bed; where eagerly his sickness
> Pursued him still: and three nights after this,
> About the hour of eight, which he himself
> Foretold should be his last, full of repentance,
> Continual meditations, tears and sorrows,
> He gave his honours to the world again,
> His blessed part to heaven, and slept in peace.

At the dissolution of the monasteries, soon afterwards, the Abbey was ruined, and the tomb of the Cardinal lost. His bones may still lie beneath the ground where the Abbey stood for four hundred years in the meadows across the river. Whilst Simon de Montfort is commemorated everywhere in Leicester, the city's sole monument, as it were, to the Lord Chancellor and last Cardinal Archbishop of England, is stamped on men's socks, and by this device both his name and his remains are trampled underfoot daily.

Out of the ruins of Leicester Abbey a mansion was eventually built by the Earl of Huntingdon, who had acquired the land. This later became known as Cavendish House. Charles I stayed in this house at the start of the Civil War, and in 1645 his troops under Prince Rupert besieged Leicester, which was on the side of the Parliamentarians. When the garrison commander refused Rupert's summons to surrender, the king's forces bombarded the Newarke walls, mounted assaults on the town from several quarters, and stormed the Belgrave Gate, taking the town in a few hours. The king stayed at Cavendish House, and when he left, his soldiers burned it down, leaving the ruin we see today. The final reversals of the king's fortunes took place at Naseby a fortnight later, and the loss of Leicester was avenged, but the town had suffered great damage in the battle.

John Evelyn passed through in the same year, and remarked in his diary that "the old and ragged City of Leicester", though large and pleasantly seated, was "despicably built, the chimney flues like so many smiths' forges".

By this time the first stocking frames were in operation in the county (it was to be another thirty-five years before Leicester itself had them). But if we see there the beginnings of Leicester's industrial revolution, as some writers have, it is a sobering thought that Europe was then in the grip of the shameful witch-craze which spread terror for over a century, supported alike by Catholic princes and Protestant theologians. Leicester was not immune to this fantasy, nor to the bubonic plague, outbreaks of which had occurred in the town three times between 1593 and 1626.

Leicester's lack of natural resources, and the need to put the poor to work, determined that manufacturing would become the town's modern preoccupation. At the beginning of the eighteenth century, its population was about six thousand, and by 1720, when Daniel Defoe passed through Leicester, hosiery manufacture was well established:

Leicester is an ancient large and populous town, containing about five parishes, 'tis the capital of the county of Leicester, and stands on the River Soar, which rises not far from that High Cross I mentioned before. They have considerable manufacture carried on here, and in several of the market towns round for weaving of stockings by frames, – and one would scarce think it possible so small an article of trade could employ such multitudes of people as it does; for the whole county seems to be employed in it.

The timber houses in the town began to be replaced gradually by brick ones. Public pumps replaced the old wells, and paved streets and street lighting appeared. The town expanded mainly to the east, and with it the town centre, which moved from High Cross to Coal Hill, at the other end of Swinemarket (now High Street). Coal Hill was so called because coal was brought by packhorse for sale there. Cow dung was still the fuel of the poorer people. The west bank of the river was left untouched by expansion and remained a quagmire until relatively recent times. In 1708, Robert Langton paid 10*d*. annual rent to the borough for "two pieces of land taken off the Common dunghill in the Lane near the West Bridge".

One of the earliest surviving brick buildings in Leicester is the Great Meeting Chapel in Bond Street, built by the Unitarians in 1708, as soon as places of worship were allowed to so-called Dissenters, by James II's Toleration Act. The building has been much altered since its foundation, of course, but it remains as a monument not only to the advent of brick, but also to the strength of Nonconformism in the town. The Quakers had built themselves a meeting-place as early as 1680, and they and the Unitarians were first among the practical reformers in Leicester at the time.

John Wesley preached a few of his forty thousand fiery sermons here, and drew large crowds, as elsewhere, helping to take the minds of the poor off their material ills. He wrote in his journal: "In the evening I preached in the Castle-yard at Leicester, to a multitude of awakened and unawakened. One feeble attempt was made to disturb them: a man was sent to cry fresh salmon at a little distance; but he might as well have spared his pains, for none took the least notice of him." Wesley preached on this occasion from the little green where the executioner's block stood in medieval times, and where Sir William Catesby was executed after the Battle of Bosworth.

The Baptists, meanwhile, had produced a native orator who attracted visitors to Leicester from long distances to hear him preach. Robert Hall was born at Arnesby, and spent the early years of his ministry at Bristol and Cambridge, but returned to Leicester for the last twenty-four years of his life. He was said to have taught himself the alphabet from the gravestones in his father's churchyard, and was preaching by the time he was eleven. All his life, however, he suffered from physical torment which was found only after his death to be due to a kidney disease. He eased his pain with opium, laudanum and tea on a phenomenal scale, and on two occasions – not surprisingly – his mental health broke down. But his eloquence was legendary, and he added great weight to the Nonconformist tradition in Leicester. Pitt went so far as to compare him with Demosthenes, and that, in the days of Burke and Sheridan, is ample testimony to the power of Dr Hall's sermons. He was also a champion of the framework knitters during the worst period of their poverty. One of Leicester's few statues is of Robert Hall, and it stands in De Montfort Square.

In 1771 the Leicester Infirmary was built by public subscription – one of the large number of charitable hospitals built throughout the country during the eighteenth century which indicate the development of a social conscience. Its entrance from Infirmary Road was at one time made through ornate wrought-iron gates, presented by Shukburgh Ashby, of Quenby. Among the new hospital's rules were a ban on swearing, indecent behaviour, playing cards, and going into the women's ward. Out-patients were directed to bring back every week their left-over medicines, as well as bottles, phials and trusses, and "whoever neglects this order will have no more medicines".

Another development took place soon afterwards for which the citizens of Leicester are still grateful, and which has become unique. This was the laying out and planting of New Walk, originally known as Queen's Walk. It ran from what is now Welford Place, and followed the line of a Roman road, known as Gartree Road, stopping just short of the London road, well outside the town, where windmills turned in St Margaret's Fields. Fashionable houses began to grow along it, and the town itself grew round and beyond it during the course of the next hundred years, but it was preserved as a quiet promenade, free from traffic, and so it remains today. Though most of the buildings are now shabby, and some new business premises have been erected which destroy its old character, New Walk is still a quiet and secluded avenue, with stylish old lamp-posts, where birds sing in the trees only a few yards from the railway station and the noisy city streets. One Victorian resident went so far as to say that New Walk was the "only solely respectable street in Leicester".

It was in this quiet avenue that a Nonconformist Proprietory School, designed in the grand manner with a four-column portico, was taken over in 1849 as the town museum. I remember a sad attendant there telling me that hardly anybody goes in nowadays, except children during the school holidays to see the stuffed animals. Another fine museum is at Belgrave Hall, a delightful Queen Anne house. Among the exhibits in the latter is the work of Mary Linwood, who lived in Leicester for most of her life, and made a name for herself with her exquisite needle-work. She copied famous pictures, using worsteds she often dyed herself, but never sold her work. She once refused three thousand guineas for her copy of Dolci's *Salvator Mundi*, and left it to the queen in her will. Catherine the Great of Russia also owned Miss Linwood's work. This busy spinster lived in Belgrave Gate until her death at the age of ninety in 1845, and she was said to be one of the last persons in England to use a sedan chair.

The former village of Belgrave was the subject of an amusing 'legend' which was undoubtedly invented by a medieval wag. It concerned a giant named Bel who undertook to reach Leicester in three leaps on his horse from a village seven miles away. He mounted his giant sorrel steed and took one prodigious leap which taxed the strength of both man and horse to the utmost. The second huge leap practically burst the giant, his girths and his horse; and the third – still a mile and a half short of his target – actually killed him. And thus came into being the village names of Mountsorrel, Wanlip, Birstall and Belgrave!

A legend with more likely ancient origins concerned a cave in the Dane Hills, in Leicester Forest. It was known as Black Annis' Bower, and a savage old woman was supposed to live there, pouncing on children who happened to pass that way, eating them and hanging their skins on a tree. Black Annis was used in Leicester to frighten naughty children into obedience at one time, before modern psychology discouraged such terrorist methods.

Some people believed Black Annis to be a witch who lived in cellars below the castle, getting to the Dane Hills by means of an underground passage. It is probable that her name – like Lear's perhaps – survived from a long-forgotten Celtic divinity, Annet or Annis, to whom the magpie was sacred. Superstition still accompanies this bird, and in Leicestershire as elsewhere children who see it may say:

> One for sorrow,
> Two for mirth,
> Three for a wedding,
> Four for a birth.

The increase of population that soon enclosed New Walk was due to the rapid growth of Leicester as an industrial centre. In the hundred years from 1700 it nearly trebled, and in the hundred after that it more than trebled again. New needs led to new communications, and in 1832 the Leicester and Swannington Railway was opened.

This was the first line in the Midlands, and its purpose was to convey coal from the Leicestershire coalfield into the town, by a faster and more direct method than by canal barge. Robert Stephenson and the local engineer John Ellis built the line, passing through a tunnel at the village of Glenfield which was then the longest in Britain. The first locomotive to run on it was the *Comet*, brought by canal for the occasion and driven by George Stephenson himself, to the sound of a band and the salute of cannon. In the following year, an engine named *Samson* collided with a cartload of butter and eggs, and a Leicester organ-builder then made the first train-whistle out of an organ pipe.

The coming of the railways proved the making of another well-known Leicester resident, Thomas Cook. Born at Melbourne in Derbyshire, and brought up as a Baptist, he soon put his missionary zeal to use in the interests of the Temperance Movement. He moved to Market Harborough, married there, signed the pledge, and managed the publications of the South Midland Temperance Association.

He moved to Leicester in 1841, and in the same year planned and arranged, for the Temperance Association, an outing by rail from Leicester to Loughborough and back, for which 570 people paid a shilling each. A band was also squeezed on to the crowded train of nine open carriages, and played music all the way.

The excursion was so successful that others soon followed, and it did not take Thomas Cook long to realize that he had laid the foundations of a thriving business. Profit proved more attractive than religious dedication (though he never deserted the temperance cause), and by the time Cook died in Leicester in 1892, Thomas Cook and Son, Travel Agents, was already a vast organization. Why so many people should have wanted to go to Loughborough in the first place, however, leaves his first venture a mystery tour, of sorts.

The need for water supplies also increased with the town's growing population. The river was useless, being notoriously polluted by domestic sewage and industrial waste, and liable to flooding which sometimes affected a fifth of the population. At one point, Leicester had the highest death-rate of any town in England, and this was attributed to the state of the River Soar, which became a national disgrace. Typhoid was high on the list of fatal diseases. It was many years before the combined benefits of a proper sewerage system, flood prevention, and reservoirs to supply water, brought modern hygiene to the town. Thornton Reservoir was the first built specially to supply Leicester, in 1853. It was followed by the reservoir at Cropston, in 1866, and that at Swithland, in 1894.

A necessary evil arising from growing population and the inevitable stress of living in a close industrial community was additional prison accommodation. The gaoler at one of the town's earlier and smaller prisons had become Leicester's greatest citizen. Daniel Lambert was born in Blue Boar Lane, and he followed his father as keeper of the town gaol. But by the time he was twenty he weighed thirty stones, and he kept on growing. He walked and swam, and drank only water, but his waist measurement grew to over nine feet, and his weight to over fifty-two stones, and he had only reached the age of thirty-nine when he died at a Stamford inn, in 1809. A wall had to be demolished to remove his body.

Lambert was a hunting and cock-fighting enthusiast, and among the stories about him it is said that he once struck a performing bear so hard with his fist, to save his dog from it, that the bear fled yelping. He was sometimes the subject of cartoons in the national press, which usually represented him as a fearsome opponent of Britain's enemies, particularly Napoleon, who is seen trembling before Daniel Lambert, mounted on Monarch, "the largest horse in the world", with the caption: "Two wonders of the world, or a specimen of a new troop of Leicestershire Light Horse".

Daniel Lambert was an amiable man, who eventually realized that there was more profit in exhibiting himself as a curiosity than in guarding the town's prisoners. Some of his clothes and other belongings are still curiosities in the city's Newarke Houses Museum.

A new County Gaol was built in 1828, in Welford Road, opposite the Infirmary grounds. The architect was William Parsons, the County Surveyor, who erected a veritable fortress with battlements and a token portcullis, as if to prevent anyone from getting in. Inside, it had a treadmill and straight-jackets. Leicester was very proud of it, and until public executions were abolished, forty years later, patients at the Infirmary were occasionally given the doubtful privilege of watching the hangings outside the gates. No records survive to tell us what effect this gruesome shock therapy had on their recovery rate. The public execution of a murderer at Leicester in 1847 attracted a crowd of about twenty thousand.

The significance of this new building was not lost on William Cobbett, the political journalist, who visited Leicester in 1830 to give a lecture. It is worth quoting him at length:

> Leicester is a very fine town; spacious streets, fine inns, fine shops, and containing, they say, thirty or forty thousand people. It is well stocked with jails, of which a new one, in addition to the rest, has just been built, covering three acres of ground! And, as if proud of it, the grand portal has little turrets in the castle style, with embrasures in miniature on the caps of the turrets. Nothing speaks the want of reflection in the people so much as the self-gratulation which they appear to feel in these edifices in their several towns. Instead of expressing shame at the indubitable proofs of the horrible increase of misery and crime, they really boast of these 'improvements' as they call them. Our forefathers built abbeys and priories and churches, and they made such use of them that jails were nearly unnecessary. We, their sons, have knocked down the abbeys and priories; suffered half the parsonage-houses and churches to pretty nearly tumble down, and make such use of the remainder, that jails and tread-mills and dungeons have now become the most striking edifices in every county in the kingdom.

Yesterday morning . . . I walked out to the village of Knighton, two miles on the Bosworth road, where I breakfasted, and then walked back. This morning I walked out to Hailstone, nearly three miles on the Lutterworth road, and got my breakfast there. You have nothing to do but walk through these villages, to see the cause of the increase of the jails. Standing on the hill at Knighton, you see the three ancient and lofty and beautiful spires rising up at Leicester; you see the river winding down through a broad bed of the most beautiful meadows that man ever set his eyes on; you see the bright verdure covering all the land, even the tops of the hills, with here and there a little wood, as if made by God to give variety to the scene, for the river brings the coal in abundance, for fuel, and the earth gives the brick and the tile in abundance. But go down into the villages; invited by the spires rising up amongst the trees in the dells, at scarcely ever more than a mile or two apart; invited by those spires, go down into these villages, view the large, and once the most beautiful churches; see the parson's house, large, and in the midst of pleasure-gardens; and then look at the miserable sheds in which the labourers reside! Look at these hovels made of mud and straw; bits of glass, or of old off-cast windows, without frames or hinges, frequently, but merely stuck in the mud wall. Enter them, and look at the bits of chairs or stools; the wretched boards tacked together, to serve for a table; the floor of pebble, broken brick, or of the bare ground, look at the thing called a bed; and survey the rags on the backs of the wretched inhabitants; then wonder, if you can, that the jails and dungeons and treadmills increase, and that a standing army and barracks are become the favourite establishments of England!

Among those who doubtless recognized the truth of Cobbett's strictures was a group of people who formed themselves into the world's first Secular Society in 1853, and in 1881 built themselves a hall in Humberstone Gate. The chief moving spirit among the local Secularists was Josiah Gimson, the founder of an engineering firm which is still in existence. Charles Bradlaugh, Annie Besant and George Holyoake (the founder of Secularism and the last man imprisoned in England for blasphemy) were present at the opening. Predictably, the Society called upon itself the kind of thunderous abuse of which Christians have always been the best exponents, but it has lived to tell the tale, and Socrates, Jesus, Voltaire, Tom Paine and Robert Owen still gaze down on unsuspecting passers-by from the rather dismal Victorian edifice of Secular Hall. Those who have spoken there include the Fabians Bernard Shaw and H. G. Wells, and the anarchist Prince Kropotkin.

George Holyoake, despite his serious speech impediment, was actually considered as a prospective Liberal candidate for Leicester, but was not adopted in the end. Holyoake first referred to the "Leicester principle of controversy", which was "to question and try all assertions".

The origins of Leicester's long-standing reputation for radicalism are obscure, but its religious Nonconformism has been noted since the fourteenth century, and secular dissent has flourished in step with it. Lollardry, Quakerism, Congregation-alism and sections of the Methodists and the Baptists all rocked their cradles in this county, and it is usual to ascribe the origins of Leicester's religious and secular Nonconformism to the period around the English Reformation. But this really begs the question "Why Leicester?", and I suspect that the true answer lies much farther back in history, and is connected with a lack of identity, deeply hidden in the 'collective unconscious' of the region, to use Jung's admirable phrase. The succession of British, Roman, Anglo-Saxon and Scandinavian influences on the population, both physically and culturally; the wedge-like advance of the invaders to the centre of the county from the east; its position near the frontier of the Danelaw; all must have contributed to Leicester's isolation from everything around it and given it a sort of nervous insecurity which made it more than ready to grasp at new ideas and new 'truths'. We have surely seen the same process taking place in America more recently, where new religions sprout like spring bulbs, and for much the same reasons.

One of the extraordinary manifestations of dissent in Leicester was its opposition to vaccination against smallpox. The out-breaks of the disease in the middle years of the nineteenth century had led the government to introduce compulsory vaccination for infants, and Leicester soon became a leading centre of opposition to the law, establishing an anti-vaccination league which maintained that isolation, not vaccination, was the answer to the problem. The 'Leicester Method', as it was called, contributed to the establishment of isolation hospitals and won exemption from compulsory vaccination for those children whose parents conscientiously objected to it.

Meanwhile, boot and shoe manufacturing was growing in importance in Leicester, giving the town's industry a diversity it badly needed, and this and the hosiery trade were to a large extent responsible for the introduction of light engineering, which has come to be one of the modern city's three great industries. Between 1851 and the end of the century the population of Leicester grew from sixty thousand to two hundred thousand, and by that time twice the number of people employed in the hosiery trade were working in the boot and shoe business.

This huge expansion brought more employment in its turn, to the building industry, to transport, and to the local traders, and Leicester was on its way to that boom which led the League of Nations to describe it in the 1930s as Europe's most prosperous city.

III

THE HUB OF THE WHEEL

THERE are citizens of Leicester who would deny truth to both Galileo and the Inquisition on the question whether the earth or the sun is the centre of the universe, and assert that it is in fact the Clock Tower of Leicester. Certainly the city, and to a large extent the county, revolves round this grotesque Victorian monument, which was erected in 1868 by public subscription. It was made in Ketton stone on a base of Mountsorrel granite.

Coal Hill, which had long ago become the centre of the growing town, had also become a bottleneck by the mid-nineteenth century, with dilapidated buildings obstructing the flow of pedestrians and traffic. After protracted debates in council chambers and the local press, demolition was ordered, and this left a large empty space in Eastgates which tended to cause even more traffic chaos than had existed before. It was soon pointed out that some refuge was needed to save pedestrians from being run over while crossing this wide area. Suggestions included a colossal statue to a local benefactor, a square tower with high relief medallions, an illuminated clock, a fountain, and a public urinal.

Opponents of the proposals argued that a large structure there would create as great a nuisance as the buildings they had just demolished, and that they did not want to provide a lounging place for idlers. But the injuries and narrow escapes experienced by pedestrians led to the adoption of a scheme to erect a memorial to four ancient benefactors. The winning design was by a local architect, Joseph Goddard, and consisted of a square tower surmounted by a spire and incorporating four clock faces, and statues at each corner, representing Simon de Montfort, William Wyggeston, Sir Thomas White and Gabriel Newton. Dates below the statues, intended as the years of the benefactors' gifts, are all wrong.

The more modern the buildings of Leicester become around

it, the more anachronistic this spectre of the Gothic Revival seems, but the people of Leicester love the monster, and its future appears secure, in spite of periodic threats of demolition or removal to a different site. It survived the construction of electric tram lines all round it in 1904, and forty-five years later saw them all taken up again. For years it served as an outsize coat-hanger for the policemen who congregated there. No doubt it will survive much more yet.

Leicester has long enjoyed a reputation for being a clean place, as industrial cities go, but on the other hand is often dismissed as being a dull and characterless red-brick city. J. B. Priestley wrote that there are many worse places he would rather live in, and Sir Harold Nicolson, who represented West Leicester in Parliament for ten years, referred to it as "that ugly and featureless city". (Winston Churchill regarded it as a "beastly place", but for different reasons – Leicester had rejected him as a Liberal M.P. in 1923.)

There is some truth in such views, but it is arguable that when we say a place is "full of character", we generally mean it is too poor to keep pace with modern progress. Leicester wastes little time in pulling down what lies in the way of new roads and buildings, and many of the historic treasures which *have* survived, such as the Guildhall or the stylish Crescent in King Street, have only been saved in the nick of time by the strength of public feeling. In any case, it may yet be that we shall come to value red brick, as the spread of concrete casts its hideous grey gloom over our towns.

One should look at the Town Hall, and the Midland Bank at the corner of Granby Street and Bishop Street. These are distinctive red-brick buildings which it would be a pity to lose. The bank is the work of Joseph Goddard, and is a very different piece of design from his Clock Tower. Among other modern buildings designed by local architects, the County Rooms in Hotel Street, built in 1792 as an hotel, have a splendid façade, and the Baptist Chapel in Belvoir Street (built by J. A. Hansom, architect of the New Walk Museum) has long enjoyed the popular appellation of 'Pork Pie Chapel' owing to its curious round shape. It is used now as an Adult Education Centre.

Meanwhile, the city continues to spread outwards. Beyond the Dane Hills, where houses now stand on Black Annis' Bower, the New Parks Estate was developed in the post-war years, and its crescent-shaped shopping centre in Aikman Avenue won an award from the Royal Institute of British Architects, though it is nothing to get excited about by today's standards.

Among the street names typical of the themes adopted all over England during the Victorian expansion, Leicester numbers half a dozen named after a motley collection of religious personalities, lined up in parallel rows of red-brick terraces as if for an identity parade – Livingstone, Luther, Tyndale, Latimer, Ridley, Cranmer. Oddly enough, it does not have a Carey Street, though William Carey, the Baptist missionary, lived in the town for a time. Perhaps the unfortunate connotations of a Carey Street in this money-minded city were too unthinkable. It does have a bag of nuts (somewhat less orderly) – Chestnut, Walnut, Hazel, Brazil and Filbert Streets. The last-named is one of the best-known streets in Leicester, since the City Association Football Club has its ground there.

It was in 1919 that George V conferred the title of 'city' on Leicester, following a visit by the king and Queen Mary, and the parish church of St Martin was eventually chosen to be Leicester Cathedral. The original church was ancient, but a great deal of alteration and restoration had made it virtually Victorian. The Herrick Chapel is a notable feature, however, commemorating an important Leicester family whose members included Abigail, Jonathan Swift's mother, who is buried here.

Swift's link with Leicestershire, albeit a tenuous one, is perhaps the county's most important connection with world literature. His maternal grandfather, James Erick, was vicar of Thornton, and married Elizabeth Imins of Ibstock; their eldest son, Thomas, became vicar of Frisby-on-the-Wreake. Wigston Magna and Houghton-on-the-Hill have both been claimed as the birth-place of Swift's mother, Abigail Erick. In fact, it seems likely that she was Dublin-born, where her parents had gone in 1634. Abigail was born in 1640, and it was in Dublin that she met and married Swift's father. On her husband's death she returned to her family in Leicester, spending the rest of her life there.

Swift frequently visited his mother, often travelling to Leicester on foot from London, and he spent six weeks with her shortly before she died, aware that her health was failing. He was in Ireland when he received the news of her end, and wrote:

    . . . my dear mother Mrs Abigail Swift dyed that morning, Monday, April 29th, 1710, about ten o'clock, after a long sickness, being ill all winter and lame, and extremely ill a month or six weeks before her death. I have now lost my barrier between me and death; God grant I may live to be as well prepared for it, as I confidently believe her to have been. If the way to Heaven be through piety, truth, justice and charity she is there.

The vitriolic dean entertained no such tender sentiments about the people of Leicester generally, however. He was well aware of the town's tradition of dissent, of course, and it was probably his contempt for Nonconformists, as well as gossip about his affairs with local girls, which led him to dismiss the natives as "a parcel of very wretched fools". A local girl named Betty Jones was one of those with whom Swift's name was linked. She married a Lutterworth innkeeper and was lost to an obscurity which was probably happier than the fame she might have won as Swift's wife.

Towards the end of the Victorian period, the Corporation of Leicester acquired the meadow in which the Abbey had once stood, and converted it into Abbey Park. It was a venture much criticized at the time, and not only because of its enormous cost. A correspondent to the local paper declared that "the very large expenditure going on and contemplated in that dank, diphtherial and febrile spot, positively gives me the shivers". But flood prevention was the main purpose of the scheme, and it worked out to everyone's lasting advantage, Abbey Park now being one of the city's most popular and attractive open spaces. It was opened by the Prince of Wales and Princess Alexandra in 1882.

At the southern end of New Walk is Victoria Park, which contains an impressive domed and arched war memorial designed by Sir Edwin Lutyens; and De Montfort Hall, built in 1913. This is of simple design for the period, with an elegant colonnade on its entrance side overlooking well-kept gardens. It was erected as a badly needed hall for public meetings, and the Corporation specified that it was to be cheap. Even then there were protests that no such building was required, but the result was a triumph. The architects produced a spacious building, seating nearly three thousand, and having first-rate acoustics, making it one of the finest concert halls in the country. Unfortunately, it is only rarely used as such, Leicester's appetite for good music being strictly limited.

Sir John Barbirolli was always a popular personality with Leicester audiences, but when he included the Fifth Symphony

of Shostakovitch in one of his programmes with the Hallé
Orchestra, instead of the standard menu of Beethoven and
Tchaikovsky, a smaller than usual audience turned up, and
rumours were soon heard that Barbirolli would not visit
Leicester again. In fact, as Sir John later assured me, he had made
no such threat. Nevertheless, he and other – less popular –
conductors were well aware that one could not take many
chances with Leicester audiences.

Ironically, this city of which Sir Thomas Beecham once
grumpily remarked "The people here don't want music" is the
headquarters of a fine and unusual organization which takes
music far beyond its home territory. The Leicestershire Schools
Symphony Orchestra was formed in the late 1940s and has
toured the continent regularly. It was the first amateur orchestra
to play in Vienna's Musikereinsaal, and a German newspaper
once hailed it as "Britain's best cultural export".

The city's reputation as a cultural desert is, nevertheless, a
long-standing one. J. B. Priestley, visiting Leicester during his
'English Journey' in the 1930s, found it "hard to believe that
anything much has ever happened there", and went on to say:
"In the whole of Leicester that night there was only one
performance being given by living players, in a touring musical
comedy. In a town with nearly a quarter of a million people, not
without intelligence or money, this is not good enough".

Mr Priestley was not to know how lucky he was. There have
been years in Leicester more recently when no live performance could be seen at all. The three theatres which were
standing in the 1930s had all been demolished by the end of
the 1950s. The oldest of them, the Theatre Royal, opened in
1836, and Henry Irving and Charles Kean had played there,
as well as Macready, who played *Hamlet* in 1845 to "a very
wretched house". One of the last productions I saw in that
theatre was Mr Priestley's own *Dangerous Corner*. Seats in the
dress circle were four shillings and sixpence then. A building
society now stands on the ground the theatre once occupied.

The Opera House, in Silver Street, was opened in 1877 and
was used as a host theatre for touring companies. A supermarket
now stands in its place. And a dry-cleaning firm occupies the
former site of the more exotic Palace Theatre, which specialized
in variety, and attempted to keep itself alive with strip shows
towards the end. It was demolished in 1959, the last of the three

to go. So, for a time, theatre in this most prosperous city in Europe was left in the hands of an amateur company, the Leicester Drama Society, who were not, in the nature of things, capable of continuous productions, although they could claim to have had a member who has become one of Leicester's few famous sons—Richard Attenborough, whose father was one of the first principals of University College.

Then there came upon the scene a small professional group which called itself, hopefully, the Living Theatre Company. It occupied a disused Sunday school, scheduled for demolition, which a national newspaper soon called "the ancestral home of the death-watch beetle". But the company, undaunted, mounted a succession of plays there which included ambitious productions such as John Osborne's *Luther,* Chekhov's *Uncle Vanya* and Tennessee Williams's *A Streetcar Named Desire.* Young actors such as Peter Blythe got some useful experience there before moving on to better things, and Kenneth Loach, famous now for his documentary-like plays in cinema and television, directed Shaw's *Candida* and himself played the love-struck poet. The actors worked for basic Equity rates, and the directors usually for even less.

The response of Leicester to this company's efforts to rescue the city's reputation was hardly sensational, but it was sufficient for the Arts Council to take a cautious interest in this theatrical graveyard, and in due course a local group of enthusiasts called the Leicester Theatre Society, using the Living Theatre as a lever which they threw away when it had served its purpose, persuaded the Council to build a more permanent theatre. The resulting Phoenix Theatre, opened in 1963, was modest, but it was a start, and it was followed ten years later by the bigger Haymarket Theatre, designed by the City Architect, Stephen George, and forming part of a new city centre development with shops on two levels. It is too early to say whether the city's bad reputation in theatrical circles will be changed by these buildings. It seems unlikely that they will ever enjoy more than local popularity, unlike the Playhouse at Nottingham, or the earliest of the post-war provincial theatres, the Belgrade at Coventry.

It is not easy to account for the city's cultural backwardness. In the theatre, a week in Leicester used to be as gloomy a prospect as Holy Week. It is too easy to describe it as a survival of the Puritan tradition. Nonconformist rejection of ritual and the use of music, on the other hand, was noted here in Elizabethan times, and we have already observed that the city's motto is "Semper Eadem" (Always the Same).

As the old theatres emptied, so did the cinemas and the churches. For a section of the community still needful of regular fellowship, ritual and faith in just rewards, the deserted cinemas have now taken over the role of the churches. In these temples built for the greater glory of Charlie Chaplin and Marilyn Monroe, congregations now bow their heads in unison and solemnly respond to the incantations of the minister, "Clickety-click, sixty-six", until one of them interrupts the ceremony with a cry of ecstasy. Bingo is the opium of some of the people.

Leicester—and indeed the whole county—is also one of the capitals of clubland, which helps to explain why Mr Priestley found but one live performance in a public theatre, and why many people have gained the impression that Leicester folk go home after work and do not come out again until next morning. Those who don't stay in and watch television go to their clubs, in its devotion to which Leicester belongs firmly to the north of England. It was one of the pioneers of the Working Men's Club movement, which arose out of growing recognition of the need for the moral education of working people, and parallel with the formation of friendly societies to protect them in times of sickness and unemployment.

The first Working Men's Clubs were founded by moral reformers to counter what they saw as the evil influences of pubs and beer shops. They were such men as Joseph Dare, a self-appointed Unitarian social worker who was in favour of temperance but not prohibition, and permitted beer to be sold in his club on the grounds that without it no one would join, and with it he could create a diversion of interests and thus reduce its responsibility for drunkenness and violence. Dare was also an early advocate of compulsory education. Only Hinckley, as far as I know, recalls him in its street names, with its Dare's Walk, not far from the town's own Unitarian Chapel, built in 1722.

Now every town and village of any size has its Working Men's Club, and there is a profusion of politically based clubs —Labour, Liberal, Conservative, Constitutional—and Miners' Welfare Clubs, Ex-Servicemen's Clubs, and what have you. The older and more ambitious purpose-built ones have their ballrooms, billiard rooms, ladies' rooms, and the smaller ones cater merely for darts and dominoes in buildings often converted from disused cinemas—always with a stage for the weekend 'turns', their inviolable rules, and that all-pervading smell of ale, most of which comes from the breweries of Burton-on-Trent.

Materialism does not breed imagination, except when it concerns money-making. Even Thomas Cook observed that "perhaps few towns present less variety in recreative attractions than Leicester". It was for many years—almost alone among towns of its size—without a free public library. Such a thing was denounced as an unjustifiable extravagance by such men as Leicester saw fit to elect to its Council. When it did eventually get one, the racing news had to be cut out of the papers in the reading room, as these columns were thought to be a source of corruption. Andrew Carnegie supplied the money for a more ambitious library, which was opened in 1905, but complaints were soon heard that, characteristically, Leicester was "the only town of importance that does not allow to the Library a full penny rate". Fifty years later, much the same complaints were being made about its lack of financial support for the theatre.

Leicester is not rich in bookshops, either. It has, in spite of itself, given birth to one or two well-known writers, chief of whom, perhaps, are C. P. Snow (Baron Snow of Leicester), who gave the language emotive phrases such as 'the two cultures' and 'corridors of power'; and Colin Wilson, who sprang, cat-like, to the top of the literary ladder in 1956 with his extraordinary book *The Outsider* (and according to some critics has been coming down, rung by rung, ever since). Professor J. H. Plumb, the historian, was born in Leicester, as well as one of the most promising of the new wave of dramatists, Joe Orton, whose early plays *Entertaining Mr Sloane* and *Loot* were great successes, but who died tragically, murdered by his flat-mate in 1967. Leicester also educated the popular and prolific novelist E. Phillips Oppenheim. who lived at Evington. All these, however, must be ascribed to those accidents which happen throughout human society, and are in no way attributable to a conscious pursuit of intellectual achievement in the city's history or aspirations.

A Collegiate School, founded in the town in the 1830s, closed down after only thirty years, but during its lifetime it had one teacher of distinction, the young Alfred Russell Wallace, who was to hit on the explanation of evolutionary processes at the same time as Darwin, and later became a leading champion of Darwinism.

Paradoxically, Leicester has been at the forefront of educational development in some other ways. Its nineteenth-century backwardness took a turn for the better when the Rev. D. J. Vaughan established a Working Men's College here in 1862, and the present Vaughan College, now allied to Leicester University, is still going strong in the field of adult education. Its modern premises flank the Roman remains in front of Jewry Wall, whence it moved from its old building in Holy Bones, where the doorway had displayed the motto Vaughan gave to it: "Sirs, ye are brethren".

The University itself is a thriving example of the 'red-brick' establishment. The University College was founded as a memorial to those who died in the First World War, and opened in 1921 in buildings which were originally the Leicestershire and Rutland Lunatic Asylum—a circumstance which led Sir Nikolaus Pevsner to write, with tongue in cheek, that "the main building of the University looks very different from that of any other in England". It achieved full university status in 1957, but like every other local advancement in cultural terms, it only did so after a long, hard struggle against the philistine principles of the businessmen who ran the city, and who considered it a waste of money.

The University's Centre for Mass Communications Research was the first unit in the country to be set up specifically for such work, and it has done some important pioneer research into the effects of television—particularly relevant in the Midlands, where people tend to watch television for more hours than elsewhere in the country.

Another controversial development was the so-called Leicestershire Experiment, introduced in the early 1960s by the then County Education Officer, Stewart C. Mason. This abolished the iniquitous '11-plus' examination and provided secondary education for all children on terms which have since been adopted nationally as the comprehensive school system. I believe it was Fenner Brockway who said somewhere that what Leicester thinks today, the nation thinks tomorrow. That is not always true, but it has been true on a good many occasions.

Radio Leicester was also ahead of its counterparts in other areas, being the first of the local broadcasting stations opened in co-operation with the BBC. As the city had by that time lost one of its two evening newspapers, the radio station was – in theory – an important supplement to the surviving and worthy *Leicester Mercury* as a source of local communication, but I have heard a few local people express some doubts, to put it no stronger, about its value.

A much older source of news and gossip of course, is the Market Place. Leicester's market is one of the largest in the country, and it has been held on the same site for at least five hundred years, and perhaps for a thousand. One of the benefits of its recent face-lift has been the removal of stalls from the front of the Corn Exchange, to reveal this building's splendid exterior staircase. The statue of the fifth Duke of Rutland, Lord Lieutenant of the County, which now stands there, was first set up in the Market Place in 1851, and has come back to its original site after being shifted from pillar to post about the town for many years. Leicester does not have many statues (it has produced no great men to erect them to), and those it *does* have, it doesn't know what to do with!

Leicester Market may not have the colourful character of the London street markets, but a wander round these stalls soon convinces one that live theatre is not to be experienced only in buildings specially designed with an auditorium and a stage. The sales patter of the stallholders is still an entertainment in itself. My own favourite used to be a man selling fabrics, who would show the women a length of curtain material and convince them that he was practically giving the stuff away. Then he would add: "Now don't tell me you don't need new curtains, ladies, because I've been round all your houses having a look." This brought shrieks of laughter from his audience, and usually had the desired effect.

I also remember a shifty-looking character whose plain-wrapped stall was always well attended by men in raincoats. He sold what were then considered to be 'dirty' books and magazines, though today they would be mild compared with even the most respectable publisher's 'breast-sellers' getting full point-of-sale display in W. H. Smith's.

Leicester Market was famous, even in the Middle Ages, for the quality of its meat, and by the eighteenth century it was said that "Smithfield market, on its greatest days, bears no sort of proportion to the beasts shown in Leicester at two or three fairs in the year". At the cattle market in Aylestone Road, one could buy a bull for seventeen shillings in the fourteenth century, before the Black Death caused massive inflation. Leicestershire cattle are still noted for their size. The grazing land of Leicestershire and Northamptonshire suits heavy animals, so that cattle produced for beef are not killed as young as in other parts of the country.

The maze of stalls has an extraordinary variety of smells, and as you wander in and out of them you catch the odour of packets of birdseed, pots of chrysanthemums, the earthy smell of potatoes and the smell of bananas in a mountainous pile on the stall, with a woman standing there, almost hidden by them, shouting: "Come on, now, gells, on'y a few left." The best ice-cream I have ever tasted is also sold here.

Weaving in and out of Leicester, bringing women into the city from the county's towns and villages to do their shopping, are the familiar buses of the self-styled "Friendly Midland Red". (All Midland Reds are Friendly, one might say, but some are more friendly than others.) Anywhere in Leicestershire you might hear a woman greet another at a bus stop:

" 'Ello, i'nt it cold?"

"Oo, perishin'."

"Y'off to Leicester, then, are ya?"

"Ar, I allus goos traipsin' off somewhere a Sat'days."

On the bus, she asks for a nineteen pence ticket.

"Nineteen?" shrieks the conductress, grinning. "Woss up wi' ya? It went up a-Monday, duck. Twenny-four now, i'nt it!"

"Gone up agen? I s'll 'ave ta stop a-comin'."

A more direct manner, at any rate, than the advertisement for "Dr Steer's Opodeldoc" (what in heaven's name was that?) which appeared in the *Leicester Journal* in 1801 – a masterpiece of prolonged suspense:

"It is with real Regret that the Proprietors of this Medicine find themselves under the Necessity of having Recourse to the same Measure which they adopted in 1795, namely that of adding Sixpence per Bottle to the Price . . ."

A few years ago many women used to come into Leicester to do their shopping and have tea and toasted teacakes at Wynn's Cafe or Simpkin and James. Both establishments have now sadly disappeared, as well as older places like the Stag and Pheasant

Hotel, which always provided a first-class meal. Leicester is as dismally backward in its provision of good restaurants as in its cultural activity, and this, again, hints at the unimaginative character of the people. Cooking tends to be of that dull variety which the men will puritanically describe as "good solid food". There is great reliance here on tinned and frozen 'convenience'-foods. Taste is not high on their list of interests.

Paradoxically, however – once again – Leicester is the home of an old-established firm making one of the county's notable contributions to the nation's famous foods – the pork pie. Walker and Son came to Leicester from Mansfield towards the end of the nineteenth century, but the business to which they gave their name had been established as long ago as 1820. It was soon famous far beyond Leicestershire, and in the days when Leicestershire did have thriving live theatres, visiting celebrities such as George Robey and Bransby Williams would always expect a Walkers' pie during their visit, and Sir Thomas Beecham would never conduct an encore at De Montfort Hall without one.

Walkers have always relied on traditional recipes for their meat products, and refused to make pies of anything other than pork. So after the Second World War, when pork was in short supply, the company decided to make potato crisps as a temporary stop-gap. Such was their popularity, however, that the crisp section of the business expanded rapidly, and a few years ago it became an American subsidiary. I learned from the Chairman that it takes a hundredweight of potatoes to make about twenty-four pounds of crisps. Meanwhile the pork section remains the independent family concern it always was, employing about a hundred people to supply its ten local shops.

At Glen Parva, one of the city's former villages, the Royal Leicestershire Regiment had its headquarters. Founded in 1688 as the 17th Foot Regiment, it became linked with the county in 1782 and was officially renamed 'The Leicestershire Regiment' a hundred years later. Its popular nickname 'The Tigers' dated from early in the nineteenth century, when the Regiment served in India for nineteen years, and it became a 'Royal' regiment after the 1939-45 war. Its battle honours included such evocative names as Sebastopol, Ladysmith, Somme, Ypres, Palestine, North Africa and Korea, and during the 1914-18 war three 'Tigers' men won the Victoria Cross.

The Royal Leicestershire Regiment gradually lost its identity in the infantry reorganizations resulting from defence cuts during the 1960s, and the old Regimental Depot at Glen Parva was closed down. Some of the buildings have since been demolished, but the remaining barracks will form part of a new Borstal institution. The Magazine, in the Newarke, has meanwhile been converted into a museum of the regiment.

Leicester is naturally the focal point of most of the county's sporting interests, apart—of course—from fox-hunting. The county's fame as a hunting centre, however, as well as its keen interest in animal development, must have been connected with the establishment of horse-racing in Leicester itself. The first mention of the sport is in 1603, when bear-baiting and cock-fighting were still among the town's popular spectacles. Later, racing took place on the present Victoria Park until the new course between Knighton and Oadby was opened, and Leicester Races still rank high in the county's sporting calendar.

Perhaps the earliest widespread native enthusiasm was cricket. A game which began its life as a rural recreation was a natural for Leicestershire, where industry was not confined to factories, and the people, being their own timekeepers, could indulge their interests more freely than in many other parts of the country. The village parsons joined in too. In fox-hunting and cricket, Leicestershire seems to have acted like a magnet to sporting parsons.

Organized cricket was first played in St Margaret's Pasture until a new ground was opened in Wharf Street, with a bowling green adjacent. The Wharf Street ground was so good, and so well placed geographically, that matches of national importance were staged there. In a North *v.* South game in 1836, the legendary Alfred Mynn was so badly battered by the fast bowlers (no pads in those days!) that he was unable to play again for two years, and there was even some talk of amputation. The ground was eventually bought for building development, and it was in 1878 that the Grace Road ground at Aylestone was opened. The road was *not* named after the famous cricketing doctor of Gloucestershire, but it is a pleasing coincidence that it should have become the site of the county cricket ground. Even so, it was felt to be too far out of the city by the end of the century, when a ground in Aylestone Road came into use and remained the county ground until 1939. After the war, the game moved back to Grace Road.

Leicestershire cricket has only recently reached the top rank among the English counties, but it has had many moments of glory throughout its history, and given a great deal of pleasure to thousands of people. Among its finest hours were those in the early years of this century, when the opening batsman C. J. B. Wood carried his bat through both innings against Yorkshire, getting a hundred in each—a record that stood until recent years when it was equalled by another Leicestershire opening bat, Maurice Hallam; or when S. Coe, a left-handed all-rounder from Earl Shilton, made the club's highest individual score of 252 not out. 'Sammy' Coe became the club's official scorer in 1931, and twenty years later was still as well known to many of the county's supporters as the players themselves.

W. E. Astill and George Geary both played for England. Ewart Astill was an all-rounder who became the county's first professional captain for a season in 1935. Geary was a medium-pace bowler from Barwell, who once took all ten wickets against Glamorgan. He retired from county cricket to become the coach at Charterhouse School, and once told a friend there that he was going to show him a future England player in the nets. The boy concerned was only fourteen then, and his name was Peter May.

The heroes of my young days were Maurice Tompkin and Jack Walsh. Tompkin came from Countesthorpe, and was a batsman of rare power favouring the driving shots. His straight drives to the boundary off fast bowlers were a joy to behold. In years when England's batting was strong, he never quite achieved the consistency needed to play for his country, until the winter of 1955-6 when he toured Pakistan with the MCC, but in September 1956, when only thirty-nine, he died suddenly. It was a great tragedy for Leicestershire cricket.

A small county such as Leicestershire had little hope of producing sufficient native cricketers to maintain a first-class county side, and Jack Walsh and Vic Jackson were Australians who played for Leicestershire after the war and formed a devastating spin-bowling partnership. Walsh was undoubtedly one of the finest left-handed googly bowlers the game has ever seen. Many were the occasions when his schoolboy admirers were delirious with joy as he bowled ball after ball to batsmen of the calibre of Bradman, Hutton and Compton and had them floundering helplessly like weekend amateurs.

A later import into the county was C. H. Palmer, who came from Worcestershire to captain the side, and in 1953 took it to joint third in the county championship—then the highest position in its history. Palmer once put himself on to bowl one over against Surrey, so that his two previous bowlers could change ends, but he carried on to take eight wickets for seven runs himself. The county has recently realized a new strength in one-day matches, under the former England captain, Yorkshireman Ray Illingworth, and in 1975 won the county championship for the first time. Native players of recent years have included M. J. K. Smith, of Hinckley, who transferred to Warwickshire and has played for England at both cricket and rugby football.

The Leicester Rugby Football Club, nicknamed 'The Tigers' like the county regiment, was formed in 1884, when the former Leicester Football Club, which organized both rugger and soccer, split itself into two separate clubs. The new rugby ground in Welford Road was soon claimed to be second only to Twickenham, and some international matches were staged there. The Tigers won the Midland Counties Cup eleven times between 1898 and 1913, establishing themselves as a side to be reckoned with, and in 1931 a combined Leicestershire and East Midlands team were the only side in Britain to beat the South African 'Springboks'. The Tigers' annual match against the Barbarians at Christmas is an important local event.

Twelve men were summonsed at Oadby in 1592 for playing football on a Sunday, and this is the first mention of the game in the county. (The case was dismissed.) The association football half of the 1884 split called itself the Leicester Fosse Club, later to become the Leicester City Football Club. Among its early financial supporters was a local draper, Joseph Johnson, who guaranteed the rent of the club's new ground at Filbert Street.

Leicester were promoted to the First Division of the Football League in 1907. The Club's fortunes have been mixed, but not a little of its success has been due to fine goalkeepers like Gordon Banks and Peter Shilton. The goalkeeper at the time of the club's entry to the first division was H. P. Bailey, who also played for Wales and was a county cricketer to boot. Another Welsh international was City's post-war right-winger Mal Griffith, who was an early and superb exponent of the art of running round one side of an opponent whilst curving the ball round the other side and meeting it behind his back. One of his team-mates was Don Revie. Leicester City were runners-up in the League Championship in 1929, and have reached the Cup Final three times, but have never won either prize so far.

One subject which is studiously ignored by the many learned professors who have written about Leicester is its reputation for having more pretty girls than other towns of its size. This seemingly flippant and unscientific claim, incapable of proof, may not be quite as frivolous as it sounds. If the general prosperity of Leicester ensures that its girls are well fed and well dressed, their racial heredity keeps them generally dark and petite – less likely to become fat, for instance, than women in the north, and without that inclination to look pale and under-nourished that characterizes the people of many factory communities. During their lunch hours in the summer, the girls of Leicester come out to sun themselves in the parks; in Castle Gardens; in Town Hall Square – anywhere they can find a few feet of grass – and it is easy to accept at such times that Leicester is unusually well endowed with glamour. Local country folk might have called them 'frem gells' at one time, 'frem' being a colloquialism for bonny or thriving. Do they share that curious preference for blue underwear which has been attributed to Midland women? Even if it is true, I doubt that any particular significance can be attached to what is probably no more than a regional accident. According to American market researchers, it is men who are strongly attracted to blue merchandise, but if that is true of England, it would imply that it is the men who purchase their wives' and girl-friends' lingerie, and *that*, in Leicester of all places, I do not believe!

What statistics *can* prove is a record of more dubious advantage, not necessarily connected with the foregoing. Since the Second World War, Leicester has had a consistently high illegitimate birth rate, usually about 10 per cent above the national average. The Registrar-General's figures for 1973 also show an unusually high proportion of legally induced abortions on girls under sixteen. Perhaps these facts are among the penalties for a community which has pursued material well-being but remained indifferent to life's deeper needs, although, here again, there is a suggestion that Midland women are inclined to hold more advanced views on sex than elsewhere.

Another social problem experienced by the city recently has

been the growing size of its coloured immigrant population, although – in spite of one or two alarms – it has handled the matter very well. The number of Ugandan Asians who came to Leicester in 1973, when the city was widely reported to be "unable to cope with any more", was less than had been expected, and those who did come settled in well. The Indian and Pakistani communities who have made the Belgrave Road area theirs, with their own shops and cinemas, have brought an element of colour and variety to Leicester that is preferable to what it replaced – shady old properties like the Blinking Owl public house, where the entertainment provided was reputedly enough to make more than the owl blink.

Nevertheless, although Leicester's unemployment figure is usually well below the national average, it had reached an all-time record for the city early in 1975, and the Community Relations Officer, reporting "strained relations", said that "with present attitudes towards immigrants in the city and the economic situation, the climate is not right for more Asians to come here to live". Such outbreaks of violence as do occur among young people are more likely to involve hot-tempered West Indians than the Asian immigrants, many of whom save enough money to move out of the concentrated 'coloured' areas like Spinney Hills. They then cause anxiety to the older residents among whom they go to live. The problems are such as only time will solve, but Leicester is controlling the situation very successfully compared with some other large towns.

Meanwhile, the city bravely continues to tear out whole areas of its older parts to provide new housing and better roads. It was one of the first cities in the country to create its own Planning Department, and it has visualized a new city centre which will – by the end of the century – have elevated pedestrian walkways and a monorail system of public transport. Already, along with flyovers, underpasses and traffic-free shopping areas, it has escalators and bridges that take pedestrians across the roads and into the shops. Its first multi-storey car park, at Lee Circle, was a major contribution towards solving the parking problem many years ago. Traffic wardens rose to prominence here, too. The Chief Constable of Leicester, when traffic wardens were established as an efficient and accepted part of city life, advocated their use on point duty to relieve the police for more important tasks, long before this principle was finally sanctioned by the

The monument to Lady Charlotte Finch
in Burley-on-the-Hill church

The butter market and stocks at
Oakham

Christianity – the church doorway at Pickworth

Paganism – the turf maze at Wing

The parish church at Melton Mowbray

The Wolds – farmland near Harston

The Wreake Valley – looking towards Ratcliffe

Belvoir Castle

The Quorn Hunt at Kirby Gate

Laying back a
hawthorn hedge

A good example o
'pleaching'

Home Office. He subsequently became the Commissioner of Metropolitan Police, Sir Robert Mark.

What I take to be one of the more impressive and acceptable examples of modern architecture in Leicester became a centre of fierce and lasting controversy early in 1975. A pair of curving air-conditioned skyscraper buildings, designed by Newman Levinson and Partners, was built at the city-centre end of New Walk, in Welford Place, and called the New Walk Centre. It added to the unoccupied office accommodation of which property developers had given Leicester more than enough. The City Council, in need of a building in which they could gather their widely scattered departments under one roof, announced that they were considering the purchase of the New Walk Centre, for a figure of five and a quarter million pounds, as a Civic Centre.

Immediately, it seemed, all hell broke loose. Irate citizens wrote to the *Leicester Mercury* deploring the "most disgraceful waste of public money this city has ever experienced", and pointing out that "impoverished ratepayers don't want a more luxurious Treasurer's Department – they want lower rates". So great was the outcry that the *Leicester Mercury*, gleefully conducting an emotional front-page debate, organized its own referendum, in which 30,000 people voted. Ninety-seven per cent of them, predictably, said "No" to the scheme. The newspaper, omitting to point out that there were at least 150,000 eligible citizens who had *not* voted, presumably because they were not sufficiently outraged by the idea, called on the Council to "heed the voice of the people". But negotiations between the Council and the developers were already well advanced, and the deal was completed in June 1975.

Professor Jack Simmons has described the New Walk Centre as "an agony" and said that concrete does not belong in a red-brick city like Leicester. But Leicester, for better or worse, is changing fast, and casting aside that rather silly old motto, which never did it much credit anyway. I am far from being a lover of concrete, but it seems to me that the material has been well used in the New Walk Centre, and that, in the long run, it made good sense for the Council to purchase it. Another ultra-modern building worth seeing, of a totally different kind, is the new Catholic Church of St Joseph in Uppingham Road.

It is always the case, of course, that the older generations do not take kindly to change, and many of the senior citizens living outside Leicester or on its fringes no longer come into the city centre as they used to. But change (and the illusion, at least, of progress) is necessary to the nature of younger humanity, or its life becomes meaningless. One of the city's social workers I spoke to deplored the apparent indifference shown towards the feelings of the old people here, who are disturbed by change, by rowdyism and by the coloured population, and whom she felt were being neglected by the powers-that-be in their greater concern for 'progress' and the young. I doubt that Leicester is worse than anywhere else in this respect, though. It is one of the major problems of civilized society we have yet to solve.

Those who prefer the old static image of Leicester can find it again just down the road, where the vast Welford Road Cemetery lies near the Royal Infirmary and the prison in a sort of eternal triangle of disease, degradation and death. The cemetery was originally intended as a Nonconformist burial ground, but there was some local opposition to this, too, and it was opened as a general cemetery in 1849.

A foggy morning in November is the best time to visit this place, when stone crosses and angels loom up out of the mist as you progress through the seemingly endless maze of memorials. Protestations of everlasting memory on the headstones are belied by the neglected graves before them, overgrown with grass and weeds, and blackened by smoke from the adjacent railway. An occasional jam jar or milk bottle holds a few wilting chrysan-themums or some other desperate glimpse of life in this immense monument to decay. The fog blanketing the sound of traffic can make it seem as if the world stands still in respectful silence when a burial is taking place there, but just as the vicar is commending the departed soul to Heaven, a train thunders past and carries it off, as it were, second-class to St Pancras, stopping at Market Harborough, Kettering, Wellingborough, Bedford and Luton.

That is the direction we will take now, leaving Leicester by the south-east, to look at that part of the county which remains the most rural and least affected by the changes of modern times, seemingly heavenly after the noise and bustle of one of the twelve biggest cities in Britain.

IV

WHERE SHEEP MAY SAFELY GRAZE

NOTHING provides a greater contrast in the Leicestershire scene than leaving the centre of Leicester by the London Road and going, within a few minutes, from a noisy concrete jungle into a lazy landscape of fields full of grazing sheep and cattle, and ash trees shimmering in the breeze. It prompts us at once to reflect on the astonishing statistic that roughly half the entire population of the county is concentrated in Leicester itself – that is, in the town and those immediately surrounding villages which, over the years, the ravenous city has crept up on and swallowed whole, including Glenfield, Braunstone, Aylestone, Wigston, Oadby, Evington and Birs all. Add to that the fact that a third of the remaining people are accounted for by Hinckley and Lough-borough alone, and it becomes clear that the sparsely populated eastern half of the county is indeed a rural paradise in which human beings are outnumbered by sheep.

It is estimated that there were half a million sheep in Leicestershire in 1870, with 60 per cent of the farmland permanently used for grazing. The vast majority of this land was in the eastern half of the county. From then until the Second World War, the amount of permanent grassland increased, although the number of sheep was gradually reduced to half the 1870 figure, giving way to a rise in the number of cattle. The war itself created an urgent need for food production and led to a dramatic increase in the land used for tillage, but half the farmland in Leicestershire is still permanent grass, supporting roughly equal numbers of sheep and cattle.

The affinities of this south-eastern area seem to belong much more to rural Northamptonshire than to other parts of Leicester-shire, not only in the appearance of the landscape, but also in the style of the houses, built of warm and mellow local ironstone, often with thatched roofs, or with tiles from Colly Weston.

The old county's most attractive villages are clustered

together in this south-east corner, near Market Harborough, and one only has to drive through them to wonder why it is that pictures of Leicestershire so rarely – if ever – appear in those calendars and books which celebrate rural England in glorious and exaggerated colour. The answer seems to be that none of the major trunk roads interferes with this peaceful corner of the county. Photographers travelling in the Midlands pass through Leicestershire on the western side, on the motorway or Watling Street, and hastily dismiss it as a flat, red-brick county of no pictorial interest, before pressing on towards Derbyshire or Shropshire. Leicestershire thus misses its share of glory, but is perhaps content to be left alone.

The prettiest of all the villages of Leicestershire is, by general consent, Hallaton, although its rustic attractions have touches of the bizarre about them here and there. The triangular village green, surrounded by thatched stone cottages, sports a strange circular 'market cross' in the shape of a cone, which it is tempting to describe as a phallic symbol. The village is the scene of a ridiculous ritual which has taken place on Easter Monday each year since 1770, and has its origins in some earlier pagan custom. It is known as Hare-Pie Scrambling. The rector is obliged by tradition to provide two 'hare' pies, bread and ale for the occasion, and to carve the pies in an open-air ceremony, when the portions are put in a sack, prior to a procession to church accompanied by a band. As if to add to the slightly sinister undertones of the proceedings, local friendly societies, such as the Loyal Farmers' Delight Lodge of Oddfellows, are officially involved.

The actual scrambling takes place after lunch on Hare Pie Hill, near the village, where the menfolk join in an uncouth scramble for a piece of the pie – a scene that has to be witnessed to be believed. This is followed by the Bottle Kicking routine, in which wooden casks containing the rector's ale are used as footballs by a Hallaton team and their traditional rivals from neighbouring Medbourne, the object being to get the casks across the village stream. It used to be part of the tradition that Hallaton should always win, but the men from Medbourne, no doubt tired of being the stooges in the affair, began playing to win, and still do so. When the game is won, the frothy ale is taken to be drunk at the market cross.

Even an unflinching atheist can feel a little sympathy for the rector of Hallaton ('Hallowed town'?) who has to follow his Easter Day services with participation in these weird customs. One rector who expressed his distaste for the ritual and refused to provide the pies found the village plastered with notices saying "No Pie, no Parson". But perhaps sympathy is misplaced for most of them, in this county of sporting parsons. It was, after all, a rector of Hallaton who, when asked to pray for rain, agreed to do so, but added that "it's no damned good with the wind in this quarter".

Even the old church clock mechanism seems to contribute to the ritualistic extravagance of the village, as it puts the weary bells into action to play a tune every three hours, day and night. There is a local rhyme to go with it:

> Old Dunmore's dead, that good old man,
> Him we shall no more see.
> He made these chimes to play themselves
> At twelve, nine, six and three!

The clock does not go backwards, as the rhyme implies, though it would be no great shock if it did, in this place.

On the other hand, it is hardly surprising, either, that this part of Leicestershire should harbour survivals of primitive practices and folklore. Three Saxon coffin-lids displayed at Hallaton Church stand as testimony to its ancient origins, and it is the area which has changed least over the centuries.

All the same, it may tax the imagination to stand in the village of Husbands Bosworth today and recall that nine local women were tried for witchcraft in 1616. A boy of about twelve, named Smythe, was thought to be bewitched. He went into violent fits, striking himself repeatedly and making animal noises. He accused the women of making the spirits of animals enter his body, and they were all found guilty of witchcraft and burnt at the stake. But the boy's fits (naturally) continued, and a few months later six more women were accused and condemned to death. It is said that it was only through the intervention of King James himself that these women were not executed also, the King having seen the boy and recognized his epilepsy. At any rate, five of them were set free, the sixth being already "ded in the gayle".

One wonders if the village population of 1755 was led to

ponder the relations between Christianity and superstition, when lightning struck the church steeple one Sabbath evening, splitting it open for thirty feet of its length and hurling huge stones on to a grave which had only just been filled in after a burial.

Great Glen and Burton Overy were the scenes of another witch-hunt in 1760, when various women were ducked, in that idiotic belief that those who sank were innocent and those who floated guilty, so that suspects suffered either way and the 'innocent' sometimes died, as well as the 'guilty'. On this occasion, two other women were made to stand in the pillory for accusing them falsely.

Among other attractive villages in this area are Great Easton, Glooston and Gumley and the modern and exclusive 'model' village of Horninghold. Many of the villages are still linked by field-paths and gated roads which did not become public at the time of the enclosures in the eighteenth century, because they were used too little to justify being taken over, and these remain as pleasant routes for the explorer on foot, who is rarely out of sight of a distant church steeple with a typical broach spire. Sometimes one sees a field where the old strips of the open-field system are still clearly visible.

A relatively new feature of the landscape which is perhaps more of an eyesore in the rural eastern half of the county, is the scar across its face caused by the slashing scalpel of that zealous surgeon of the early 1960s, Doctor Richard Beeching. Cuttings and embankments now wind through the countryside like mysterious prehistoric earthworks, but occasionally these, too, can make interesting walking routes.

Gumley Hall was the home of Joseph Cradock, who was that rare being, a country gentleman interested more in culture than in sport. His father had defied popular opinion in Leicester by having his son inoculated against smallpox, and young Joseph thrived, and came into a fortune when his father died. He went to London and became a man of fashion, indulged his passion for the arts, and became a friend of Garrick and other celebrities of the day.

David Garrick visited Gumley, and it may be that Johnson did too, although the excellent Squire Cradock recorded that whenever the possibility of such a visit was mentioned to his wife, Mrs Cradock replied that she only wished to be certain of

Dr Johnson's near approach, as "that would be a sufficient signal for her to retreat to Merevale". A sensible woman, I fancy.

Cradock spent so lavishly that eventually he had to sell his library and give up his home, and for the twenty years before his death he was an invalid. He told a friend that he had entertained "two of the most absurd notions in the world: the one was that independence was honourable: the other that literature was its own reward". But it was said of him that he was "respected by people of all parties for his worth, and idolised by the poor for his benevolence".

Gumley and Foxton have been famous for centuries for their fox earths, and the latter village got its name from the fact. (Although 'Fox' is a surname widespread throughout England, the older survival 'Foxon' is particularly common in Leicestershire.) Between these two villages there is a hill which obstructed the route of the Leicestershire and Northamptonshire Union Canal, which was first proposed in 1793 to link the River Soar near Leicester with the Grand Junction Canal near Northampton, and thus to provide navigable waterways from the Trent to London. Construction of the canal had begun in the following year, but had been held up, mainly because local landowners fought a vigorous campaign against the proposed route, convincing villagers that damp and fog would kill the elderly inhabitants, and alarming them about the behaviour of the 'navvies' who were carrying out the work.

Eventually the company was forced to make a diversion and build the half-mile-long Fleckney tunnel, and the high cost of this, together with the necessity of building another tunnel through the hill between Foxton and Gumley, again brought the work to a halt, this time for thirteen years. The village of Fleckney is a dreary industrial place which looks as if it had broken from its moorings and drifted into waters where it does not belong, but it was here that the well-known Wolsey Company had originated.

Work on the canal was resumed in 1810 by the newly formed Grand Union Canal Company, and by that time the great engineer Telford had suggested a means of avoiding a tunnel at Foxton, by building instead an ambitious flight of locks, which became one of the engineering triumphs of the period. Ten locks, in two ranks of five, lifted the canal over the hill by raising the water level 75 feet, and a narrow-boat and butty could negotiate the locks in about three-quarters of an hour. The chief cargo was coal, going from the Midland coalfields to London, but granite was also carried, from Mountsorrel, and in the opposite direction there was regular transportation of chemicals to Boots at Nottingham.

At the turn of the century an inclined plane was built, to replace the locks by speeding up the passage of the vessels. Boats were hauled up a ramp in movable docks, and the lift could be completed in twelve minutes. But operating costs were high, and the lift frequently broke down, so it was abandoned in 1911, and dismantled in 1927.

By this time, competition from the railways was rapidly reducing the usefulness of the canals. Forty thousand tons of traffic passed through Foxton Locks in 1911, but ten years later this had dwindled to eight thousand tons, and by the end of the Second World War the canal was practically redundant. It has been kept open as a waterway for pleasure boats, however, and the Foxton Staircase is still one of the county's popular summer attractions. Walking along the towpaths of the canals in Leicestershire is one sure way of enjoying the country without interference from traffic, and every so often one comes to an attractive little bridge, built for the benefit of the farmers whose land the canals cross.

At the foot of Foxton Locks, a branch canal runs to Market Harborough, which long ago replaced Hallaton as the economic capital of south-east Leicestershire. It was an important staging post for coaches travelling between London and the north, and the A6 passing through it today is the only trunk road through this part of the county. The wide main street immediately impresses the visitor with its aura of the old market town, and the Three Swans Hotel, with a long stabling yard at the rear, sports a fine wrought-iron inn-sign made in the eighteenth century. The Angel and Peacock Hotels also add to the pleasant atmosphere of the town, which provides at least one of Leicestershire's best eating-places.

The Angel used to be a stopping-place for the Royal Mail coach, where ostlers would hurriedly change the horses which had brought the coach from Leicester by nine o'clock in the morning, and with a great clattering of hooves and grinding of wheels on the cobbled yard, send the fresh team on their part of the fast gallop towards London.

The state of the roads in those days was notorious. A traveller from Berlin wrote that he would remember a post-coach journey from Leicester to Northampton in 1782, as long as he lived. As the coach was full at Leicester, he had to travel on top, and said: "The getting up alone was at the risk of one's life", and, "the moment that we set off, I fancied I saw certain death await me". He went on: "Every moment we seemed to fly into the air; so that it was almost a miracle that we still stuck to the coach and did not fall off". The poor fellow was almost a nervous wreck by the time the coach reached Harborough.

Market Harborough became a market town in the early years of the thirteenth century, and its church, the steeple of which is the town's architectural glory, was dedicated to Saint Dionysius, the Scythian monk who worked out the system of reckoning the Christian era which we are stuck with, even though it was wrong. The steeple consists of a Decorated tower surmounted by a tall broach spire, built of grey limestone, and of such splendid proportions that Pevsner has called it "one of the finest in England".

In the little square beside the church stands a unique structure, the old Grammar School. This quaint building was founded by Robert Smythe, a wealthy native, in 1614. It is of timber-framed construction, with arches and pillars of oak, resting on stone piers and supporting the upper floor. This was the schoolroom, and the shady open space below it was used as a butter market. The building was restored in 1868, but we can still imagine it in Stuart times, with the women gossiping there on market days, and the boys studying Latin above, though surely finding it hard to concentrate with all that 'canking' going on below.

It was from Market Harborough that Cromwell sent his despatch to the Speaker announcing the total defeat of the royalist army at Naseby, after a battle lasting three hours. The New Model Army took five thousand prisoners, and the king fled to Leicester. Charles passed through Market Harborough again, later, on his way to his trial and execution. Since then, the town has gone quietly about its business, providing meat, making corsets, agricultural machinery and soups, and growing mushrooms. It is also the capital of the Fernie Hunt country, the kennels of which are at Great Bowden, a village close to the town.

Market Harborough always seems to me to retain a warmth of character that many other old market towns have lost long ago. Its streets and buildings, though marred to some extent by factories, shop-fronts and other modern intrusions, always hold the promise of large open fires on cold winter days, and it can be a bright and cheerful haven for the weary traveller today, just as it was centuries ago.

One of the few jarring notes in the peaceful rural landscape of the area is Gartree Prison, just outside Market Harborough. It was built on the site of a disused airfield which had been a bomber base during the war. Opened in 1966, the establishment was originally a closed prison, built on the new H-plan principle, but its purpose has now been changed to that of a dispersal unit for medium-sentence prisoners. It accommodates nearly 300 men.

Lutterworth, almost at the point of Leicestershire's heart-shape, is notable only for the fact that Wycliffe was rector here, under the protection of John of Gaunt, for the last few years of his life. He was a Yorkshireman, but his most important work was done during his years at Lutterworth. His outspoken opposition to papal abuses was bad enough from the Church's point of view, but when he attacked the doctrine of Transubstantiation his heresy got him expelled from his teaching post at Oxford. Then, what was even worse, he instigated the translation of the Bible into English, making it available to anyone who could read, and thus destroying the tyranny of Latin, exercised by the Church in exploiting the public ignorance.

Wycliffe died suddenly in 1384 and was buried in his church, but in 1428 the Council of Constance excommunicated him and ordered that his body should be taken up and burnt, "to the damnation and destruction of his memory". His ashes were thrown into the little River Swift, whence, as his sympathizers observed, they were carried as an emblem of his doctrine via the Avon and the Severn into the sea, and "dispersed the world over". But the furnishings in Lutterworth Church became the objects of precisely that veneration of relics which Wycliffe had attacked, and I dare say American visitors still come out of the church believing they have touched Wycliffe's chair and his pulpit!

Wycliffe's supporters, known as Lollards, became concentrated among the poor people of the Midland counties, and they were persecuted, and many burnt at the stake, until Lollardry was absorbed into Protestantism at the Reformation. The importance of this movement in Leicestershire can scarcely be estimated, for Leicester itself was, along with Oxford, the cradle of Lollardry. Why it should have become so is far from clear, but its rapid growth as "the metropolis of heresy" was due in no small part to the preaching of William Swinderby, known as "the Hermit" because he lived (for security) in Leicester Forest. He enjoyed the hospitality at one time of Leicester Abbey, where one of the canons, Philip Repton, was an early convert to Wycliffe's doctrines. Repton subsequently recanted, however, and in due course became Abbot of St Mary's and Bishop of Lincoln. Swinderby was called to appear before an ecclesiastical court at Lyddington, in Rutland, but failed to attend. Then when the outraged friars of Leicester called for his death, he, too, recanted, not being the stuff that martyrs are made of, but he evidently continued to preach, and through his influence the impact of Wycliffe was felt in many of the towns and villages of Leicestershire, while the city itself was set on its long course of leadership in religious dissent.

The tower of Lutterworth Church originally bore a spire, which collapsed in fierce gales in 1712 and was never replaced. If the spire had not already been removed by the wind, it might have been removed by an earthquake which occurred one Sunday morning early in the autumn of 1750, during divine service. It was felt over a wide area of the south-east quarter of the county, from Leicester and Narborough down to Lutterworth and Market Harborough, and including Hungarton, Noseley, Stonton Wyville and Rolleston. It caused great fear and some panic everywhere, with a sound like overhead thunder. At Narborough Church, the congregation fled, leaving the vicar alone in the pulpit, vainly calling for them to come back. Faith is no substitute for self-preservation when the roof is falling in.

The most southerly tip of the county is guarded by the villages of Catthorpe and Swinford, now separated by the M1 and M6 motorways as they streak through the county like an angry two-headed viper. Swinford has a story of an eccentric parson worth telling. He was so strict that he used to lock his servants in the house in the evening to prevent them from getting into mischief. Worse still, he chained a dog to each of his apple trees to prevent 'scrumping' by local children. One morning, he went out early to release his dogs, leaving the servants still locked up, but the excitement of his fifty-eight dogs caused him to fall into his pond and as no one could get out to rescue him, he drowned.

On the border of the county, east of Swinford, is Stanford Hall, a fine house built at the end of the seventeenth century by Sir Thomas Cave, whose notes on local history contributed to Nichols' mammoth work. It was in the grounds of Stanford that Percy Pilcher, one of the pioneers of flying, took off on his fatal demonstration of his flying machine. Stanford village is over the border in Northamptonshire, separated from the hall and its park by the River Avon.

Of the two villages of Peatling Magna and Peatling Parva, the latter is now ironically the larger, but the thirteenth-century church of All Saints in Peatling Magna is the more interesting, containing monuments to the Jervis family. One of them, christened Elizabeth in this church, became the second wife of Dr Johnson; the famous 'Tetty' whom he adored, notwithstanding that she was twice his age and very ugly, according to Garrick. Johnson was too short-sighted to see her properly; not that he was a handsome figure himself!

Nearby, Willoughby Waterleys is sometimes called 'Waterless' (absurdly since it stands between two arms of the Whetstone Brook). This interesting village is worth seeing for some fine houses of red brick built in the eighteenth century, and there are other good brick houses in the Welland valley, probably built by prosperous farmers.

A group of villages in the open unspoilt country north of Market Harborough is known as the Langtons, and consists of Church Langton, East Langton, West Langton, Thorpe Langton and Tur Langton. The 'metropolis' of the group is Church Langton, and the church there, with its lofty tower, has had two rectors of note. One was Polydore Vergil, the Italian historian, who came to this country at the bidding of the Pope, stayed for twenty-eight years and wrote a history of England. He was a friend of Erasmus and Sir Thomas More, and an enemy of Wolsey, who imprisoned Vergil for calling him ambitious!

The second notable rector of Church Langton was himself ambitious, and made no secret of it. He was the Reverend William Hanbury, whose ruling passions were music and horticulture. In 1759 he organized a great music festival at Church Langton, for which a London orchestra was hired. Every spare bed in Market Harborough and the surrounding villages was taken by the multitude of visitors, and the Duke of Devonshire had to spend the night in a local tradesman's house. Ham pies a yard in diameter were made for the occasion, and prices rocketed. And the purpose of all these goings-on was to publicize the rector's views on the planting of trees and shrubs, and to advertise the plants available in his nurseries. He fondly believed he was going to make a fortune, out of which he would build a library, a hospital, a picture gallery and heaven knows what else. Perhaps it was fortunate for Church Langton, and indeed for all this quiet corner of Leicestershire, that these extravagant plans never came to pass. The only hint of such wild ambition in the village today is the surviving Georgian rectory, which was built by Hanbury's son. The churches of the Langtons are of the warm local ironstone one sees everywhere in this area – except, that is, for the one at Tur Langton, which is a more modern building of red brick. It comes as a surprise if one visits the other Langtons first.

At the extreme south-east corner of the county, between Medbourne and the Eye Brook, there was once a village called Holt, which was deserted we know not when or why. It was on high ground overlooking the peaceful valley of the Welland and the Northamptonshire countryside beyond. Little is left now but a few houses and a mansion which is joined to the village church, standing in a park. Because it was owned and enlarged by the Nevill family, the place became known as Nevill Holt. In the eighteenth century, it enjoyed a brief reputation as a spa, and a Doctor Short from Sheffield catalogued some of the sick who attributed cures to the medicinal waters there:

A worthy young lady of thin habit and hectic disposition, having been some years married, etc.

The effect this water had on a clergyman's lady was really wonderful, etc.

A young gentleman, whether from a venereal affair or being run through the body in a Rencounter, or both, etc.

The mind boggles! A modern advertising copywriter would be hard put to improve on these typically vague inflations of the brand image. Despite these outrageous testimonials, or possibly because of them, Nevill Holt water did not work its magic for long.

Later the Hall was owned for nearly forty years by the Cunard family, but in 1919 the estate was sold, and the Hall was bought by Rev. C. A. C. Bowlker for a preparatory school. The establishment is closely associated with Uppingham School, and accommodates about ninety boys, twice the population of the remaining village. The church can be visited, and it contains memorials to Sir Thomas Nevill and his daughter Jane.

Not far from Nevill Holt, the Roman road, known now as Gartree Road, passed by on its way to Leicester. It is sometimes referred to as the Via Devana, but the authority for such a name is very doubtful. However, if we follow its route we come eventually to a place called Great Stretton, where a diminutive church, once at the centre of a village, remains in a field. Fifteen families lived here in Elizabethan times, but the village was gradually deserted and the church began to fall into ruin. It was repaired in the nineteenth century, and now stands a lonely sentinel over the buried foundations of the houses which once surrounded it. Great as Great Stretton undoubtedly was, Little Stretton is now the greater.

The neighbouring villages of Galby and Kings Norton, standing in beautiful unspoilt country, are also interesting mainly for their churches. The one at Galby, which was restored in 1960, has a tower built in 1741 by John Wing of Leicester, and it is surmounted by four eccentric pinnacles like Chinese pagodas, each one bearing a weather-vane. When I last saw them, they were all pointing in different directions, subject to a breeze that passeth all understanding.

The church of St John the Baptist at Kings Norton is altogether different. This one was built by Wing's son, and is a restrained expression of the Gothic Revival, both inside and out. The tower originally bore a spire, but it was struck by lightning in 1850, and crashed down, destroying the original font. This is a village church with all the dignity and imposing appearance of a great cathedral.

There are numerous lost village sites in this area, and one of them, Hamilton, is in flat, open countryside not five miles from the centre of Leicester, just north of Scraptoft. Another, Ingarsby, lies beside the road from Houghton-on-the-Hill to Hungarton. Professor Hoskins, the leading expert on Leicestershire's lost villages, has described Ingarsby as the best site of its kind in the county, and indeed the high, uneven fields that mark its position do make its layout easier to trace than many other sites which can only be seen clearly from the air. Ingarsby was founded by the Danish settlers in the ninth or tenth century, and was a village of considerable size. Once it had a castle, and an ancient road from Stamford to Leicester passed through the village. Eventually it became the property of Leicester Abbey, and was enclosed for pasture land in 1469 and depopulated. Perhaps the Black Death had already reduced its inhabitants drastically, making the task easier. Cattle now graze over the foundations of the houses and the courses of the village streets. It cannot be said that humans were always on the winning side in the fight for living space. Sometimes, as at Ingarsby, the animals won.

There used to be a little railway station at Ingarsby, serving the surrounding villages, on the only line to cross the area of High Leicestershire between Market Harborough and Melton Mowbray. A signpost still points to it, but neither line nor station is any longer there, and a station building converted to a private house is all that Ingarsby has to show of its long history, apart from its old hall, perhaps built originally as a bailiff's house.

Another lost village is Wistow, which lay a little to the north of Fleckney. Only the church and the hall survive here. Wistow Hall was the home of the Halford family, whose monuments adorn the church. Sir Richard Halford supported Charles I and received the king at Wistow the night before Naseby, which cost him dear when Cromwell won. At length the estate passed by marriage to one of the Leicester Vaughan family, Sir Henry, who changed his name to Halford by Act of Parliament. Sir Henry was President of the College of Physicians for twenty-four years, and attended four successive monarchs, George III and IV, William IV and Victoria. His first royal patient called the physician an "infamous scoundrel" when Halford tried to disabuse the mad monarch of his notion that he (the king) was married to Lady Pembroke, who was in fact his mistress of long standing. Such delusions led Halford to advocate – among other things – sitting the king in a warm bath and pouring cold water on his head, a procedure approximating to that which the Chinese had discovered centuries earlier and found to be very effective in sending men mad! Whether oriental inquisitors were wiser than Western physicians is a nice point, but even nicer is the question whether Halford might have done better to stick needles in his patient, like oriental physicians.

From Hungarton, a long drive reaches Quenby Hall, one of the finest architectural treasures to have eluded the county's conscientious demolition experts. It is a splendid Jacobean mansion of red brick, with mullioned and transomed windows, built about 1620 by the Ashby family on high ground overlooking the undulating countryside around it. In more recent years it was owned by Sir Harold Nutting, who was Master of the Quorn Hunt from 1930 to 1940, and Quenby is still a favourite meeting place for the Quorn. The house is now the property of the Squire de Lisle. The fine wrought-iron gates originally belonging to Quenby Hall, which were presented by Shuckburgh Ashby to Leicester Infirmary, now grace the grounds of the Newarke Houses Museum in Leicester. The former village of Quenby was depopulated, as well as that at Lowesby nearby, probably by the Ashby family to enlarge their estate. At Lowesby, only the church and hall remain. Lowesby Hall is a fine Georgian mansion of red brick, much altered in the early years of this century.

Travelling through this countryside further east, one comes to Leicestershire's highest village, Tilton-on-the-Hill, 700 feet above sea level. Its little church is charming. It contains work of various periods, the oldest parts being late twelfth century. Large clerestory windows give to the interior an unusual degree of light, and both inside and outside there are stone carvings of human heads and animals, including some interesting gargoyles. Inside are some impressive monuments to members of the Digby family buried there.

It is but a short distance from Tilton to the lovely valley which houses Launde, very close to the former Rutland border. One passes between two hills, one of which is Whatborough Hill – the highest point in the eastern half of Leicestershire – and the other bearing the curious name of Robin-a-Tiptoe. Whatborough Hill used to have a village on its flat top, but not a stone is left. The reason for its desertion is uncertain, but probably its exposed site made it inhospitable and the people gradually moved elsewhere. They are fond of telling you, in the southern parts of Leicestershire (as if proud of their misfortune), that the winds blowing here come unimpeded from the Urals in Siberia, and it is true, I believe, that if you travel east from Whatborough Hill you will not reach higher ground until you come to the borders of Asia. It is not surprising, therefore, that the wind was harnessed to provide power in this area, as in East Anglia, and a few of the old windmills survive here and there, in varying states of dilapidation.

"Item to remember. Myself for Launde." The note was made in his diary by Thomas Cromwell, Henry VIII's henchman in the suppression of the monasteries, when he came, saw, and coveted the Priory of Launde, standing in its own secluded little valley in one of the county's quietest parts. The name means a grassy level between woods – hence our word 'lawn'. It had been a wealthy priory for Augustinian canons, founded in 1125. The last prior considered the visiting agent of the king "a man of prying eyes and gripple hands", and sure enough, when the time came, "*Malleus monachorum*" ("the Hammer of the Monks") took the place for himself.

Cromwell did not enjoy it for long, however. He was beheaded in 1540, having served the king's purpose, and Launde then passed to his son Gregory, Lord Cromwell of Okeham, who married Jane Seymour's sister, but died without issue eleven years after acquiring Launde.

The Cromwells built out of the old priory a gabled house of stone, with crenellated bay windows, and incorporating part of the priory church. The building has been altered and restored since, but the chapel, which can be visited on application, contains a monument to Gregory Cromwell, made in local stone, which Pevsner describes as "one of the purest monuments of the early Renaissance in England".

The house is now an Anglican retreat, and retains an air of Elizabethan peacefulness far removed from the twentieth-century world a mile or two away. Approaching Launde is like taking a step back in history, and it is easy to see why Cromwell wanted it as soon as he saw it. It is a piece of England which is itself like "a precious stone set in the silver sea", and it is an appropriate spot from which to cross over into the former county of Rutland.

V

TOWARD THE UNKNOWN REGION

THE only fact about Rutland known by everyone is that it was England's smallest county. It was not, however, one of the counties established by the Danelaw, being then partly in Lincolnshire and partly in Northamptonshire. Edward the Confessor bequeathed the land known as Roteland to his wife Eadgyth, sister of Harold, who succeeded his brother-in-law. The royal owner's name is preserved in one of the county's villages, Edith Weston.

During King John's reign, Rutland became a separate county, with its capital at Oakham. The new county had a population of about three thousand. It was a totally agricultural area, and it remains so today. The only signs of industry on the horizon, as you walk or drive along its quiet roads and lanes, are the three chimneys of the Ketton cement works. The whole of the former county possessed only one set of traffic lights, even though the traffic roaring along the Great North Road, which passes through the eastern half of the area on its way between Stamford and Grantham, seems a harsh reminder of twentieth-century facts of life.

The western part of Rutland is very much a continuation of the rolling hills of east Leicestershire, and is nearly all pasture land. The River Gwash rises in these hills and flows eastward to join the Welland, which forms the southern boundary of the whole county right down to Market Harborough. The Gwash passes through the valley in which Oakham lies, called the Vale of Catmose, then runs into a flatter area where the predominant rock is oolitic limestone. The land usage then changes from grazing to arable land, and Rutland's most profitable crop, barley, is much in evidence here. The extreme east of Rutland has been one of England's best barley-producing areas for centuries. The majority of the annual crop goes to those breweries at Burton-on-Trent which supply the county with most of its beer.

Rutland is a land of scattered villages, many of them having fine churches and houses of mellow stone. The red brick and Welsh slate of west Leicestershire have fortunately not penetrated here to any great extent, though there is plenty of it in Oakham, and in odd villages like Langham and Whissendine, which seem strangely out of character. The fact is that the population of Rutland never grew at a pace which demanded an extensive and economical building programme such as happened in the rest of Leicestershire.

The proposal to absorb Rutland into Leicestershire was first made by the Parliamentary Boundaries Commission in 1961. The county immediately mounted a fiercely argued and spectacular publicity campaign against the merger which aroused local feeling to such a pitch that the Minister of Housing and Local Government overruled the Commission's recommendation. But the reprieve was to prove only temporary. The Local Government Act of 1972 laid down that Rutland was to be incorporated in Leicestershire on 1 April 1974.

The county began its fight all over again, and a Rutland M.P. asked in the House of Commons that a 'preservation order' should be put on the county. Over 85 per cent of the population were said to be opposed to the amalgamation. The Leicestershire County Council, which had maintained close administrative co-operation with Rutland for many years anyway, was anxious not to be cast in the role of a takeover bidder, and said cautiously that "the spirit of independence and cohesiveness of Rutland is worth preserving".

Soon, however, Rutland's champions found themselves arguing over a red herring – that the name of Rutland should be preserved by making it a separate administrative district within the new county – a point which the Government magnanimously conceded in its own good time. The local agitators were reduced to making emotional amendments to the old county boundary signs, adding beneath 'Rutland' such slogans as 'Rat Race Ends Here'. Anyone who knew Rutland knew this already, unless caused to doubt it by the noise of the campaign.

Just as the fire seemed about to die out, it was fanned into flame again by the Post Office, which issued a statement saying that as Rutland no longer existed, its use in addresses would render letters liable to be treated as second-class mail. Residents flew into a fury, and threatened to return, unopened, any letters addressed to them merely as 'Leicestershire'. By the time this fresh cloud of dust had settled, the amalgamation was a *fait accompli,* and Rutland sat back in its new chair and found it less uncomfortable than it had feared.

Oakham, the former capital, was a small market town in medieval times, when it passed from the possession of the crown to the Ferrers family, who built the castle there. Its weekly market dates from the reign of Henry II, and the old Market Place with its butter cross and its ancient stocks is still the centre of the town. Comparison of the growth of the separate counties of Leicestershire and Rutland throws some light on the modest development of Oakham in contrast to the explosion of Leicester's area and population. It is estimated that at the end of the seventeenth century Leicestershire's population was eighty thousand and Rutland's sixteen thousand. But a hundred years later, as manufacturing industries spread, the population of Leicestershire had leapt to a hundred and thirty thousand against Rutland's slow crawl to sixteen and a half thousand. During the next century, Leicestershire's rural population was left as a mere quarter of its total, whilst Rutland's remained as high as three-quarters. Little wonder that while Leicester's population grew about twelve-fold, Oakham's only doubled. Leicester changed, and Oakham remained the same. If Leicester had wanted to seal its new and closer relationship with Oakham by some token, it could hardly have done better than to make a present of its old motto, for which the city has no further use.

Of the twelfth-century fortified house known as Oakham Castle, only the Great Hall still exists, but like Leicester's, it is one of the finest of its kind in England. The pillars supporting its splendid Norman arcades have carved capitals so similar to those in the chancel of Canterbury Cathedral that it is assumed the same craftsman was responsible for both. Most visitors to Oakham Castle come to see the collection of horseshoes. It is a long-standing tradition that any peer of the realm passing through this little town for the first time must present a horseshoe to the Castle, and here they are hanging round the walls of the Hall – surely the most magnificent array of good luck symbols ever assembled. There are large ones and small ones, wooden ones and rusty ones, one presented by Queen Elizabeth I, and one by Queen Elizabeth II.

Those who appreciate the fine stone carving in Oakham

Castle should not miss that in All Saints' Church. The capitals in the nave are carved with all sorts of unusual figures and animals, including a fox with a goose. Here also is the Oakham Bible, written on vellum at about the time of Magna Carta. Oakham Church is a good example of the fine parish churches one finds all over Rutland, unspoiled and standing proudly over the villages of which they are the noble ambassadors. One of the oldest weather vanes in England has told Oakham men the wind direction for centuries past. Perched on top of the church's lofty spire, it is known as Cock Peter.

One native of Oakham who saw which way the wind was blowing was the infamous Titus Oates, born here in 1649. He had been a clergyman in the Church of England, but had led such a disorderly life that he had brought upon himself the condemnation of his superiors. He then professed himself a Roman Catholic, but his new church welcomed him no more warmly than his old. At this point his malignant imagination conjured up the so-called Popish Plot. The Papists were, he said, planning a massive uprising in which the king was to be assassinated, all the shipping in the Thames burnt, and the Protestants massacred. A French army was to land in Ireland and leading statesmen of the country were to be murdered.

The story was pure fantasy, but in the agitated state of relations between Protestant and Catholic at the time, it was like putting a match to petrol. The country reacted with panic, and many innocent Catholics were murdered or thrown into prisons. The psychopathic Oates, temporarily a hero among the Protestants, won their further gratitude by declaring that he had overheard the queen consent to her husband's assassination.

If Titus Oates was one of the most evil-minded Englishmen ever to draw breath, the punishments he suffered, when the nation had calmed down and brought him to trial for perjury, were among the most evil inflicted in the name of justice, and the whole episode was as shameful in its culmination as in its perpetration.

Another native of Oakham, born a few years before Oates, was Jeffery Hudson. Leicester gave birth to one of the largest men who ever lived and Oakham to one of the smallest, for Jeffery Hudson was a midget. His father worked for the Duke of Buckingham at nearby Burley-on-the-Hill, and the duchess treated the dwarf child like a pet poodle, dressing him up and showing him off to visitors.

When Charles I and Henrietta Maria came to Burley, a surprise was prepared for the royal guests. A huge cold pie was placed on the table before them at dinner, and when the pie was opened, out jumped Jeffery Hudson. At least one writer has declared absurdly that it was a "piping hot" pie. That would account for Hudson's small size – done down in the cooking, with puff pastry, no doubt, to account for his inflated self-regard! Now wasn't *that* a dainty dish to set before the king! The queen thought so, because the duchess gave Jeffrey to her, and off he went to London. It is said that at the age of nine, Hudson was only eighteen inches high, but we may take that with a pinch of salt. Portraits of him (by Van Dyck, among others) show him to have been about three feet.

At any rate, he became a popular toy at court, and compensated for his small size – typically – by developing an outsize ego, which made him enemies, one of whom he killed in a duel with pistols, Hudson being too small a target for his opponent. He was captured twice by pirates whilst crossing the Channel, and was sold as a slave in Barbary. Ransomed by his former master, the Duke of Buckingham, he returned to Oakham for a while, but then went back to London and was eventually thrown into prison, accused of being involved in the Popish Plot conjured up by Titus Oates. This remarkable little man died at the approximate age of sixty-three, and the approximate height of three feet six.

Burley-on-the-Hill, where George Villiers, the Duke of Buckingham, lived at this time, was the second house on the site. The first had been built for Sir James Harington in about 1573, and it was sold to the duke in 1620. He rebuilt it on a larger scale, and his stables were said to be "where the horses were the best accommodated in England". The house was occupied by Cromwell's troops, who burnt it down when they left. The property was then bought by Daniel Finch, the second Earl of Nottingham, who built the present house at the end of the seventeenth century, using Clipsham stone. It is the finest country house in Rutland, its north front being flanked on either side by Doric colonnades which are a copy of St Peter's in Rome.

In the grounds is one of those extraordinary (not to say weird) variations on the grotto ornament beloved of landscape gardeners of the time – a hermit's cell where a long-haired hermit, kept by the owner like a monkey in a cage, lived for some years, no doubt bringing a flutter of excitement to the earl's aristocratic female guests as they toured the gardens. The past owners of Burley evidently had a taste for the bizarre, and we have not finished with the Duke of Buckingham yet. Perhaps I should add that Burley-on-the-Hill is not open to the public, and should not be confused with Burghley House, the Marquess of Exeter's home near Stamford.

The church at Burley contains the kneeling figure of a beautiful girl. It is a memorial, full of pathos, to Lady Charlotte Finch, carved in white marble by Sir Francis Chantrey. Lady Charlotte, the great-granddaughter of the notorious Judge Jeffreys, was governess to the children of George III. We can hardly blame her for the excesses for which the Prince of Wales developed a taste, though she had charge of him in his formative years. Queen Caroline thought very highly of her.

Some writers have implied that the memorial in Burley Church is actually a statue of Lady Charlotte, and one has gone so far as to say that it is "a genuine likeness of the lovely and virtuous lady". However, she died at the age of eighty-eight, and the memorial was not made until seven years afterwards, Chantrey himself being then under forty, so we may assume that the statue is meant to represent her spirit rather than her flesh. It is none the less beautiful for that.

Proceeding further along the road leading from Oakham to Burley, we come to Cottesmore, which has given its name to one of the oldest hunts in Britain. Its kennels are now at Ashwell, a little to the west. At Ashwell Church is the grave of the first clergyman to be awarded the Victoria Cross. He was an Irish padre named Adams who, single-handed and under heavy fire, saved a number of men of the 9th Lancers from certain death in India.

The large church at Whissendine contains, in the south transept, the screen which was originally presented to St John's College, Cambridge, by Margaret Beaufort, the mother of Henry VII. It was brought here when Sir Giles Gilbert Scott built a new chapel for the college. The church at Teigh (pronounced 'tee'). has a very high pulpit over the entrance, and an odd arrangement of reading desk and clerk's desk flanking it, accessible from the tower. As only two parsons served the village from 1830 to 1914, notwithstanding the long climb to the pulpit, one supposes Teigh to be a healthy place to live.

Roman coins and Anglo-Saxon ornaments have been found at Market Overton, which was granted its weekly market in the twelfth century. Also found here was a clepsydra – a primitive water clock used by the Anglo-Saxons to mark the passage of an hour. It consists of a bronze bowl with a hole in the bottom. The bowl was placed on the surface of the water, and it took (more or less) an hour for enough water to leak through the hole to make the bowl sink. Market Overton, along with Uppingham and other villages in the area, used to be known for the custom of giving Valentine Buns to children on Valentine's Day. They were oval buns, and were once called 'Plum Shittles'.

Isaac Newton's mother came from Market Overton and the sundial on the wall of the church tower is said to have been presented by Sir Isaac. The village green still sports the ancient stocks and whipping-post which were being used in Sir Isaac Newton's time. It is surely one of the more peculiar aspects of modern life that we can look upon such relics of the past and include them among the 'quaint' attractions of our old village greens, to be preserved at all costs. It would be better for us to reflect on the suffering and degradation that used to be inflicted there, and congratulate ourselves that, whatever the ills of our society, we are not generally as brutal and ignorant as our forbears were. Imagine some poor villager – mentally defective, perhaps, and called the 'village idiot' – sentenced to sit in the stocks for some petty misdemeanour, to be jeered at and hit by rotten vegetables thrown by peasants and their screaming urchins, to say nothing of worse indignities. Imagine a felon, tied to that whipping-post and flogged till blood ran from the stripes on his back, in full view of an audience of his village neighbours. Such events on the village greens of England degraded society as a whole, not just the wretches who suffered in them. There was nothing much good about those old days.

Not far away from here is a place called Thistleton Gap, where originally the three counties of Leicestershire, Rutland and Lincolnshire met. Here in 1811 a famous bare-fist fight took place, between Tom Cribb, the English champion pugilist, and Tom Molineux, the U.S. negro champion. Some say that twenty thousand people turned up to see it, sitting or standing on the grass, climbing trees for a better view, or standing on the saddles of their horses. Cribb knocked the negro out after a bloody battle of twenty minutes, in which he broke the American's jaw and two of his ribs, and for those who derive satisfaction from this sort of thing, England had a world champion.

Humphrey, Duke of Gloucester, who fought at Agincourt with his brother Henry V, was lord of the manor of Stretton, which lies beside the Great North Road, called by the Romans Ermine Street. It is a far cry indeed from its ancient origins to the inn which stands upon it now, called the Ram Jam Inn. Not that Pakistani immigrants have followed the Roman invaders into Rutland. The old coaching inn was originally called the Winchelsea Arms, and was changed when an eighteenth-century landlord who had been to India became well known for the potent concoction called 'Ram Jam', which he served to travellers whilst their horses were changed there. We can smile indulgently at the alternative and more picturesque explanation of the name, which concerns a traveller who offered to show the landlady how to draw mild and bitter from the same barrel. Leading the simple soul down to the cellar, he drilled a hole in one side of a barrel, and asked her to ram her thumb in it; then he drilled a hole in the other side and bade her jam her other thumb in that. Then he departed without paying his bill.

Close to the Lincolnshire border is Clipsham, where the quarries have been worked since the thirteenth century. Clipsham stone was used at Burley-on-the-Hill, in various cathedrals, and in the House of Commons when it was repaired after wartime bomb damage.

On the north-eastern border here is a tiny village named Pickworth. If you drive through it hastily you will notice nothing that appears to justify a pause. It looks like a rather isolated agricultural community, scattered about a crossroads, without even the usual church steeple to its name. But do not be deceived. Pickworth once had a very fine church spire, which could be seen for miles around, and in a bumpy little field by the roadside is a fascinating piece of evidence.

Before the Wars of the Roses, Pickworth was a thriving village with a century-old church. Then in 1470, where a wood called Bloody Oaks now stands by the Great North Road, Yorkists and Lancastrians joined battle. The Lancastrians were soundly beaten, and according to legend, the fleeing soldiers threw away their tunics to avoid being recognized – hence the battleground is known as Losecoat Field.

In 1491, Pickworth was reported as having no parishioners, and it is generally supposed that the rebel troops destroyed the church and the village. It is not certain that this is what happened, because another nearby village, called Hardwick, was devastated *before* this battle – no doubt a total casualty of the Black Death. Whatever the reason for Pickworth's desertion, however, the remaining steeple of the church was demolished in 1731, so that the stone could be used for building bridges in the locality.

As the village began to live again, a farm grew up on the land where the churches and houses had once stood, and in 1821 a new church was built, not far from the old, but it was never completed. Then some of the farm buildings were converted to cottages. Gradually Pickworth was repopulated, and new houses built. But the village had gone west, and the site of the old community remains inhospitable; the farm cottages again derelict on the uneven ground where grass covers the foundations of the medieval community. One reminder of its past is still there. A solitary stone arch, through which the villagers once entered their church, stands near the road in front of the deserted cottages. It somehow seems more touching, in its lonely five hundred years' defiance of the desolation surrounding it, than grander and more beautiful ruins elsewhere.

John Clare, the Northamptonshire nature poet, knew this Gothic arch. He had come into Rutland from Helpston near Peterborough, where he was born to the wife of a poor labourer, and at a farm near Great Casterton he met his own future wife, known to his readers as Sweet Patty of the Vale. He came to Pickworth to work as a burner in a lime-kiln, whilst writing his poems descriptive of rural life. He needed a pound to get a prospectus of his poems printed, and managed to save it with great difficulty out of his scanty wages here. It earned him publication, and the attention of some wealthy patrons who tried to provide him with a better means of livelihood, but his sensitive and humble spirit could not cope with the practical business of life, and his mind gradually gave way. For twenty-seven years, until his death in 1864, he lived in asylums, where poor Patty could never bring herself to visit him, and eventually she deserted him. "If life had a second edition," the lonely and tormented poet wrote to a friend, "how I would correct the proofs." But he left behind him some fine poetry, in which we can recognize the local countryside:

> Meet me at the sunset
> Down in the green glen,
> Where we've often met
> By hawthorn tree and foxes' den,
> Meet me in the green glen.

I remember being delighted by his poem 'Little Trotty Wagtail' as a small child, and in his work are to be found words that are common in Leicestershire as well as Northamptonshire. He makes 'agen' serve not only for 'again' but also for 'against', and he refers to the flower of the Kidney Vetch as 'lambtoe'.

Clare also worked on a farm at Ryhall, which stands beside the Gwash and has a delightful little square with an old inn, The Green Dragon, where there is a vaulted cellar dating back to the thirteenth century, which gives this place some claim to be the oldest inn in Leicestershire. In the village church there is a memorial to a child who died in 1696 at the age of two, and who is eulogized as having "a most pregnant wit" (he must have been an insufferable little brute!).

Tolethorpe, nearby, is notable as the birthplace of Robert Browne, who may be regarded as the first formal Dissenter. He founded the Brownists, who subsequently became the respectable Congregationalists, but in those early days the penalty for printing Browne's works was death by hanging, and Browne himself suffered much imprisonment before eventually returning to the Church of England.

Back towards the Great North Road, and the Roman Castertons, great and small. Great Casterton, where the Romans built a fort beside their important road to the north in the first century A.D., remained astride Ermine Street for centuries, while the marching footsteps of Roman legions were replaced by the roar of modern traffic. Then the Stamford bypass was built, and Great Casterton got a little well-deserved respite. The Roman town here, the name of which is not known, covered about fifteen acres, and halfway to Little Casterton, beside the river, a villa was built, probably as a farmhouse, which was later burnt down. A hoard of ninth-century coins was found buried here, and it seems likely that the owner was taking precautions against possible attack by the Danish invaders.

The little church at Tickencote, though much restored, has a

Norman chancel arch which is famous among connoisseurs of church architecture, although it is, as Pevsner says, "wildly overdone and in addition incompetently constructed". It consists of five carved divisions, the central one of which has interesting grotesques of men and animals.

Dominating the skyline to the south of these villages, in startling contrast to the honey-coloured limestone church spires everywhere else in the area, usually built in stone from the Ketton quarries, are the chimneys of the Ketton cement works. Yet, ironically, the church at Ketton itself, although one of the largest and finest village churches in the East Midlands, is not built of Ketton stone but of Barnack stone, from quarries six miles away in Huntingdonshire (as it was then). Who can tell why? Perhaps the medieval masons were heartily sick of the local stone, and wanted to work in something different for a change, no matter how slight the difference. Whatever the reason, they built a splendid monument to their skills, with an impressive west front and tower, though personally I find its much praised broach spire a bit top-heavy. It is surrounded by houses built in the local stone which has graced great buildings from York Minster to the Tower of London.

To get to the village church at Tixover, you have to walk beyond the end of the village and over the fields towards the River Welland. The twelfth-century church originally served a village which disappeared, probably as a result of the Black Death, and later inhabitants built their new village further north, leaving the church standing alone.

If we travel west towards Seaton, we come to a knotty conglomeration of used and disused railway courses, with cuttings and embankments crossing the roads – and one another – by means of bridges, and tunnels through which no trains now pass. But here, carrying the still-existing line across the river into Northamptonshire, is the Welland Viaduct, an imposing piece of industrial architecture. It was built in 1878, and consists of eighty-two brick arches, totalling over three-quarters of a mile in length, carrying the railway 70 feet above the river.

The chief interest of Lyddington, an attractive village with many old stone houses and a worn old cross on the green, is the Bede House beside the church. The present building dates from the late fifteenth century, but long before that the house there had been the residence of the Bishop of Lincoln. The rebuilt house was converted into an almshouse in 1602 by Thomas Cecil, Earl of Exeter, and is now in the care of the Department of Environment. It has a superb banqueting hall with richly carved oak panelling in the ceiling.

The church at Lyddington contains some rare clay acoustic jars, set high in the walls of the chancel, whilst Caldecott, in the southernmost corner of the former county, has yet another church which was struck by lightning. It set the spire on fire, and cracked walls and windows, during a storm in 1797.

Near the Eyebrook Reservoir, which was opened in 1940, lies the tiny village of Stoke Dry, where there is another of Rutland's delightful village churches. This one has some interesting Norman carvings, and monuments to more members of that Digby family we first noticed at Tilton-on-the-Hill. The best known of the Digbys, however, has no monument either at Tilton or at Stoke Dry, for though he was born here, he was hanged in St Paul's Churchyard, London. Sir Everard Digby financed that Catholic revolution, which he planned with Robert Catesby and others, culminating in the Gunpowder Plot. When Guy Fawkes was captured beneath the House of Lords on 5 November 1605, he revealed the names of the conspirators, under torture, and all were soon disposed of, including Digby, who had been knighted only two years before by the king he sought to blow up.

And so to Uppingham, Rutland's second largest town – though that is not saying much. At its centre is a delightful old market place, little changed in centuries. It does not stretch the imagination too far to stand here and visualize minstrels and bear-baiting. Seventeenth-century shop fronts, and the Falcon Hotel, with Elizabethan inn buildings behind its façade, give the place a special rare atmosphere not much encountered these days.

The entrance to the church of St Peter and St Paul is also in the market place, and yet from its south side one looks out at the open country. The church has undergone much restoration, but its pulpit is Elizabethan, and a famous preacher once stood in it. Jeremy Taylor, that learned and literary divine who became chaplain to Archbishop Laud and Charles I, was made Rector of Uppingham in 1638 and remained so for about four years, marrying his first wife in this church. In those times of great trouble, which twice landed him in prison, he consistently preached toleration, but like all idealists, discovered that he could not always practise what he preached. He wrote a number of books, one of which contains my favourite piece of ecclesiastical logic: "As our life is very *short,* so it is very *miserable,* and therefore it is well it is *short."*

What makes this little market town a place to be reckoned with far beyond the boundaries of Leicestershire, and indeed of England, is its famous school. It was founded in 1584, together with Oakham School, by Robert Johnson, Archdeacon of Leicester, and until 1853 it was merely a local grammar school. Then the Reverend Edward Thring was appointed headmaster, and he stayed there for thirty-four years, transforming the little grammar school with twenty-three boarders into one of the most famous public schools in England. The school has over six hundred pupils today, and its many buildings dominate the town, to say nothing of its vast playing-fields, but the original school building, with its inscriptions in Hebrew, Greek and Latin, can still be seen near the churchyard where Rev. Thring lies buried.

The land sloping down to Wardley Wood and the Eye Brook, to the west of Uppingham, is called Beaumont Chase, and it was undoubtedly a hunting preserve of one of the Beaumont earls of Leicester. To the north, Ridlington and Preston are extremely attractive stone-built villages, looking down on the River Chater, and making us wonder, once again, why the colour photographers so rarely explore this part of England. Preston, particularly, has some fine gabled ironstone buildings of the Stuart period and presents a very sunny and pleasing aspect to the visitor.

The original headquarters of the Cottesmore Hunt was Exton Park, a little to the east of Burley-on-the-Hill, where the Earls of Gainsborough lived in an Elizabethan mansion, approached through splendid wrought-iron gates. The house was badly damaged by fire in 1810, and a new one built, with a Catholic chapelattached to it. This house is nstill lived in by the Noel family. The original house on the site was built by the Haringtons, who also built the first house at Burley-on-the-Hill. They were an old and respected family, but their claim to lasting remembrance is the fact that one of their number – not a Leicestershire man – was the inventor of the water closet. In Exton village there is a little street which used to be called Pudding Bag Lane.

The glory of Exton, which is a fairly large village, is the church, dedicated like Uppingham's to St Peter and St Paul. Few churches in England can claim such a splendid collection of sculpture as Exton has in its monuments to the Haringtons and the Noels. The most ambitious of them is to Baptist Noel, the third Viscount Campden, and is by the incomparable Grinling Gibbons. It is made in black and white marble, and has life-size figures of the viscount and his fourth wife, and reliefs representing his other three wives and their children. There are also monuments by Joseph Nollekens, that businesslike Royal Academician who amassed a fortune of nearly a quarter of a million pounds.

Empingham, on the Gwash, also has a famous church, one of the largest and most beautiful in the county, though you would hardly think so from its squat little crocketed spire. But recent developments in Rutland give this village another, more mundane interest. South-west of the village, the river has been dammed to create the new Empingham Reservoir, to supply water to the Northampton and Peterborough areas, as well as to the south-east corner of Leicestershire. This giant undertaking – which was opposed by the former Rutland County Council – is the responsibility of the Anglian Water Authority, and it is not only the largest man-made lake in Britain, but is nearly equal in size to England's largest natural lake, Windermere. The small River Gwash is obviously not able to supply all the water for such a vast reservoir, and the majority is pumped in from the Welland and the Nene.

No other single undertaking since the Enclosure Acts has wrought such immense changes in the Leicestershire landscape, and the reservoir is undoubtedly destined – with its sailing and fishing facilities, picnic areas, and nature reserve – to put this unknown region on the map as a tourist centre. It has also added to the county's lost villages. The hamlet of Nether Hambleton, and part of its neighbour Middle Hambleton, have been submerged beneath thirty million gallons of water. Upper Hambleton stands now on a peninsula created by the fortuitous horseshoe shape of the reservoir (the horseshoe being the heraldic symbol of Rutland), and the roads that led to the surrounding villages now lead only to the water's edge. Half of Hambleton Wood is now under water, as well as the site of the village lost in the eighteenth century, Normanton. Sir Gilbert Heathcote, who was a Governor of the Bank of England and a Lord Mayor of London, built an estate here, and his son destroyed the village to enlarge the park, in 1764. His great house was demolished many years ago, and all that was left of Normanton was the rebuilt church. This attractive little church, which contains a monument to Sir Gilbert by Rysbrack, in the form of a cherub holding an oval medallion with his portrait on it, has been saved from the rising waters, and is accessible by a causeway linking the church, on its own little island, to the south shore of the reservoir, which is to be officially named Rutland Water.

The new lake laps the threshold of Edith Weston, an attractive village rendered rather less accessible than hitherto by the reservoir. It has a gabled seventeenth-century rectory, and used to have a church clock of similar age which, until it was replaced recently by a new clock, told villagers and visitors, single-handed as it were, the approximate time of day.

There are other interesting houses and churches in this part of Leicestershire, at Manton, a village with a railway tunnel running beneath it, and at Barrowden, Glaston, Morcott, and North and South Luffenham. Robert Scott was rector at South Luffenham for a few years, prior to his election as Master of Balliol in 1854. With his contemporary Henry George Liddell, Dean of Christ Church, he compiled the Greek Lexicon, for which the two Oxford scholars are famous. (It was for Dean Liddell's daughter that Lewis Carroll wrote *Alice in Wonderland*).

Bisbrooke has a relatively new church. It was built in 1871 after the twelfth-century village church had been demolished. A vicar of Bisbrooke, Samuel Palmer, shocked his parishioners in 1578 by lying in the church with his wife Ellen "from Christmas until Candlemas Day last, and abused that place too shamefully to be writed". Since the vicarage had been demolished in 1575, however, the vicar and his wife doubtless had nowhere else to lie! Nor is that all the shocking history of this innocent-looking village. It was once called Pisbrook. The Victoria County History coyly gives a slightly less graphic variation of the spelling – Pysbroke – whilst Arthur Mee avoids mentioning the place altogether.

I have already remarked on the exceedingly attractive village of Preston. Wing, a mile away, will not bear comparison as a tourist attraction, but suddenly this village thrusts itself on our attention, like Hallaton, with hints of mystery and magic. Just outside the village, beside the road to Glaston, is an ancient circular turf maze, only a few inches in height and about 40 feet in diameter. Its design is the same as mosaic patterns in the floors of Chartres Cathedral and other French churches. However, the oft-repeated supposition that it was a Christian invention for making sinners do symbolic penance is certainly wrong. Such mazes are rare, but Wing's is not unique, and these devices were, like maypoles and kissing under mistletoe, pagan survivals which Christian countries perforce tolerated and then embraced, though Cromwell suppressed the fertility rite of dancing round the maypole in England, and the church still forbids mistletoe.

These mazes were brought across Europe and into Britain by Celtic invaders, for whom the spiral, like the ash tree, had magical significance. (Robert Graves has pointed out that when we 'touch wood' it should, strictly speaking, be ash). The origins of the maze go back at least as far as the Minoan civilization of Crete. It was connected with ideas of resurrection – the centre represented death, to which one went and then made one's way out of. The story of the labyrinth of King Minos, in which Theseus slew the Minotaur, embraces this theme, and may explain its origin. In Britain, on mazes such as this one at Wing, a spiral dance called 'Troy Town' used to be performed in some villages at Easter, and this was the maze's purpose – the enactment of an ancient ritual, possibly arising from the delivery of the Athenian maidens from the dreaded Minotaur. Why the mazes were later called Troy Town is not clear, but it was possibly because of the old tradition that heroes from Troy founded Britain and France, where the mazes occur. (Later and more elaborate mazes such as the famous one at Hampton Court were merely constructed in grand gardens for entertainment, their designers probably being ignorant of their true origin.)

A similar turf maze exists at Alkborough, in Lincolnshire, and half a dozen other turf mazes survive in various parts of England from Yorkshire to Hampshire. The plan of the maze at Alkborough is repeated in stone in the church porch, in one of the stained-glass windows, and in a headstone in the shape of a Celtic cross in the village cemetery, and it is the frequent proximity of turf mazes to churches that gave rise to assumptions of their Christian origin and purpose. In fact the Church almost certainly embraced their magical significance in its own myth-ology, using them to ward off evil spirits, which could only travel in straight lines. There were a great many turf mazes in Britain at one time, but most – like the one on Priestly Hill near Lyddington – have disappeared under the plough after long neglect; a fact even in Shakespeare's day, for he refers to them in *A Midsummer Night's Dream*:

> The nine-men's morris is fill'd up with mud;
> And the quaint mazes in the wanton green,
> For lack of tread, are undistinguishable:

This is not the place to enquire into the significance of references to mazes and nine men's morris in a play featuring Theseus and a man with an animal's head, but we might note that nine men's morris was a once-popular game played on a basic labyrinth design, and on the Isle of Wight it was called 'Siege of Troy'.

If you should entertain doubts about this little village's involvement in magic, let us digress for a moment to consider Amelia Woodcock. She was a labourer's wife who became known as 'The Wise Woman of Wing'. She had a wide reputation for curing every imaginable disease, including cancer, with her herbal remedies, and she was visited by so many people, both rich and poor, that they often had to take lodgings in the vicinity until she could see them. Now it may very well be that if Mrs Woodcock's 'cures' could be examined by modern scientific methods, they would be declared useless. But it is one of the delusions of modern times that fact is always superior to fantasy. Plenty of Leicestershire women have age-old remedies for a variety of complaints, which they consider more reliable than doctors' prescriptions, and they usually work, simply because people *believe* they will. As Voltaire said, the doctor's function is to keep the patient happy while nature cures the disease. Is it any wonder that this former county, which has never become industrialized, should harbour ancient superstitions which have been driven out of more sophisticated areas? We have noted earlier that the village names here are older than the Danish ones which are predominant in other parts of Leicestershire. Those horseshoes in Oakham Castle are more than just a quaint tradition.

I have said that the mazes were brought to Britain by Celtic invaders. There is sufficient proof of that in the fact that such maze patterns are known in Cornwall, in Wales and in Ireland. In Wales they were known as 'Caerdroia' – Troy Town, as in

England. Mazes carved on rocks in Ireland and Cornwall have the same pattern as the labyrinths shown on some Cretan coins, and the Easter dance performed on the turf mazes in Britain until the nineteenth century was known (by different names, of course) to the ancient Greeks and to the Romans. On the island of Delos a spiral dance called the 'Crane Dance' was performed in imitation of the extraordinary courtship ritual of these birds – also sacred to the Celts as well as to the Greeks. It seems likely that the children's game of 'hopscotch' is a survival of pre-Christian maze dances, and is linked with the fertility ritual of the Crane Dance.

Julius Caesar noted that the Druids of Gaul employed Greek characters for their secular business, that they indulged in human sacrifice, and incidentally, that they regarded Chartres as the centre of Gaul. The Romans were able to drive the Druids out of Britain, but they were not able to suppress the beliefs and customs which the Celtic priests left behind. Easter, which is the Sunday following the first full moon on or after 21 March, is named after Eostre, a Celtic dawn-goddess, and 'Easter eggs' are derived from a Druidic ritual in which eggs were painted in a ceremony honouring the sun, which 'hatched' or renewed the world each year as it rose in the east at the beginning of spring. To Eostre, as to the Greeks, a certain animal was held sacred, and in ancient Britain, as elsewhere, there was a strict taboo against hunting it. Because of its prolific breeding habits it was associated with spring and fertility, and much ancient ritual surrounded it. What was this animal? Lo and behold—it was the hare!

The magical significance of this animal was respected by everyone—not only the Druids. When Boadicea led her people into battle against the Romans, it is said she took a hare with her, to strike fear into her enemies. Eating hare is expressly forbidden in the Mosaic Law: "And the hare, because he cheweth the cud, but divideth not the hoof; he is unclean unto you." (We may observe, in passing, that the Lord was mistaken in speaking thus unto Moses – the hare doth *not* chew the cud.)

Eventually, hare hunting became the subject of symbolic ritual at Easter, with highly erotic undertones, and taking many forms. Witches said they transformed themselves into hares to be chased by the Devil in the form of a greyhound. The paper-chase called 'Hare and Hounds', very popular at one time (it is described in *Tom Brown's Schooldays*), called for two boys representing hares to lay a trail of paper to be chased by the other participants, representing hounds. On Easter Monday in the Dane Hills, outside Leicester, a ritual hare hunt used to take place in which a dead cat represented the hare, and which traditionally ended at the door of the Mayor's house. This ritual, I need hardly add, was associated with that cannibalistic hag Black Annis, who was also known as Cat Annis. Is it pure coincidence, one wonders, that the dead cat was customarily sprinkled with aniseed? By now, no one will be surprised to learn that Bel (remember that legendary giant?) was also a Celtic god, and that Anna or Annet was his sister! And even these ancient gods may have been adopted from the earlier Syrian deities Baal and his sister Anat, she being one of the early Near Eastern mother-goddesses.

Hares were once believed to change sex, and are traditionally responsible for 'laying' the Easter eggs which are still sometimes hidden in gardens and hedges for children to find. And the old superstition that it brings good luck to say 'hares' on the last night of the old month and 'rabbits' on the first morning of the new is connected with the changing phases of the moon. Samuel Pepys was among those who kept a hare's foot about him for luck, or as a protection against bodily ailments.

Here then, are the 'pagan' origins of that Hallaton ceremony of Hare Pie Scrambling, in which two men walking abreast and carrying the hare pies lead the procession to the scene of the hunt. The fact that the pies are nowadays made of meat other than hare does not matter any more than that the old Dane Hills ritual used a dead cat. It is the thought that counts, and the thought is a symbolic rape; the ritual chase after a token of virility, which has lurked in the darkest recesses of man's unconscious despite centuries of change. What Christianity has for centuries loudly condemned as 'paganism' is not a primitive and wrong-headed religion which Christianity has conquered and replaced, but a layer of folklore and myth which has been overlaid by that of the Christian faith itself, and if anyone doubts that the earlier beliefs survive, in any significant form, they can be found alive and well, and living in Leicestershire.

Some readers may not have noticed that we have, in deference to the ancient gods, progressed through Rutland on a more or less spiral course to Wing. For those who are superstitious, there is nothing else for it but to retrace the whole course and go out at the point of entry, near Launde. The rest of us can cheat, however, by going back through Preston and Ridlington, along the roller-coaster road to Brooke, and thence to Braunston, and soon the twin prominences of Whatborough and Robin-a-Tiptoe welcome us back to the motherly bosom of old Leicestershire.

VI

THE WAY OF THE WOLD

ANY discussion of the north-eastern quarter of old Leicestershire must start at Burrough Hill, which is slightly less high than Whatborough and Robin-a-Tiptoe, but historically much more important. The clearest and most impressive Iron-Age earthworks in the county are to be seen here, and it is possible that this hill fort was the capital of the Coritani before the Romans came. The hilltop commands fine views in every direction except to the south, where the higher hills block the distant scene, and its windswept old trees remind one of the blasted heath in *Macbeth*.

The hill has been a place of pilgrimage for centuries. I use the word 'pilgrimage' deliberately because, although scarcely anyone (other than the occasional archaeologist) visits the hill in conscious homage to the ancient Britons, these prehistoric habitations have a strange sort of magnetism which does not derive only from their situation as fine viewpoints. We learn, for instance – with no great surprise – that running, wrestling and dancing used to take place there on Whit Mondays, and people came from miles around to enjoy the festivities. Burrough Hill retains an unconscious significance in local folklore, though this would probably be denied, to a man, by the crowds that flock there during summer weekends.

The hill has long been a natural location for steeple-chasing, and the village of Burrough-on-the-Hill extended its hospitality on occasion to the late Duke of Windsor, when he was Prince of Wales. Burrough Court, which was burnt down during the Second World War, entertained the Prince when he rode with the Quorn, or in the point-to-point races, and it was there that the course of English history was somewhat altered by his first meeting with the future Duchess, Mrs Wallis Simpson.

Of the group of villages which surround Burrough Hill, Owston, to the south-east, is often said to be the most remote hamlet in Leicestershire. This is arguable – particularly since

Rutland became part of the county – but Owston is certainly tucked away from major roads, on the highest parts of east Leicestershire, in beautifully wooded countryside. It once had an Augustinian priory, which owned Knossington village, and at the dissolution both became the property of Gregory Cromwell.

Somerby is the largest village of the group, and it has given us two notable medical men, William Cheselden and Sir Benjamin Richardson. Cheselden was born in 1688. He was an eminent surgeon, who attended Queen Anne and Isaac Newton, and invented the lateral operation for the stone. He is said to have died from a surfeit of ale and hot buns, but one wonders whether the physician who diagnosed the cause of death was quite as expert a medical man as the victim himself. Richardson was born in 1828, and although a physician of considerable reputation, he is remembered primarily as a champion of teetotalism.

A contemporary of Richardson's who lived at Somerby House at one time was Colonel Frederick Burnaby, the son of a local vicar, and a soldier adventurer of gigantic stature who could carry a small pony under one arm. He crossed the Channel in a balloon, and became famous for his book *Ride to Khiva,* in which he described his journey, mainly on horseback, across Russian Asia, with a Tartar dwarf as his only companion. He died under a shower of Dervish spears whilst fighting in the attempt to relieve Khartoum in 1875.

The church of St Andrew at Twyford is in every respect but one a modest little village church of no great significance. The exception is its north arcade, a piece of twelfth-century work by the same hands that were responsible for the hall of Oakham Castle, and probably for some of the carving in Canterbury Cathedral. Further west, the village of Beeby is hardly more than a mile from the probing tentacles of the octopus Leicester, yet it retains an air of isolated rustic peace which is only disturbed by the spectacle of its ridiculous church steeple. The tower is surmounted by the beginnings of a spire which was never built, and remains a stump, like a felled tree. Legends grow where facts are thin on the ground, and one explanation of the 'Beeby tub' is that the builder despaired of rivalling the splendid crocketed needle spire at Queniborough, and threw himself off the tower. Whatever the true reason for its unfinished state, it would have been better to demolish what *was* built, if the money could not be found to finish it, and leave the little church with a modest but respectable tower, instead of the appearance of an outsize coffee pot.

South Croxton has another of those ill-fated Leicestershire churches which have been shattered by lightning. The rector of the time saw the medieval spire struck and ruined, with masonry crashing through the roof, and much restoration was needed as a result. Gaddesby, fortunately, has escaped this unhappy fate, for it has one of the county's finest churches, with an elegant broach spire. The church belonged to the Knights Templar of Rothley, who were no doubt responsible for its lavish decoration, particularly in the south aisle. Gaddesby Church's only misfortune has been the depositing there of a pretentious monument to Colonel Cheney, of the Scots Greys, who lived at Gaddesby Hall. As a young ensign at the battle of Waterloo, he had five horses shot under him, and the monument depicts one of these incidents in nearly life-size marble, completely overwhelming the other attractions of this stylish village church.

The 'capital' of the Quorn country, and of this corner of Leicestershire, is Melton Mowbray, a small market town standing on the River Wreake, which separates the Wolds from High Leicestershire. Although it is a little larger than Market Harborough, Melton appears, by comparison, rather cramped, and its heavily congested little streets hardly make it an endearing place – especially on market days. But Melton is famous throughout England, for more than one reason.

Perhaps it is best known to the public at large as the home of the traditional English pork pie – one of Leicestershire's few but precious contributions to the nation's gastronomic delights. Coincidentally, it also became the centre of the Stilton cheese-making industry, and the home of Europe's largest manufacturers of animal foodstuffs. It seems odd that Melton should have become so important in the food line, when pre-dating all these industries was its devotion to the 'uneatable'. Melton Mowbray is the capital of fox-hunting, as decidedly as Lords is the capital of cricket, and we shall have occasion to return here with the hunting fraternity in the next chapter. Suffice to say here that many of the large houses in Melton, now occupied by public bodies or private companies, were originally built as hunting lodges by the aristocrats who came here for their sport, and it was not unusual for over a thousand horses to be stabled in the town during the winter season, when millionaires and monarchs descended on the place after their summer in Monte Carlo.

As for Stilton cheese (the name of which, by curious circumstance, associates it with Huntingdonshire, when in fact it is one of Leicestershire's greatest gifts to mankind), there has been much dispute about its true origin. One book may say that it was first made by Mary Beaumont of Kirby Bellars; another that Mrs Paulet of Wymondham was responsible; another that Elizabeth Scarbrow of Quenby invented it, and yet another that Mrs Orton of Little Dalby was the venerable lady to whom we owe this marvellous cheese. In fact, Elizabeth Scarbrow and Mrs Orton were one and the same person. Miss Scarbrow was housekeeper at Quenby Hall until she married Mr Orton and went to live at Little Dalby. It seems that she learned how to make the cheese whilst at Quenby, but it was already known there as Lady Beaumont's recipe, and in fact Mrs Paulet of Wymondham was the daughter of an earlier housekeeper at Quenby. How a Lady Beaumont enters the story is not clear, unless – as Professor Hoskins suggests – she had been a guest at Quenby and gave her hostess the recipe. But the identity of the Lady Beaumont in question is itself a mystery. The Squire de Lisle has suggested to me that she may have been Elizabeth Hastings, who married Sir John Beaumont of Grace Dieu in the sixteenth century, but if this were the case, the cheese must have remained practically unknown for about two hundred years – very difficult to believe! So we cannot trace, with any certainty, who invented it, and Quenby Hall's claim to being its place of origin must remain open to question. At an early stage in its career, however, the cheese came into the hands of the publican of the Bell Inn at Stilton, in Huntingdonshire, and it was there that it became widely popular and where it got its name.

To confuse matters a little more, the well-known Leicester red cheese, originally made in the south of the county, is now also made at Melton Mowbray. It is not what it used to be, though. At its best it should be dry and crumbly. Years ago, Leicester Market used to have a Cheese Fair every September, when stacks of Stilton and Leicester cheeses were sold. Nowadays, it is as much as anyone can do to avoid buying the stuff wrapped in polythene which passes for cheese in supermarkets. Modern methods have reduced the maturing time for Stilton from eighteen to four months, but it still takes seventeen gallons of milk to make a fourteen-pound cheese.

Melton's history goes back at least to Roman times, and its second name comes from the Mowbray family who were lords of the manor in the twelfth century. One of its best-known buildings is the fifteenth-century so-called Anne of Cleves' House, now a restaurant. It was once called the Priory House, and was probably a chantry house belonging to the nearby church. Although it was part of the manor granted to Anne of Cleves by Henry VIII when he had finished with her, there is no evidence to suggest that the ex-queen ever visited it, let alone lived there.

In Scalford Road is Elgin Lodge, where John Ferneley lived and died. He was one of Leicestershire's few artists to achieve lasting fame, and remains the best known of them today. He was born at Thrussington in 1782, the son of a wheelwright, and moved to the town when he was thirty-two. He exhibited frequently at the Royal Academy, and his hunting pictures and other horse paintings became very popular. Ferneley originals command good prices today, and one of his works hangs in the Tate Gallery.

There is a monument to Ferneley in St Mary's Church, which is acclaimed as one of the most beautiful parish churches in England. Pevsner calls it "the stateliest and most impressive of all churches in Leicestershire", and serious consideration was given to making it the cathedral of the new Diocese of Leicester, in 1926, in preference to any of the churches in Leicester itself. This church, too, has been struck by lightning, during a service, but only minor damage was done. No doubt if it had had a tall spire the consequences would have been more serious. One wonders if the practical wisdom of building churches with spires in thunderstorm areas ever crossed the minds of medieval builders. They obviously knew that lightning strikes the tallest object in the vicinity, but doubtless believed that God would protect the churches from hazards which were merely natural. How appalled those masons would be now to discover the powerlessness of faith against natural disasters (to say nothing of incompetent workmanship – in 1675, the spire of the church at Great Dalby had come crashing down into the nave without assistance from a storm). Melton's congregation of 1776, when the lightning struck, had more respect for nature – they promptly fled in panic. It is hardly surprising that a company specializing in the manufacture and erection of lightning conductors exists in the area, at Nether Broughton.

The vicar of Melton Mowbray at that time was the celebrated Doctor Ford, who was noted for his almost fanatical devotion to Handel's *Messiah*. He used to sing it whenever he rode from Melton to Leicester, and always contrived to reach the end as he entered Belgrave Gate. Once at a performance of the oratorio he could not resist accompanying the choir from the auditorium, and a fellow member of the audience objected that he had not paid to hear Doctor Ford sing. "Then you have got that into the bargain," the vicar retorted.

Dr Ford was not the only well-known Melton interpreter of *Messiah*. Sir Malcolm Sargent, born at Stamford, spent ten years as organist at St Mary's Church, during which he obtained his Doctorate of Music and conducted the Leicester Symphony Orchestra. This, of course, was in his younger days – long before he became known as 'Flash Harry' and encouraged the nearest thing to violent nationalism we have in England – the Last Night of the Proms.

Burton Lazars, just outside Melton on the road to Oakham, got its name from a lazar house, or leper hospital, founded by Roger de Mowbray, who was also partly responsible for building Melton's parish church. The hospital disappeared at the dissolution, but for four hundred years it was the most important lazar house in England.

To the east of Melton are the villages of Wymondham and – close to the former Rutland border – Edmondthorpe. Wymondham is an ancient market town, interesting now chiefly for the fact that its old grammar school was founded by the lord of the manor, Sir Charles Sedley, one of the Merry Monarch's merry men, who only left the delights of court for Leicestershire in order to escape the plague, which was then raging in London. Most would call Sedley dissipated, but Arthur Mee, that reverent guide round the more spinsterly aspects of the King's England, felt sufficiently repelled to call him "depraved".

Edmondthorpe's church of St Michael contains a monument to Sir Roger Smith and his two wives and sons. Smith was a name to be reckoned with in Edmondthorpe for hundreds of years, and legend embraces Sir Roger's second wife, Ann Goodman, whose image lies here with a gash on its wrist. She is supposed to have been a witch, who appeared as a black cat, after her death, to a cook at Edmondthorpe Hall. The cook, not to be intimidated by a spook moggy, went for it with a kitchen knife and cut its paw. Hence the slashed wrist on the alabaster figure. And if people would rather believe that than accept that the gash is only a natural vein in the alabaster, who is to convince them otherwise? The relief of Lady Smith is not among the urgent topics of conversation in the village. Nor does the lady herself look much concerned, as she lies here nonchalantly with her elbow supporting her head – a study in indifference.

Halfway between Melton and Edmondthorpe is Stapleford Hall, set in a large park where once the old village stood. Now only the church remains, in which numerous monuments bear witness to the fruitful virility of the Sherards, who built the house and the church, and peopled both with their progeny, alive in the one, and dead in the other. The most attractive member of the clan was Lady Abigail Sherard, the wife of Sir William, and formerly Abigail Cave of Stanford Hall. She was evidently responsible for much seventeenth-century improvement and extension of the house, part of which is known as Lady Abigail's Range. She found time to bear her husband eleven children, nevertheless, and all are represented with their parents in the splendid monument of black and white marble in the church. The Sherards became Earls of Harborough and the line lasted until 1859.

One of the earls of Harborough was the chief promoter of the Oakham Canal, and he was naturally put out when the canal's trade was threatened by the coming of the railways. So incensed was he, in fact, that he had traps laid to hinder the railway engineers. Blood flowed on more than one occasion, and the incidents became known locally as "the battles of Saxby".

I cannot pretend to much personal enthusiasm for Stapleford, but it has a fine collection of Staffordshire pottery figures, a popular miniature railway, and – for those who wish England was Africa – a lion reserve. (The decline of the circus as a popular entertainment has at least led to better conditions for animals and ringmasters. The animals have more space and freedom and the ringmasters occupy stately homes. Only the spectators are worse off. Instead of the animals being safely enclosed in small cages, the spectators are safely enclosed in small vehicles.)

Before venturing into the area of the Leicestershire Wolds, it is time to introduce the reader to a Leicestershire man whose practical influence has been immense, not only in Leicestershire but throughout the agricultural world, and though he is little known to the general public, he was perhaps the greatest man ever born on Leicestershire soil. Jonathan Swift wrote in *Gulliver's Travels* his famous dictum that "whoever could make two ears of corn or two blades of grass to grow upon a spot of ground where only one grew before, would deserve better of mankind, and do more essential service to his country, than the whole race of politicians put together". Robert Bakewell, who lived up to that high ideal, was born in Leicestershire in the very year when Swift was preparing his great work for the press.

Bakewell was born at Dishley Grange, near Loughborough, where his father and grandfather had farmed the 400 acres of land before him. Robert helped his father to irrigate his fields by spreading the flood-waters of the Soar over them, and the seeds of scientific agriculture were sown in his young mind. Later, he developed a more sophisticated irrigation system of his own and, typically, made the canal which fed it serve a dual purpose. Instead of loading turnips from his fields on to carts and having them pulled by horses to his storehouse, he threw the turnips into the canal as they were lifted from the fields and they floated down to the barn, arriving already washed.

Bakewell's fame rests on his scientific breeding of livestock. His first experiments were conducted with the longhorned-red cattle then common in the area. They were primarily draft animals used for meat only in their old age. With the dawn of the Industrial Revolution and the increase in urban population, food production was of paramount importance to the nation, and by inbreeding, Bakewell raised cattle with smaller bones and higher meat content. He also bred the forerunner of the great Shire horse, which is, next to the elephant, the world's strongest animal. Bakewell's greatest success of all, however, was with sheep. The type most common then were big-boned animals bred mainly for their long wool. By inbreeding, Bakewell produced the New Leicester sheep, which was barrel-shaped, with short legs and smaller than average head and bones, and increased meat and fat content.

So great were his improvements in the quality of livestock that important visitors came to Dishley from all over the world to learn about his methods, and bachelor Bakewell and his sister entertained there on such a lavish scale that he eventually went bankrupt. But his knowledge and experience were his greatest assets. He leased his bulls, stallions and rams to other farmers at high prices, instead of selling them, and one of his bulls was described as "the greatest stock-getter the Midland district ever knew". Bakewell kept specimen bones and other parts of his best animals in pickle when they died, as a sort of primitive genetic museum, but he was cautious in explaining his methods to casual visitors. The superstitious thought inbreeding immoral, because incest was supposed to lead to degeneracy and insanity.

The changes in agricultural priorities since Bakewell's time have led, as we noted in an earlier chapter, to a huge decline in the number of sheep in the county, but thousands still graze on the Wolds in this quarter, as well as the larger numbers of dairy cattle. Ironically, scientific progress since Bakewell's day has advanced the methods of breeding cattle and pigs much more than sheep. Bakewell was also an advocate of small enclosures, having proved the economic advantages of using small fields in rotation. His practice was followed throughout the Midlands, but today, with the large and powerful agricultural machinery in general use, small fields and hedges are inconveniences, and new methods are again bringing changes to the landscape.

The villages of the Wolds, starting from Walton-on-the-Wolds near Loughborough to Croxton Kerrial and Sewstern near the Lincolnshire border, are small and sleepy farming villages, generally less attractive than one might perhaps expect. Sewstern gave its name to an ancient drove road which forms the border between Leicestershire and Lincolnshire for some miles here. Its older name was Sewstern Lane, but it was later called The Drift. It was almost certainly a prehistoric trackway, running along a high ridge between the valleys of the Welland and the Trent, and its silent and deserted green remains provide a fine walking route, where one can easily imagine the medieval drovers with their cattle on the long, slow journey to the London markets.

John Nichols, who seems to have believed anything that would add a few lines to his voluminous history, remarks that the spire of Buckminster Church can be seen alike by mariners in the North Sea and by people at Hinckley. A likely story! Buckminster and Knipton are 'estate' villages, neat and rather formal, and though less exclusive than Horninghold in the south, still give the visitor the impression that strangers are not particularly welcome there. Even the Knipton Reservoir is now more or less inaccessible. This was made by damming the little River Devon, to supply the Nottingham and Grantham Canal, abandoned long ago.

Eastwell has a very curious old church, and it once had a very curious old rector. The church is of ironstone, and the crumbling stonework of the tower is capped by what looks like a later addition of limestone battlements. Hoskins says that Eastwell has one of the most appealing country church interiors in the East Midlands, but I find it peculiarly unattractive, with its ugly wrought-iron lectern and green benches, like a dismal Victorian schoolroom - hardly to be compared with the church at Croxton Kerrial, which is graced by forty-two carved fifteenth-century benches. (Note, by the way, that the names Croxton and Sproxton are pronounced Crowston and Sprowston. But Leicestershire nonconformity extends even to the pronunciation of place-names. Owston is pronounced Ooston!)

Eastwell's curious old rector was the Rev. Edward Bullen, one of Leicestershire's sporting parsons. He was rector here for fifty-four years, dying when he was eighty-nine, and it is said that he followed the Quorn until well into his eighties. Because he was poor and could not afford a sound horse, he could only enjoy the gallop in the early minutes of the hunt, and this circumstance earned him the nickname 'Spurting Bullen'. Another sporting parson, of more recent memory, was incumbent at Ab Kettleby until he resigned to try his hand at training horses, and the Rev. Parkes is said to have trained over a hundred winners in three years.

Holwell is notable for its contribution of heavy industry to this unlikely area, for rich iron ore deposits were worked here from the late 1870s, and at one time the Holwell iron works was producing 600,000 tons of ore a year, and soon had five blast furnaces at Asfordby Hill, close to what was once described as a pretty little village. Holwell's church is built of the local ironstone.

Nestling below the escarpment of the Wolds, Nether Broughton, Old Dalby and Wymeswold stretch themselves out close to the Nottinghamshire border. Wymeswold is the largest of them. Its church was drastically restored by Pugin in the nineteenth century when the Reverend Henry Alford arrived there and found it in a badly neglected state. "The chancel," he wrote, "was devoted to the girls' Sunday School, the space within the rails to parish meetings. In that area, connected in every Christian's mind with the most holy rite of his religion, sounded the obscene brawls and blasphemous oaths of the village farmers." Alford collected £3,500 for the restoration of the church. He afterwards became Dean of Canterbury.

Can it really be true that Old Dalby was one of the first places in England where Beethoven's music was heard? In 1793 Old Dalby Hall was bought by the Hon. Mrs Bowater, a lady of musical tastes, who was hostess there to an Abbé Dobler. The Abbé had evidently brought some of the young Beethoven's music with him to England, and as Mrs Bowater was inclined to go into the woods to play music in the open air with her friends, it may be that the earliest compositions of the genius from Bonn filled the air around this Leicestershire farming village before they were heard in the concert halls of the metropolis. Alas, even the more traditional country matters associated with the woods scarcely disturb the wild life there now, and the music of Beethoven is heard in villages like Old Dalby today – if at all – only via the multitudinous aerials which occupy those modern stations of the cross, the roofs of thatch, tile or slate.

Prestwold consists only of hall and church, the village having disappeared long ago. The Packe family, who still own the estate, and to whom there are numerous monuments in the church, acquired it in 1650, when it was bought by Sir Christopher Packe. He was a Parliamentarian, a Lord Mayor of London and Governor of the Company of Merchant Adventurers. He was among those who urged Cromwell to assume the crown, and at the Restoration, retired here to pass his remaining years, barred from public office by the king.

Of all the buildings in Leicester and the county which have been the victims of neglect and then of demolition gangs, the one whose passing is to be most strongly deplored was Ragdale Hall. It was built in the sixteenth century by one of Leicestershire's great families, the Shirleys, and stood beside the church of this peaceful little village on the edge of the Wolds. The pattern of rebellious eccentricity which ran through the Shirley family was evident in Sir Henry Shirley, who enlarged Ragdale Hall early in the seventeenth century. Claiming descent from that "valiant Shirley", falconer of Henry IV, whose death at Shrewsbury is mentioned by Shakespeare, Sir Henry married Dorothy, the daughter of Robert Devereux, Earl of Essex, the favourite of

Swithland Reservoir

The Campanile in Queen's Park, Loughborough

Staunton Harold
Hall and church

The interior of
Staunton Harold
church

The ruins of Bradgate House

Hastings brick – Kirby Muxloe Castle

Hastings stone – Ashby Castle

Swithland slate cottages at Woodhouse Eaves

Coal-mining at Bagworth – miners' houses and colliery

Hosiery manufacturing at Hinckley – former framework knitters' cottages and modern factory

Inside a modern knitting factory

A framework knitter at work

Queen Elizabeth. Hawking seems to have been a family tradition, for Sir Henry got into trouble with his hawks, and his grandson, who was created Earl Ferrers in 1711, is said to have kept his hawks in the parlour at Ragdale. Sir Henry's troubles came when the Earl of Huntingdon denied him the right to hawk on his land, and Sir Henry was sent to prison over the matter, defiantly proclaiming that he cared nothing for a lord in England, "except the Lord of Hosts".

A later Earl Ferrers built a new hall, which still stands, now a 'health hydro' farther away from the village, towards the place known as Six Hills. (I must digress here to explain that there are not, and never have been, six hills here. The name is evidently a corruption of Seggshill, 'segg' being an old local word for sheep.) The Old Hall became a farmhouse, and was then divided into two, and in course of time began to decay. It was a very fine timber-framed Tudor mansion, with gables, tall star-shaped chimneys, and mullioned and transomed windows. Sir Henry Shirley's coat of arms was on the projecting stone porch, and a pillar inside bore his and his wife's initials with the date 1631. Ragdale Old Hall had become so ruinous by 1958 that it was demolished, and Leicestershire thus carelessly and disgracefully lost one of its finest architectural treasures. Now the little old ironstone church, which had the Old Hall as its close companion through the centuries, is itself crumbling to dust, and will soon be in ruins also. We have not by any means, however, heard the last of the Shirleys. Hang about, as they say.

South of Ragdale, by the River Wreake, is Brooksby, the village which begat that Duke of Buckingham whom we have met briefly at Burley-on-the-Hill, where he had Jeffery Hudson served to the king in a pie. And if the reader thinks *that* episode ludicrous, he has heard nothing yet! The Villiers family had been connected with Brooksby at least as far back as the thirteenth century, when an Alexander de Villiers held land there. His descendant, Sir George Villiers, married a Beaumont, and George, the future duke, was their second son, born in 1592. After the death of his father, George was sent by his mother to France to learn some 'useful arts', and it was soon after his return that he first met the homosexual King James I—"that false Scottish urchin", as Elizabeth had once called him. If James was a specialist in extravagance, he met his match in George Villiers.

The young man was possessed of an effeminate beauty, and

when King James met him it was a case of love at first sight. Villiers was taken to court as a cup-bearer, and within seven years had rocketed to a dukedom. Lift-off was in 1616, when he was made Master of the Horse, Knight of the Garter and Viscount Villiers, all in the same year. He went into orbit as Earl of Buckingham in the year following that, then became Marquess, and finally Duke, in his thirty-first year of life. If the king had but lived long enough, George Villiers might well have been deified.

James called him "Steenie", apparently on the grounds that he resembled Saint Stephen, and once remarked: "Christ had his John, and I have my George." Self-exaltation can scarcely fly higher than that, and the duke was only too willing to pander to the king's ridiculous whims. If James could end a letter with "God bless you, my sweet child and wife, and grant that ye may ever be a comfort to your dear dad and husband"; then Villiers could respond with "Your Majesty's most humble Slave and Dogge, Steenie."

Nor was the rest of the Villiers family left out of account in this undignified royal farce. All the Villiers snakes suddenly ran up all the court ladders. George's avaricious mother became a duchess and his brother John became Viscount Purbeck. His two half-brothers were made baronets, and his sister's husband an earl. Buckingham himself married Lady Catherine Manners, daughter of the Earl of Rutland, and she also enjoyed the king's favour, and kept him informed of every detail of their domestic life: "I hope my Lord Anan has tould your Majestie that I did mean to wene Mall very shortly. I would not by any mens a don it, till I had furst made your Majestie acquainted with it . . . I think she is oulde enufe, and I hope will endure her wening very well; for I think there was never child card less for the brest than shee dos."

If all this were simply an episode in the private lives of the senile monarch and his favourite, we should simply squirm and pass on. But the Duke of Buckingham became one of the richest and most powerful men in the kingdom, and it is his conduct in affairs of state which makes him a significant son of Leicester-shire. He had cultivated the friendship of the young Prince Charles as assiduously as that of James. The fatuous expedition of the two young men to seek the hand of the Infanta of Spain was Buckingham's idea, and his influence over Charles continued when the prince became king. It was Buckingham who arranged the marriage of Charles to Henrietta Maria, and he was thus largely responsible for the king's downfall and the subsequent fate of England. When he led the nation into pointless wars with France and Spain, he was finally impeached as a menace to the realm, but before he could be called to answer the charges against him, he was assassinated.

As he left his breakfast table one morning, a Suffolk man named Felton approached him, drew a long knife and thrust it "with great strength and violence, into his breast and under his left pap, cutting the diaphragma and lungs, and piercing the verie heart itself. The Duke, having received the stroke, instantlie clapping his right hand on his sworde hilt, cried out, 'God's wounds, the villaine has killed me!' " Felton steadfastly maintained that he had done the deed for the public good. Although he was mentally unbalanced, it may be that he *did* have the public good in mind, but he was hanged at Tyburn, even so.

The Villiers family remained at Brooksby until early in the eighteenth century, and the Duke of Buckingham's descendants continued their involvement in court affairs. His son, the second duke, provided Charles II with the mistress who became Duchess of Cleveland. His daughter, Lady Mary Villiers (she in whose weaning James I had taken such a close interest), married three times into noble families. William III made Elizabeth Villiers his mistress, and married her off to the Earl of Orkney when he had finished with her. Brooksby Hall is now an agricultural institute, but among its occupants after the Villiers had left were the Earl of Cardigan and Earl Beatty.

Frisby-on-the-Wreake, a short distance up-river from Brooksby, is one of those unchanging villages of Leicestershire which goes about its daily life almost untouched by the great world beyond. It has an old village cross, the odd thatched cottage, and a little church Norman in origin. The Children's Corner in the church has an oak screen made in 1930 of timber from an old windmill at Seagrave, and the local man who made it, Cyril Smith, has recorded his memories of the village in the early years of this century, when a doctor from Melton used to visit the village and tie up his horse in the yard of the inn, and the village boys used to give the barrel-organ man a push up the hill towards Leicester, before the modern road bypassed the village altogether.

Those days have gone for ever, when the local blacksmith was also the church sexton, who rang the pancake bell on Shrove Tuesday to let the children out of school for a holiday; and a farmer who made Stilton cheese founded a village brass band. But Frisby is typical of many quiet and attractive farming villages in Leicestershire, which have changed only slowly, and retained an atmosphere of old-world calm, far removed from the national catastrophes perpetrated by the nobs at neighbouring Brooksby.

All the more surprising, therefore, that Frisby-on-the-Wreake was once front-page news. An eighteenth-century rector here, the Rev. William Wragge, suddenly startled the village by announcing that he would marry any couple who came before him, without banns or licence. When the news got abroad he did a roaring trade for a time, but eventually the law caught up with him and he was sentenced to fourteen years' transportation, for performing an illegal marriage ceremony. By that time, however, he was too old for the sentence to be worth carrying out. He faded into obscurity, and the Leicestershire Gretna Green once more became a quiet farming village. The railway line separates the village from the river, but there is no station here now, and both road and rail pass Frisby by. Hens sit placidly in the lane leading to the river, and an old wooden footbridge over it was guarded by a friendly donkey when I was last there.

Frisby seems infinitely more tranquil than its neighbours simply by virtue of its layout. The village of Hoby is peaceful enough, but drive (very slowly) through its zigzag street and then come out giddy into the straight to find yourself deep in water at Thrussington, when the Wreake has overflowed its banks and flooded the road, and you may momentarily try to recall if you have been drinking. One wonders if drink was the defence put up a couple of centuries ago, when the local rat-catcher, one Samuel Letts, was sent to the county gaol for stealing two turkeys. ("Honest to Gawd, yer honour, ah thowt they was rats!")

Most of the disused railway stations, like Frisby's, have been demolished or converted, but one or two remain, here and there, isolated and derelict. Taking the hint from Professor Hoskins ("The country all round here is very hilly and picturesque, worth exploring slowly, in all directions"), I decided to start from the old station at East Norton, near Tugby, and follow the cutting for a while. The hunts sometimes use the old railway cuttings now, and I believe have bought some of the land from British Rail. But I was in for a shock at East Norton. The cutting here has been turned into a huge rubbish tip, directly beneath the Leicester-Uppingham road. The stench rose to meet me as I approached to look over the bridge at the old station, and thousands of scavenging gulls settled on the mounds of refuse or circled screaming in the air, whilst in the trees hundreds of crows perched like vultures waiting for their turn at a rotting carcass. This area was not to be explored, slowly or otherwise, in any direction.

It seems a pity that guides like Arthur Mee had to concentrate so much on churches at the expense of other buildings which played their part in the story of the king's England. How well Mee could have given us a record of these forgotten railway stations, with their own distinctive style of architecture, lying alone like the ruined churches of deserted villages. "Raised by the men of the Victorian age," he might have written, "it stands bare and melancholy, stranded by the receding tide of national affairs. Its canopied little platform, where for more than a century local travellers commenced their journeys, sometimes to the farthest corners of the empire, now stands deserted before a straight and narrow path to nowhere. The broken windows in these wooden walls let wind and rain into the tiny room where for more than twenty years the last faithful old servant of the company handed tickets to those who came here seeking adventure in distant places. The pools of water on the bed of the former track bespeak the neglect of our own times, but among the forlorn fragments of the past brought to light here was a small but thrilling thing – a rusty sign reminding us of days that are no more. When its excited discoverer had cleared the mud and grime from the treasure in his hand, he found himself just able to make out the time-honoured inscription: 'Do not pull the chain while the train is standing at the station'."

If writers on Leicestershire have failed us in this respect, however, a few artists have more than made up for them, and the great age of the railways, in particular, has been the preoccupation of David Weston, of Kirby Bellars, who has captured the atmosphere of vanished transport systems with a flair that has extended also to many of the county's lost buildings, such as Ragdale Hall and Leicester's Opera House.

Kirby Bellars derives its strange name from Roger Beler, a

medieval lord of the manor, whose canopied monument is in the south aisle of the village church. The church is a little distance away from the present village, as the original habitations were deserted and the village grew up again on a new site. Kirby Gate, beside the Leicester-Melton road, is the traditional scene of the Quorn's opening meet of the season, on the first Monday of November, and at the southern approach to the village, also on the main road, an inn called The Flying Childers is named after a famous eighteenth-century racehorse.

Further down the Wreake valley, Ratcliffe has the first Catholic college built in England since the dissolution of the monasteries. It was begun by Pugin, and contains a crucifix which is said to have been brought to England by the Duke of Wellington. It formerly belonged to Syon Abbey in Middlesex, but was taken away by the nuns at the dissolution. South of the village, beside the Fosse Way, is Shipley Hill, which Arthur Mee, following the Victoria County History, reverently describes as "a huge mound raised by the men of the Stone Age". It is really just a natural spur created by erosion, and had been established as such even when Nichols produced his history. There is precious little evidence of any Stone Age settlement at all in Leicestershire.

The erosion of Sileby is anything but natural. This is one of Leicestershire's dreary red-brick industrial villages on the wrong side of the Soar, and we may be grateful for the light relief offered in the churchyard, in rhyming epitaph to a long-dead sexton, Edward Barradell:

> For fifty-two revolving years
> Devoutly he attended prayers,
> With mellow voice and solemn knell,
> He sang the psalms and tolled the bell.

One wonders that all those revolving years didn't make him too giddy to do anything!

Cossington stands near a confluence of waterways which seem like a tangled ball of string one would like to unravel. The Soar is joined by the Wreake, a bit of the Grand Union Canal, and one or two tributary streams, flanked by Wanlip and Syston (another desperately uninviting industrial village). Cossington has one of the finest of the interesting old water-mills on the Soar north of Leicester. It is now a restaurant, but corn was ground here as long ago as the thirteenth century. There are also some very old cruck cottages in the village, which is the home of another famous Leicestershire doctor, Isobel, Lady Barnett.

Cossington is without doubt one of Leicestershire's most peaceful and attractive villages, which is remarkable in view of its close industrial neighbours, another of which is Barrow-upon-Soar. Barrow's limestone deposits, which have been worked for centuries, have yielded skeletons of our prehistoric ancestors in well-preserved states, a twenty-foot long plesiosaurus among them – a monster reptile which swam in the waters here before even the dinosaurs appeared on the earth. Modern man's visions of a Loch Ness Monster seem to bear some resemblance to this old serpent.

Beyond the Wolds, the beautiful Vale of Belvoir stretches out ~thern extremity of the county and into Nottingham-
~olnshire. Standing sentinel over this territory is

within sight of Nottingham Castle and Lincoln Cathedral, and occupies the most spectacular castle site in England, excepting Windsor alone. Having said that, however, I must add that it is best seen from a distance. Closer inspection of its architecture reveals a lamentable confusion of towers, battlements, pinnacles and turrets, sham-Tudor or mock-Camelot in style – everything that nineteenth-century builders considered romantic.

The hill on which the castle stands is partly artificial. As Leland wrote: "The Castelle of Bellvoire standith in the utter part of that way of Leicestershire, on the very knape of an highe hille, stepe up eche way, partly by nature, partly by working of mennes handes, as it may evidently be perceived. Whether there were any Castelle there afore the Conquest or no, I am not sure, but surely I think rather no than yea." It was in fact Robert de Todeni, the Conqueror's Standard Bearer at Hastings, who built the first castle, and his heirs owned Belvoir for 150 years. It passed by marriage into the de Ros family, and then, in due course, to the Manners family, who adopted the peacock as their family crest. By that time, the castle's condition was ruinous, as a result of protracted disputes following the Wars of the Roses, and it was rebuilt by Sir Thomas Manners, who was created Earl of Rutland in 1526.

In 1603, the fifth earl entertained James I at Belvoir, and the castle's commanding situation led the king to remark: "By God, what a traitor the man would make!" He was sufficiently impressed to make forty-six knights before breakfast on the morning of his departure. The earl's household consisted of more than two hundred people at that time, and he owned thirty thousand acres of Leicestershire. Nevertheless, during the Civil War, Belvoir was forced to surrender after a siege lasting four months, and the castle was ordered to be demolished. The eighth earl then built a new mansion on the site, which was a most imposing piece of classical architecture, but this was also demolished when the fifth duke decided to rebuild the house on the lines of a medieval castle, evidently to please his wife.

To whom should he entrust this task but that master of the mock-heroic in stone, James Wyatt! Wyatt was the dreaded bogey-man of architectural purists and was nicknamed 'The Destroyer' after his neo-Gothic restorations of various English cathedrals. He worked on Belvoir Castle and Ashridge House, in Hertfordshire, at the same time, and there is a great deal of similarity in many of the details in the two buildings. In 1813, before he had finished either, Wyatt died of shock when his coach overturned, and the completion of Belvoir was entrusted to the Rev. Sir John Thoroton, the vicar of Bottesford and chaplain to the duke. This amateur architect had the assistance and encouragement of the duchess herself, who was also responsible for the layout of some of the gardens. In 1816, a great fire broke out which destroyed much of Wyatt's work, as well as valuable pictures by Titian, Van Dyck and Reynolds. Thoroton then supervised the rebuilding, and the castle we see today was completed by him in 1830. To my mind, it is far less impressive than the mansion which was destroyed to make way for it, which had been designed by John Webb, the pupil and successor of Inigo Jones.

The treasures of Belvoir, which is Leicestershire's most opulent showplace and one of the most popular tourist attractions of the Midlands, include a series of magnificent Gobelin tapestries, and paintings by Poussin, Murillo, Holbein, Hogarth and Reynolds, among others. There is also a hunting scene by John Ferneley, showing the fifth duke and his brothers at full gallop across the Vale with the castle in the background. The castle also houses the museum of the 21st Lancers, the regiment raised by the Marquis of Granby, the son of the third duke and hero of the Battle of Minden. It was the Lancers whom Lord

Car... ...amous Charge of the Light Brigade,
and th... ...holy relics can see the bugle which
sounde... ...trous event.

The st... ...kes of Rutland are many and
varied (th... ...ke by Queen Anne in
1703), but... ...noblemen and
generous lan... ...itchcraft
should have ra... ...all
places, in the sev...
earl, employed tv...
Philippa Flower. M...
and was dismissed. ...
Bottesford and was re...
the earl and countess. ...
were gloves belonging to...
was dipped in hot water b...
pins, and within a week th...
brother's glove was buried in...
a curse was put on the earl and countess rendering them sterile.
So when Sir Francis died, the earldom passed to his brother.

Five years elapsed after the deaths of the Manners boys before
the Flower women and three local accomplices were arrested,
and the trial of the 'Witches of Belvoir' took place at Lincoln
soon after the execution of those other 'witches' at Husbands
Bosworth. Joan Flower asserted her innocence by challenging her
inquisitors to give her bread, saying that if she were guilty it
would choke her. The bread was brought and – no doubt to
everyone else's surprise, to say nothing of her own – she instantly
choked and died. This alarmed the other women so much that
they could hardly wait to incriminate one another, and bizarre
details of their practices poured forth. They related descriptions
of orgies, of familiar spirits which sucked beneath their breasts
and ears, of Joan Flower's satanic cat Rutterkin, and of meetings
of their coven on a hill below the castle. The five women were
condemned to death and hanged at Lincoln Gaol. How much
of the story was truth and how much fiction we shall never
know, but we may surmise that imagination played the greater
part in the minds of the women and their accusers in believing
they had caused the deaths of the heirs to the earldom. (Flower
power is not what it was!)

The more traditional feminine charms associated with Belvoir are worth pausing over. The heirs to the Manners titles seem to have been singularly adept at marrying and begetting women of extraordinary beauty. Charles, the fourth duke, married Lady Mary Somerset, the daughter of the Duke of Beaufort, who was said to be "the most beautiful woman in the kingdom of high rank . . . combining in her figure the variety of points that Apelles is supposed to have sought throughout Greece". Possibly so, but she can hardly have been more ravishing than the fifth duchess, unless the latter's painters and sculptors unduly flattered their patron. She was Elizabeth Howard, daughter of the Earl of Carlisle, and it is said that when she married John Henry, the fifth Duke of Rutland, she remarked on their honeymoon that she must have a castle! Well, I can forgive her share of the responsibility for James Wyatt being let loose on this hilltop if she looked like that. But is this fair goddess, so appropriately proud as a peacock, whose full-length portrait greets us on the staircase, the woman who was an amateur architect, and a farmer and stockbreeder, as well as a wife and the mother of eleven children? It is indeed. She was eighteen when she married John Henry Manners, whose statue stands in Leicester Market Place. No wonder he was so popular! But the duchess died a week after her forty-fifth birthday of an obstruction in the bowels, and if her obituary sounds a little fulsome to modern ears, I believe every word of it, even so: "England may boast of women of dazzling beauty – of women possessing great taste for the arts – and of many a fond mother, . . . but qualities so various, never met together in any individual, till they were united in the person of the lovely, and ever to be lamented Duchess of Rutland." Another well-known beauty of the Manners household, Lady Diana Cooper, the daughter of the eighth duke, was once described by Cecil Beaton as creating "the effects of all the lights being turned on when she enters a room".

The large village of Bottesford is the most northerly in Leicestershire, and its church, with the county's tallest steeple – 210 feet high – contains memorials to the eight earls of Rutland – a collection of monumental sculpture which is unique in England. The church itself, apart from its crocketed needle spire, is not exceptional, though it is one of the largest village churches in the country. But even if it were a church of outstanding beauty, its charms would be swamped by the Rutland monuments, which overwhelm the chancel and practically hide the altar from the congregation in the nave. As well as the earls and their wives, a vast number of offspring are represented on the monuments. (Manners maketh man!).

A mausoleum was built at Belvoir in 1828 by Thoroton, and the tombs of the dukes were transferred there, which is just as well. As it was, Bottesford Church had to be 'adjusted' to accommodate those which are here now. Walls were taken down, and the chancel roof shoved upwards to take the tomb of the sixth earl, a vulgar mass of masonry which is famous and unique because of its attribution of the deaths of the earl's sons to "wicked practice and sorcerye". It was this same earl whose daughter Catherine married 'Steenie' Buckingham.

The seventh and eighth earls' monuments are almost certainly by Grinling Gibbons, though they are not to be counted among the great works of that master carver. The earlier monuments are the most impressive—the third and fourth earls' by the Flemish mason Janssen Gerard, and the fifth by Nicholas, his son. Records show that the fourth and fifth earls' tombs were made in London, transported to Boston in Lincolnshire by sea, and then brought across country on carts pulled by ninety horses.

George Crabbe, that realistic poet of nature, was appointed domestic chaplain to the fourth duke, and published his first important work, *The Village,* whilst at Belvoir Castle. He became rector at Muston soon afterwards but was unpopular there, as any preacher was bound to be who attacked Nonconformism in Leicestershire. Personal tragedy added to his own unhappiness. His wife Sarah lost her reason when five of her children died, and after her death, the poet himself descended into melancholy, and gratefully left Muston when another living was offered him. The villagers were so glad to see him go that they rang the bells for his successor before he had left.

A string of villages stretches out along Leicestershire's narrow strip of the Vale of Belvoir, from Bottesford and Muston, down to Hose, via Redmile, Barkestone, Plungar and Harby. They are linked together not only by attractive narrow country roads, but also by the old Nottingham-Grantham Canal, opened in 1793. You may feel very far away from Leicester as you explore this peaceful and relatively unknown vale, though in fact the city centre is but twenty miles distant. It is easier to imagine that the lords of Belvoir Castle still rule here, than that any such thing as a county council plays a part in local affairs. The peacock has pride of place here rather than the running fox. But ominous breezes of change waft through the clear air of the Vale of Belvoir at the time of writing, for it is said that massive coal seams lie beneath this tranquil land.

It was the eighth Earl of Rutland's wife, the well-proportioned daughter of Lord Montague of Boughton, who brought Thomas Daffy to Redmile as vicar in 1666. And like many a Leicestershire parson, he was more renowned for his non-professional activities than for his sermons. This particular cleric was the inventor of 'Daffy's Elixir', a miracle cure which, it was claimed, was "a Sovereign and never failing Remedy" against every conceivable ailment, and gave "immediate Ease in the most Racking Pains of the Cholick", prevented miscarriages, destroyed worms and "changeth the Whole Mass of Blood". There was no Trade Descriptions Act to prevent such advertisement in those days, not that one was needed in Leicestershire, where the women had their own answers to bodily ills. It was in sophisticated London where the Reverend Daffy's potion found its gullible customers.

Barkestone is a tinier and sleepier village down the road, with a bellcote on the village school and a slender spire on the village church; whilst Plungar and Harby are larger, but just as unconcerned with the frantic pace of the modern world. The road from Harby to Waltham-on-the-Wolds is exceptionally wide in places, and was an old drovers' road, probably very ancient in origin, because it joins The Drift to the south-east, and was no doubt used as a direct route to and from Nottingham.

A border that is not to be found on any Ordnance Survey map crosses the land hereabouts. It is the line dividing the territory of the Belvoir Hunt from that of the Quorn - reputedly the two most distinguished hunts in England. What better point at which to pause and look more closely at this sport for which Leicestershire has long been famous, or, if you like, notorious.

VII

FOR'ARD, FOR'ARD!

HUNTING of the fox in Britain probably began as a substitute for stag-hunting, when deer were becoming less plentiful in the deforested countryside. It was a casual pastime for as long as two hundred years, possibly, and did not become an organized sport until relatively recent times. A hunting horn which belonged to Thomas Boothby of Tooley Park bears the legend: "With this horn be hunted the first pack of hounds then in England for fifty-five years. Born 1677. Died 1752." There is doubt about the accuracy of the inscription on two counts. One is that Boothby's date of birth is at variance with the records in his parish church; the other that packs of hounds existed earlier than this, but probably were not used exclusively for hunting foxes. At any rate, it is generally accepted that fox-hunting was established on an organized basis at the beginning of the eighteenth century.

The pre-eminence of what were called 'The Shires' in fox-hunting was soon established. The term was usually taken to include Leicestershire, Rutland and parts of Northamptonshire, but hunts from the Shires operated beyond these confines, as they do today, and hunts from outside also ride in Shires country. The hunts which include parts of modern Leicestershire in their territories are the Quorn, Belvoir, Cottesmore, Fernie, and Atherstone, and all except the last of these are Leicestershire based. Let us look at the facts first, and ask the inevitable questions afterwards. I have no intention of ignoring the moral issue, as some writers on Leicestershire have done, but it would be well to know what it is we are talking about.

One of the most famous names in the history of hunting is Hugo Meynell, often referred to as "the father of English fox-hunting". Meynell married Thomas Boothby's grand-daughter, the sister of the last Boothby to own Tooley Park. This Boothby was a snob and a spendthrift, the first trait earning him the nickname 'Prince' Boothby, and the second causing him to

sell the neglected estate and to commit suicide in the following
year. Tooley Park, which no longer exists, was north-east of Earl
Shilton in the parish of Peckleton, and had once been called
Shilton Park. It was one of the best-known estates in the county.
The Boothbys were people of substance in London, and Horace
Walpole and Henry Fielding enjoyed their society. Fielding is
said to have based certain characters in *Tom Jones* on members of
the Boothby family. At Tooley Park, however, the earlier
Thomas Boothby kept his hounds and made what must have
been one of the first specially created fox coverts in the country,
still known as Tooley Spinneys. One of the stories told of
Boothby was that a vicar informed Mrs Boothby that her
husband had a mistress. Boothby took his revenge by inviting the
parson to go fishing with him, and then pushed him into Groby
Pool.

When Hugo Meynell married into this family, he acquired
the hounds as well as a wife, and in 1754 he bought Quorndon
Hall, where he built stables 300 feet long. He developed Thomas
Boothby's pack of hounds on a scientific basis, possibly with
advice from his contemporary Robert Bakewell, and became the
true founder of the modern Quorn Hunt, raising it to a quality
which it has maintained since, making it still the world's most
famous hunt. In the early days there were but few subscribers,
but things soon changed. Meynell entertained on a lavish scale at
Quorndon. He was a man of wit, and once remarked, after
struggling through a meeting with a group of Frenchmen who
spoke no English, that he "wished we were safe at war again". He
was described as being "like a regular little apple-dumpling on
horseback", and in 1800, a few years before his death, he said that
"hunting can't last another ten years".

In Rutland, meanwhile, a pack of hounds created in West-
morland by Lord Lowther became the property of the Earl
of Gainsborough at Exton Park, and this eventually became the
Cottesmore Hunt. The aristocratic Belvoir Hunt was founded in
1730 by the famous Marquis of Granby, whose bald head appears
on so many inn signs. The hunt is still known as the Duke of
Rutland's, though the present duke does not hunt, and the
Belvoir hounds, kennelled at Belvoir Castle, have long rivalled
the Quorn as the finest pack in the world. The Fernie Hunt was a
later development. The Billesdon Hunt, which had been
established originally as a branch pack of the Quorn to hunt the

country round Market Harborough, was taken over by Charles Fernie of Keythorpe Hall from Sir Bache Cunard of Nevill Holt, and Mrs Fernie succeeded her husband as Master when he died. It has been known ever since as Fernie's Hunt, and it is the only one of the four Leicestershire packs to hunt entirely within the county boundary.

The territories of the Quorn, the Belvoir and the Cottesmore meet at Melton Mowbray, which has long been the metropolis of the hunting set – not always an enviable position. Hair-raising stories of the goings-on at Melton during the season, when the night air "trembled with the sighs of adulterers", have become part of the sport's literature, most of which was inspired by the 'great days' of hunting in the nineteenth and early twentieth centuries. It was an exclusive society, in which champagne flowed like water and the talk was of nothing but horses and hunting. George Whyte-Melville, the sporting novelist who lived in John Ferneley's house for a time, and died in a hunting accident, wrote:

> Who that has ever spent a season in the cosy, cheerful, joyous little town, but would wish to turn the stream of time, and live those golden days and pleasant nights over again? – would wish to be galloping his covert-hack once more through the fragrant air and under the dappled sky of a February morning, with a good horse to ride from Ranksborough Gorse or Barkby Holt, as his day's amusement, and a choice of at least a couple of invitations, offering him the pleasantest society and the best dinner in England for his evening's gratification?

Large houses were needed to accommodate those wealthy visitors whose thousand horses were stabled in the town, and among those who built or owned lodges in Melton as head-quarters for hunting were the Earl of Wilton, the Marquis of Hastings, the Countess of Warwick, the Duke and Duchess of Cleveland, the Earl of Plymouth, the Marquis of Worcester and the Maharanee of Cooch Behar. The sporting guests of these hosts make an even more illustrious list. Edward VII slept in beds in most of these houses at one time or another, among them the Countess of Warwick's. Then there were the Dukes of Wellington, York, Gloucester and Cambridge, Earl Beatty, the Earl of Oxford and Asquith, Winston Churchill, and so on, *ad infinitum*, changing to *nauseam*, perhaps, only when it comes to the notorious Marquis of Waterford.

Wherever high jinks among the young bloods of the Leicester-shire hunting set got out of hand, there would the third Marquis of Waterford be, often accompanied by one of the Villiers clan. The marquis was Henry de la Poer Beresford, who had suc-ceeded his father to the title at the age of fifteen, in 1826. He was a generous landlord and devoted husband, evidently handsome and chivalrous. But away from his Irish estate, he was a wildly eccentric and hard-living hunting fanatic. At Lowesby Hall, he amused himself by shooting the eyes out of all the portraits on the walls, and for a wager of a hundred guineas, brought his favourite horse indoors and jumped a five-barred gate in the dining-room. At Melton one night in 1837 he and his friends painted the White Swan Inn red. He thought it a great joke to reverse all the signposts in the vicinity so that visiting sportsmen could not find the way home. Once he put a donkey in an unsuspecting victim's bed, and painted aniseed on the heels of a clergyman's horse and set bloodhounds after him.

The upper-class louts who toadied to this 'noble' gang-leader sometimes ended up in court with their hero. The 'Mad Marquis' and his friends were fined a hundred pounds each at Derby Assizes on one occasion for disturbing the peace at Melton by challenging an old nightwatchman to a fight, overturning a caravan, and breaking open the lock-up to release one of the prisoners. The objectionable tenor of the marquis's pranks led to his comeuppance at the hands of a bass-singer. Outside the Bell Inn at Leicester he challenged the travelling minstrel to a fight and provoked him with a tap on the nose. The singer then proceeded to give the marquis a sound thrashing, to the dismay of his hangers-on. It was said that the marquis always paid generously for any damage he did during his drunken revelries, but his reign of terror came to a sudden end in 1859 when he fell from his horse and broke his neck.

Rowdyism continued at Melton, during the season, long after the marquis left the scene, but never with the same malicious fervour. In 1890 Lady Augusta Fane invited her guests to take part in a midnight steeplechase over a course lit by railway lamps, and wearing ladies' nightdresses over their hunting gear. The race was won by Algernon Burnaby, a later Master of the Quorn, wearing Lady Augusta's own pink gossamer nightie. Second was Count Zborowski, the Polish millionaire who was killed in a motor race in France in 1909, and was buried in

Burton Lazars churchyard. The future Commander of the Fourth Army in the Great War, General Lord Rawlinson, also took part, as well as three members of the well-known Paget family. This ridiculous but relatively harmless spree outraged local opinion, and on the following Sunday the vicar condemned it in a sermon on the text: "Have no fellowship with the unfruitful works of darkness."

This vicar, clearly, was not one of the sporting parsons who contrived to get livings in Leicestershire in order to take a day off now and then to ride with the hunts. Leicestershire has always shown a measure of tolerance towards sporting clerics, of whom Sydney Smith remarked, characteristically: "If anything ever endangers the Church, it will be the strong propensity to shooting for which the clergy are remarkable. Ten thousand good shots dispersed over the country do more harm to the cause of religion than the arguments of Voltaire and Rousseau."

One bishop took a vicar to task over the matter, saying: "This is a tattling world and they tell me that you hunt." "It is indeed a tattling world," the vicar retorted. "They say your Lordship goes to the queen's balls." The bishop replied: "It is true that when I am invited by Her Majesty I do not think it proper to decline. But I am never in the room in which the dancing is going on." "That is just my case, my lord," the vicar said triumphantly. "I have only one old mare, and I am never in the field in which the hounds are."

Sporting parsons, steeplechases, hunt balls and aristocratic pranks, however, are merely the by-products of the serious business of fox-hunting, and I mean 'business', for in Leicestershire hunting was – and is – a very expensive sport. It used to be said that a man with five or six hunters could make a respectable appearance with the 'Provincials', but to hunt every day with the cream, in the Shires, he would need at least ten sound horses, which might cost him a thousand pounds each. Today, it may cost an enthusiast two hundred pounds in subscription alone to ride with the aristocrats of hunting for one day a week during the season.

The rich winter residents of Melton provided John Ferneley and other artists with frequent commissions for portraits of their horses or themselves. Sir Francis Grant, President of the Royal Academy, who lived in Dalby Road, painted one picture of the Quorn in which Lord and Lady Wilton, the Count d'Orsay, the

Dukes of Beaufort and Rutland, and the Earls of Chesterfield, Plymouth and Cardigan appear, among others. But though Grant was fashionable, Ferneley was the better artist, and a canvas for which he may have charged two thousand pounds is worth at least ten times that amount today.

The larger hunts have perhaps eighty or ninety hounds (the Quorn has 128) and hunt four days a week in the season, using dogs and bitches separately. Hounds, as well as horses, are bred scientifically, to a very high standard, and are exercised regularly for long periods when they are not hunting. The cost of keeping a top-class pack of hounds is phenomenal today, and almost all British hunts now have joint masters, although the masters no longer bear the whole burden of the cost of keeping the pack, as they used to.

The object of all the care and expense lavished on horses, hounds and wardrobe is the small native animal *Vulpes vulpes,* the common or red fox. When the fox replaced the hare and the deer as the quarry of the huntsman, European foxes were imported to swell the native population, and early in the nineteenth century, a thousand foxes a year were passing through Leadenhall Market to be set free in different parts of the country. During this period, in hunting territory, foxes were encouraged to breed in specially created coverts, and Leicester-shire is dotted with such dens, many of which are famous in hunting circles, among them Ashby Pastures, Cradock's Ashes, Botany Bay, Thrussington Gorse and Barkby Holt. But the fox breeds fairly prolifically, a vixen generally producing five to eight cubs a year, and it was not long before there were far too many foxes. The cubs are usually born in April, after a gestation period of about two months, and are classed as adults by the time the hunting season starts in November.

It has been estimated that something like fourteen thousand foxes a year are killed in Britain by hunting alone. I find it difficult to reconcile this figure with the statements of hunting people that, more often than not, the foxes they chase get away. There are about two hundred packs of fox-hounds in Britain, and if they hunt, on average, three days a week during the season, they cannot account for anything like fourteen thousand foxes unless they catch most of those they set up. Nevertheless, although animal lovers may be appalled at this vast number of victims, all the evidence seems to indicate that the fox is thriving.

I think it is beyond dispute that hunting has helped to preserve the fox population, though whether that is a good or a bad thing is another question. Before the animal was hunted for sport, it was regarded as vermin to be exterminated, like the rat, by any possible means. The hunts safeguarded the fox zealously, and it became almost a cardinal sin to shoot or poison foxes in hunting country.

Generally speaking, farmers are in favour of the hunts and often ride with them, though they have a lot to put up with in damage to their hedges and fences, particularly on the days when hundreds of riders turn up at a fashionable meet. But Leicestershire's pre-eminence in hunting is due to its superb terrain for cross-country riding, and as the land has influenced hunting, so hunting has influenced the landscape.

The quick-growing hawthorn was the ideal hedging plant for the Midland counties when fields had to be enclosed in the eighteenth century. It is extremely hardy, unfussy about soil, and soon makes a dense hedge. But left alone, hawthorn will reach a height too great for any horse to jump. So the riders' dreams of glorious gallops across country were likely to be foiled every time they reached a hedge, or a 'bullfinch' as they called such overgrown hawthorn barriers. (In hunting parlance every barrier is a 'fence' regardless of whether it is of natural growth or man-made.) The solution was in the discovery of the art of 'laying-back' hawthorn hedges, which was made and perfected in Leicestershire, and is now used wherever hawthorn is common.

Laying-back or 'pleaching' of hawthorn hedges is a craftsman's job if it is to be done properly, and it is carried out in the winter months, every few years. Apart from its obvious advantage to the hunts, it prevents the hedges from exhausting themselves by over-energetic growth, keeps them tidy and solid, to prevent livestock from straying, and incidentally – in Leicestershire at least – preserves the distant view, which would be blocked almost everywhere in the county if it were not for the farmers' care of their hedges.

The hedge-layer often works alone, and his only tools are a very sharp bill-hook and perhaps a mallet. The bill-hook is a curved hatchet with a point, and with this he trims off all the branches of the hawthorn, leaving only the main stem. This is then cut half through, not more than a foot above ground level, and bent over. Knowing how to make the cut is one of the secrets, for it must be done so that the sap still rises in the uncut half of the stem.

The line of the hedge is staked, perhaps with ash, and the bent-over stems of the hawthorn are then woven into the stakes, overlapping one another, and the tops of the stakes bound with bramble or hazel. At the same time, the workman will be clearing the hedgerow of unwanted growth which might choke the hawthorn, and if there is a ditch, he will clear that too. It is easy to see the difference between a hedge which has been properly laid by a craftsman and one which has been cut back by an amateur. There are fewer of the old craftsmen about now, of course, but also fewer hedges to be laid, with the arable farmer wanting larger fields and wire fences to make economical use of agricultural machinery. There is an increasing tendency now for hawthorn hedges to be hacked back as if they were privet, making an unsightly mess of them.

The hedge-layer will be at work early in the morning, in rolled-up shirt sleeves, waistcoat and cloth cap, in spite of the cold, when the hunt comes down the lane, between the hedgerows, with the morning dew still hanging in sparkling beads on the spiders' webs. The sound of the horses' hooves, at walking pace, slightly muffled by the mist, greets you first, but the well-disciplined hounds and the huntsman precede the master into view, breath rising in the cold air, and then the fine hunters of bay, chestnut and grey, carrying the 'field' in scarlet or black – more often black than scarlet these days. And suddenly the crisp morning air is alive with colour and warmth and an excitement shared by men and animals.

It takes, I believe, a singularly soulless campaigner to remain unmoved by a scene like this. I am not for a moment suggesting that the means justifies the end, but the human mind is sadly limited by its inability to embrace opposing ideas. We too readily adopt a point of view and then throw aside everything that does not fit it. The man who has no soul and sees – with the mind of an accountant – all the wonders of the world merely as figures on a balance sheet, is unable to cope with contradictions, and if he has his way he will give us Bertrand Russell's appalling vision of a world reduced to mathematical formulae. Offer him the seven pillars of wisdom as credits and the seven deadly sins as debits and he will solemnly declare, having examined the accounts, that human life is a viable proposition. So let us not turn our backs on this colourful winter scene yet, whatever opinions we may hold about its purpose. It is a fact of English country life, and if the moral accountant fails to enter the spectacle in his ledger on the credit side, we may reasonably suspect him of cooking the books.

The fox's scent is a powerful one on a good day and when he breaks cover, the hounds will not lose him unless he misleads them or puts a barrier in their way. He will readily take to water, or run through a herd of cattle, or along a railway track. He cannot run as fast or as long as the hounds, but he knows the country better and will use it to his own advantage. The Pytchley Hunt in Northamptonshire once lost some hounds when a fox led the pack on to thin ice covering a lake. The ice supported the weight of the fox, but when the hounds ran on to it, it gave way, and left the hounds floundering in the icy water while the fox got away. Ten of the hounds were drowned. The fox probably knew exactly what it was doing. "If thou dealest with a fox, think of his tricks", says an old proverb, and although a thousand legends have exaggerated the fox's cunning, he is certainly an animal of exceptional alertness and resourcefulness. The frequency with which a pack of hounds, gaining on a fox, suddenly changes course to go after a different one, has led to suggestions that the original quarry, knowing his territory well, has deliberately set up one of his neighbours – a fresher fox – to let himself off the hook.

The matter of the fox's scent is one of some mystery to huntsmen and naturalists alike. It is believed that the scent the hounds follow is not the body scent of the fox, but the scent emitted from the glands on its pads, with which it impregnates the ground it runs over. But there are days when scent is very hard to pick up – in bright sunlight, heavy rain, strong wind or fog – and sometimes a fox will just 'disappear', leaving no traces of scent for the hounds to follow.

Meanwhile, the 'field' gallops after the pack and the countryside is alive with the noise of the hounds, the hunting horn, the shouts of the riders and the thud of the horses' hooves on the turf. It is for the thrill of the ride that so many hundreds turn up at meets all over the country, and Leicestershire offers rides which are unequalled elsewhere. To the real enthusiast, however, the uncertainty involved in hunting a live animal provides much of the excitement of the sport, and cannot be replaced by substitutions like drag-hunting.

The hunting literature abounds with stories of long rides and cunning foxes. Some of the tales are as tall as the fishermen's 'ones that got away', but among the most famous in the annals of the sport was the 'Billesdon Coplow run' which took place in February 1800, during Hugo Meynell's mastership of the Quorn. The fox broke cover at Billesdon Coplow and was chased on a spiral course (a fox of Celtic descent, perhaps) to Aylestone, via Tilton, Skeffington, Galby and Great Stretton. At Aylestone the hounds changed their fox, and the chase ended at Enderby Gorse, on the other side of the Soar. The run lasted two hours and fifteen minutes and covered a distance of twenty-eight miles. Only four riders were up at the finish and two of them were named Smith. Charles Lorraine Smith, the Squire of Enderby, weighed fourteen stones and was the only one to get across the river on horseback! Thomas Assheton Smith, who was noted for his superb riding of cheap horses, and wittily boasted that there was not a fence in Leicestershire he could not get over with a fall, did the run on a horse he had bought for twenty-six pounds, and sold it next day for four hundred.

Almost as challenging an obstacle as the Soar was the Whissendine Brook, a tributary of the River Eye which rises in the uplands of East Leicestershire and can swell rapidly with the winter rains. Charles Apperley, the sporting squire who wrote under the pseudonym 'Nimrod', has a nice piece about it:

> "We shall cross the Whissendine brook," cries Mr. Maher, who knows every field in the county, "for he is making straight for Teigh." "And a bumper too after last night's rain," holloas Capt. Berkeley, determined to get first to four stiff rails in a corner. "So much the better," says Lord Alvanley, "I like a bumper at all times." "A fig for the Whissendine," cries Lord Gardner, "I am on the best water jumper in my stable." . . .
>
> "Yooi, over he goes!" holloas the Squire, as he perceives Joker and Jewell plunging into the stream and Red-nose shaking herself on the opposite bank. Seven men, out of thirteen, take it in their stride: three stop short, their horses refusing the first time, but come well over the second, and three find themselves in the middle of it. The gallant "Frank Forester" is among the latter; and having been requested that morning to wear a friend's new red coat, to take off the gloss and glare of the shop, he accomplishes the task to perfection in the bluish-black mud of the Whissendine, only then subsiding after a three days' flood. "Who is that under his horse in

the brook?" inquires that fine rider and good sportsman, Mr. Green, of Rolleston, whose noted old mare has just skimmed over the water like a swallow on a summer's evening. "Only Dick Christian," answers Lord Forester, "and it's nothing new to him." "But he'll be drowned," exclaims Lord Kinnaird. "I shouldn't wonder," observes Mr William Coke. But the race is too good to enquire . . .

Undertones of snobbery colour all such stories, and among the oldest of Leicestershire hunting jokes is the one about a young man who was bragging of his Melton acquaintance. Eventually someone asked him if he knew Barkby Holt. "Yes, of course," the young man replied instantly, "I dined with him last week."

However, it is time to be serious. Those impatient reformers will soon accuse me of evading the issue, which is the death of the fox. I have heard it suggested that if only a few of those sincere lovers of animals had seen the bloody carnage wrought by a fox in a hen-house, they would lose their sympathy for the animal at once. That may well be so, but it is perhaps doing the fox an injustice. Some naturalists believe that foxes usually kill only what they need to eat, and that a fox which gets into a chicken run, sent berserk by the panicking, squawking and flapping birds all around it, behaves wildly out of character. Farmers and huntsmen are inclined to dispute this theory, but such hard evidence as is available suggests that the fox is not nearly such a menace to the farmer as is usually believed. Although foxes will take young lambs, for instance, when vixens have their cubs to feed, they do not account for nearly as many sheep and lambs as are destroyed by domestic dogs, which are messy and indiscriminate killers.

In any case, the fox's bad reputation as a killer is beside the point. The fact that it is a nuisance does not justify cruelty. But is fox-hunting cruel? As to that, facts are few and opinions plentiful (and often extreme). There is, on the one hand, the confident assertion that the terrified fox is chased until he is too exhausted to run any further, and is then torn to pieces, while still alive, by the hounds. At the other extreme, there is the statement sometimes made by hunting enthusiasts that the fox actually enjoys being hunted. This ludicrous idea displays such an ignorance of nature that one wonders that its proponents are capable of sitting on a horse.

Since few riders are ever on the spot at the moment of the kill, descriptions of what happens must be treated with some caution, and as I have never seen a fox killed myself, I cannot side with the dogmatists on one side or the other. It seems to me very unlikely that, if a number of hounds reach the fox at the same time, the fox does not suffer before it dies. If one hound reaches the fox ahead of the other, it may be that a quick, clean bite at the back of the neck kills it at once. The attribution of a human emotion such as 'terror' to a fox or other animal is, I am sure, a mistaken one. It is doubtful if animals anticipate pain, and certainly not death, and I am assured by those who have seen them that foxes are quite calm – even casual – whilst on the run, although of course if there were not some kind of instinctive fear they would hardly bother to run at all. The rituals of the kill, which many opponents of hunting profess to find so offensive – such as 'blooding' first-time hunters – have generally been abandoned.

What I am sure of is that there is some cruelty involved in fox-hunting, as there is in fishing and bull-fighting, and I doubt that the *degree* of cruelty really matters. Men and domestic cats hunt for sport because, in both cases, it is in their nature to hunt for food, but the artificial environment they live in now has created a kind of schizophrenic existence in which both are supposed to have changed their natures for the better. But that is asking too much of them.

Man is essentially a carnivorous animal who has gained superiority over others by his extra brain-power; but his capacity for self-examination and speculation has misled him into monstrous megalomania since he began to aspire towards what he is pleased to call 'civilization'. Those idealists who say, in effect, that man's superior intelligence gives him a moral responsibility for the welfare of other animals, which he betrays if he hunts them for pleasure, have an argument which is valid and admirable. But the hunters can make the equally weighty point that the fox population has to be kept down, and if those fourteen thousand foxes a year are not killed by hunting, the alternative methods are even more cruel. It may be that, in purely logical terms, those alternative methods would be preferable because, being a necessary evil, they would absolve man from the charge of immorality. Fox-hunting as a sport is not, after all, 'necessary'. People do it because they want to, not because they have to.

My own view – to come to the point at last – is that blood-sports do not advance the cause of civilization. But I believe also that man does himself little credit by raging and demonstrating against such comparatively trivial activities, when there are so many more worthy targets for his wrath. The ardent campaigners against hunting are, in fact, doing precisely what the fox-hunters are doing – choosing an easy target at which to loose off their surplus aggression.

Modern man's greatest dilemma is his inability to abolish violence despite his urgent need to do so. Why should the domestic cat, with all the juicy food it needs carefully prepared for it at Melton Mowbray and presented to it on a plate, still go to such trouble to kill birds and mice? So, alas, it is with man. He cannot escape his own nature, and if he is not quite Dean Swift's misanthropic conception of "the most pernicious little odious vermin ever suffered to walk upon the face of the earth", well, neither is he that noble upright character that so many well-meaning idealists like to imagine. There are numerous massive priorities to be dealt with in man's aspirations towards a civilized condition, and the abolition of fox-hunting is not one of them.

Besides, hunting will die without assistance from reformers, if they will only be patient, although I ought to add that people have been confidently predicting the end of hunting ever since Meynell made his forecast in 1800. Mounting costs will put hunting beyond the purses of increasing numbers of people. More land will go under the plough, too. The days when you might "find at Melton Spinney and run to Billesdon Coplow and not cross a ploughed field", have gone for ever. The Second World War put an end to that, when the amount of farmland used for tillage in Leicestershire was more than doubled in five years. And there is the modern preference for larger fields bounded by wire fences rather than troublesome hedges and ditches. All these things are against the interests of hunting.

The biggest danger of all facing the sport at present, however, is the possible spread here of fox-rabies from Europe. In spite of a massive extermination programme, the dread disease continues to spread west across France at the rate of about thirty miles a year. If it crosses the Channel, which it is most likely to do by means of a rabid animal being smuggled into the country by one of those very animal-lovers who are so opposed to hunting, it could mean that hundreds of thousands of foxes and other wild animals, as well as domestic pets, would have to be slaughtered urgently on a scale recalling the Black Death, and fox-hunting could be transformed overnight from a traditional English country sport into a suicidal prank.

If the end of fox-hunting should come about, by this or any other means, I shall not be among those who lament its passing, but in the meantime, I see no reason to get apoplectic with rage over a sport which merely substitutes hounds for bullets or poison.

VIII

ACROSS THE RIVER AND INTO THE TREES

THE village which was the home of Hugo Meynell, and gave half its name to the celebrated hunt, is properly called Quorndon, and we can reach it by crossing the river at Barrow-on-Soar. Its church contains the chapel of the Farnham family, who have lived there continuously since the thirteenth century, and built both the grand houses, Quorndon Hall and Quorndon House. The hall now belongs to Loughborough University, and reminds us that we are but a stone's throw from that large town where industry and red brick face us for the first time since we left Leicester in Chapter Three. Let us look the other way for a while, and brace ourselves for the encounter by taking the air on the fringes of Charnwood Forest, although we will postpone the chief pleasures of that delightful area until later.

Immediately south of Quorndon is Buddon Wood, a pleasant wooded hill which has at its foot Swithland Reservoir. This is an attractive spot for a pause before grappling with weightier considerations, and at the other end of the village, Swithland Wood, a place of great beauty, is well known locally for its spectacular carpets of bluebells in the spring – one of the county's natural delights. In the middle of this peaceful wood, however, are the huge water-filled pits from which the famous Swithland slate was quarried for many hundreds of years. The quarries – rather eerie now in their woodland setting – were worked in Roman times, and the material was used for roofing until the nineteenth century, when the cheaper (and much duller) Welsh slate caused the abandonment of the Swithland quarries. One can still see cottages in the forest villages with roofs of Swithland slates gleaming beautifully after a shower of rain, and their variable size and colour give them a distinction which the Welsh product has entirely destroyed elsewhere.

Another major use of the slate was for headstones, and a great many of these can still be seen in Leicestershire churchyards. In

the eighteenth and nineteenth centuries, Swithland slate headstones were often shaped and engraved to elaborate designs with
ornate flowing inscriptions, and the craftsmen who made them
were true artists, although inclined to be ostentatious as their
skills increased. It is said (I have not counted them) that there
are a thousand Swithland slate headstones in the churchyard at
Loughborough, and that St Mary de Castro and St Margaret's in
Leicester also have well over a thousand between them, quite
apart from the smaller numbers in a great many village
churchyards in this part of the county. Some modern student
should adopt them as the subject for a thesis. A thorough,
systematic study of their shapes, designs and inscriptions would
be a worthwhile undertaking, for they will not lie in these
churchyards for ever. S. H. Skillington's essay in the *Transactions
of the Leicestershire Archaeological Society* would be a useful
starting point.

Among the most elaborate slates in the churchyard at
Swithland itself are those in a sarcophagus to Sir Joseph Danvers,
M.P., who died in 1745. It is built partly inside and partly
outside the churchyard, apparently on the grounds that Sir
Joseph wanted to be buried with his favourite dog, which could
not be admitted on consecrated soil.

Of much more interest to me in Swithland Church is a curious
fifteenth-century brass with a 3-foot-high figure of a veiled
woman, Agnes Scott, said to be a hermit of the forest. Why she
should have been so commemorated is not known, but Robert
Graves identifies her with Black Annis of the Dane Hills, and
says she became a nun. He took the hint from Nichols,
apparently, but I think the evidence for this interpretation is
slender, to say the least, and it is hard to believe that a church
brass is inscribed to one who inspired a piece of Grand Guignol
verse by a local poet:

> Tis said the foul of mortal man recoil'd
> To view Black Annis' eye, so fierce and wild;
> Vast talons, foul with human flesh, there grew
> In place of hands, and features livid blue
> Glar'd in her visage; whilst her obscene waist
> Warm skins of human victims close embrac'd.

Mountsorrel is also famous for its quarries, but what a contrast
to the subtle beauty of the Swithland slate! Here, out of a hillside

but three miles from Swithland Wood, is quarried granite of such hardness that until quite recent times there was no known way of dressing it. The granite is thought to have been formed during earth movements some three hundred million years ago, and some of its exposed surfaces were polished by fierce winds which blew up sandstorms during the glacial periods. It supplied road metal and kerbstones to London and other parts of England, as well as millstones, and since 1812, when it was discovered how to work the granite, it has been used also for building purposes. The church of St Peter in the village is built of it.

The village itself, overshadowed by the cliff face where a Norman earl built a castle, is an untidy place. At its centre is a market cross in the form of a domed rotunda, on eight columns. This was put here in 1793 when Sir John Danvers took the original medieval cross from Mountsorrel to ornament the grounds of Swithland Hall, where it stands to this day. Let us move further down the road, to Rothley, which has a figure of more worthy achievements to offer us.

A pleasant enough place, Rothley has become one of the most popular commuter villages for the executives of Leicester and Loughborough, and between the village and the inevitable golf course is a hotel where they can dine out with friends. But long before the hotel business started there, it was a private mansion of very ancient origin, called Rothley Temple. It was built in the thirteenth century as a preceptory of the Knights Templars, and in Tudor times it came into the hands of the Babington family, whose memorials are in the village church. The place has been considerably altered since those days, but its interest for us lies in the fact that, in 1800, a pregnant relative of the Babingtons, in London, was invited to stay here in the country for her confinement. The baby she gave birth to, on St Crispin's Day of that year, was Thomas Babington Macaulay.

The infant became a child prodigy. He grew up at Clapham, but regularly visited Rothley, where he would sit at a window and translate Dante aloud for the benefit of anyone who cared to stay within range. Once, while still a small boy, his leg was scalded with hot coffee, and when a lady asked him later how it was he replied: "Thank you, ma'am, the agony is somewhat abated." And when a servant swept away some shells with which he marked his little patch of the garden, he burst into the drawing-room crying: "Cursed be Sally, for it is written, cursed be he that removeth his neighbour's landmark." When he grew up, his prodigious memory and his unceasing talk were the wonders of the age. Sydney Smith, that admirable parson whom Macaulay called "the Smith of Smiths", said that Macaulay was "laying society waste with his waterspouts of talk; people in his company burst for want of an opportunity of dropping in a word". He once remarked to Macaulay after one of the latter's extended monologues: "Now, Macaulay, when I am gone you will be sorry that you never heard me speak."

Meanwhile, Macaulay had taken the reading public by storm with his essay on Milton in the *Edinburgh Review,* and had entered the House of Commons after practising law. He held various important government posts, while continuing to write poetry and essays, and commencing his great *History of England,* which he worked on until his death but did not complete. He was raised to the peerage in 1857, and took the title Baron Macaulay of Rothley. He died two years later, and was buried in Westminster Abbey.

Lord Macaulay's politics prevented his *History* from being as impartial as it should have been, but it is one of the great monuments of English literature, nevertheless. Macaulay's writing, like his conversation, is like a river which continually bursts its banks, and anyone standing near is swept along in a flood of memorable phrases of which my own favourite is: "We know of no spectacle so ridiculous as the British public in one of its periodical fits of morality."

Macaulay's nephew and biographer, the historian Sir George Trevelyan, was also born at Rothley Temple, and in his youth was one of his uncle's favourite companions. He tells us that Macaulay loved the place of his birth to the end of his life, and always spoke of it with affection. So Leicestershire contributed something valuable to the character of this great Englishman, as it did to another, who was born just down the road at Thurcaston.

Hugh Latimer was the son of a tenant farmer, who sent the boy to school – we know not where – brought him up to be "as obstinate a Papist as any in England", and taught him how to use bow and arrows. But while he was at Cambridge, Hugh Latimer's study of the New Testament led him to new beliefs. He had been born perhaps a couple of years after Martin Luther, and his mind absorbed the religious ferment of the time. He became a priest, and his forthright sermons in support of the reformed doctrines soon brought him to the notice of Henry VIII, who appointed him chaplain to Ann Boleyn, and then made him Bishop of Worcester.

Latimer's sermons – homely and often humorous, though always outspoken – soon made him famous throughout England, and the village of his birth rarely saw him, but he preached in the county often enough. Melton Mowbray Church has a record of a man being paid twopence for "ringing the great bell for Master Latimer's sermon", and he was heard at Leicester and at Bradgate. But he was bound in the saddle of his beliefs to gallop towards the precipice of religious controversy, and he refused to draw the reins to save himself. He was imprisoned in 1539, resigned his bishopric, and was imprisoned again in 1546. Then, almost as soon as Bloody Mary came to the throne, she had him committed to the Tower, and in the following year he was sent with Ridley and Cranmer to Oxford, to defend his opinions before the university divines, who condemned them all to be burnt alive for their heresy.

Latimer and Ridley were led out to the stake at Oxford on 16 October 1555. The two weak old men – Latimer was about seventy – were stripped and shrouded, and again exhorted to recant. When they refused, the fire was lit, and in that moment Latimer spoke his famous words to his companion: "Be of good comfort, Master Ridley, and play the man. We shall this day light such a candle, by God's grace, in England, as I trust shall never be put out."

With that Leicestershire spirit in our minds, we can no doubt face anything – even Loughborough! It is the second largest town in the county, and thrives mainly on engineering (particularly electrical engineering) and hosiery manufacturing. It was the first place in Leicestershire to have a power-operated factory for textile manufacture, and now the whole town is so much like a power-operated factory that it is impossible to imagine what it was like before industry claimed it. It is here, for the first time since we left Leicester itself, that we enter the dreary conglomeration of red brick on a large scale. Loughborough is an old market town, but you would never guess it from looking around. Even its ancient and solid parish church was so transformed at the hands of Sir Gilbert Scott that it adds to the atmosphere of heavy Victorian industrialism, and to complete one's impression of Loughborough as a forbidding and forsaken place, one needs only to be here when Nature switches off her house-lights to stage a thunderstorm of spectacular dimensions. The town even seems reluctant to put its street names up, with the result that its residents hardly know the place any better than strangers. I asked an obvious native the way to a street which turned out to be quite near, but he said: "Sorry, I couldn't tell ya, me duck."

In fact, though, Loughborough has music to lift the heart out of its lowest depths. Over these terraced rooftops of dull Welsh slate sounds the sweet song of forty-seven home-made and perfectly tuned bells. They are housed in the town's unique war memorial in Queen's Park – a brick-built campanile, 150 feet high, erected to the memory of the local men who died in the 1914-18 war. It was completed in 1923, and the *carillonneur* of Bruges come from Belgium to play the first recital, which included a Memorial Chime specially composed for the occasion by Sir Edward Elgar. The bells range from one 7 inches high, weighing a little over 20 pounds, to one 5 feet high, weighing over 4 tons. When you have heard the bells of Loughborough Carillon, you can immediately forget the town's other deficiencies. But what gave Loughborough, of all places, this particular distinction?

In 1839, before Scott began his restoration of All Saints' Church, a man named John Taylor was engaged to come from Oxford to recast the church bells. It happened that, whilst he was working here, he took a liking to Loughborough and decided to stay and start a foundry in the town. So Oxford lost a craftsman and Loughborough won an industry. For John Taylor and Company have been casting bells in Loughborough for nearly 140 years. I called at the firm to find out more about them, and was greeted by Mr Paul Taylor, the great-grandson of the founder. Surrounded by portraits of his ancestors, Mr Taylor tapped out his pipe in a miniature inverted bell on his desk, and told me about Great Paul, the largest bell in the British Commonwealth, in St Paul's Cathedral. It was made by Taylors in 1881, measures $9\frac{1}{2}$ feet across its mouth, and weighs 17 tons. It was taken to London by road, and took ten days to get there, with the director of the transport contractors leading the way on a tricycle.

The old method of making a bell, in simple terms, was to form a clay mould of the inside shape of the bell, then build up a layer of beeswax round this, and enclose it all in an outer clay mould. The whole was then baked, so that the clay hardened and the wax melted, and the bell metal was then poured into the resulting space between the two moulds. The metal used is approximately four parts of copper to one of tin. Any other mixture, Mr Taylor pointed out, might *look* like a bell, but it wouldn't ring! He told me that there are not more than a dozen real bell-founders in the world and they are all in Europe. (There are those who claim to make bells, who merely make gongs!) Taylor-made bells can be heard ringing in every corner of the Christian world, in cathedrals, universities and town halls from the United States to Australia, and including India and Singapore.

Loughborough's only other claim to fame – and it is no inconsiderable one – is its University of Technology, the first in England. It began as a small technical institute early in the century, and gradually grew in size and importance until it was well known all over the country. Students come here from far and wide, both for its technology and for its colleges of education and art, and the university's main building is named after Dr Herbert Scholfield, the principal of the college between the wars, who built up its high standing in the world of technology.

Dishley Grange, where Robert Bakewell lived and died, lies beside the A6 road just beyond Loughborough to the north. Dishley was once a village belonging to Garendon Abbey, but was deserted long ago except for the famous farm. The village church, in which Bakewell was buried, is a forgotten ruin, instead of the place of pilgrimage it ought to be. When I went there a huge flock of pigeons took off from the conifers surrounding the shell of the church and circled noisily until I left. A simple memorial plaque to Bakewell has been put on the north wall, but the gravestones of other forgotten men and women lie beneath the thick grass, just showing through here and there, but scarcely legible. One of them was covered with the feathers of one of those pigeons, taken by a cat in an unwary moment, I dare say.

At Dishley was one of the entrances to Garendon Park, where a Cistercian Abbey was founded in 1133 by Robert le Bossu, Earl of Leicester. At the dissolution of the monasteries, the first Earl of Rutland acquired the estate. It was there that Lady Catherine Manners met George Villiers, the Duke of Buckingham, and it was part of her dowry when she married him. Then it was bought by Sir Ambrose Phillips, King's Serjeant to Charles II, and one of his descendants built a splendid Georgian mansion on the site of the abbey. Disraeli visited Garendon Hall, and described it in his novel *Coningsby* under disguise of the name 'St Geneviève':

> In a valley, not far from the margin of a beautiful river, raised on a lofty and artificial terrace at the base of a range of wooded heights, was a pile of modern building in the finest style of Christian architecture. It was of great extent and richly decorated. Built of a white and glittering stone, it sparkled with its pinnacles in the sunshine as it rose in strong relief against its verdant background. The winding valley, which was studded, but not too closely studded, with clumps of old trees, formed for a great extent on either side of the mansion a grassy demesne, which was called the Lower Park: but it was a region called the Upper Park that was the peculiar and most picturesque feature of this splendid residence. The wooded heights that formed the valley were not, as they appeared, a range of hills. Their crest was only the abrupt termination of a vast and enclosed tableland abounding in all the qualities of the ancient chase, turf and trees, a wilderness of underwood and a vast spread of gorse and fern.

The house was demolished in 1964, and now the M1 motorway thunders through its 'verdant background'.

The occupant of Garendon in Disraeli's time was Ambrose Lisle Phillips, who appears in *Coningsby* as Eustace Lyle. He became a Catholic convert at an early age, and was responsible for the foundation of Mount Saint Bernard Abbey, near Whitwick. This was the first Catholic abbey built in England since the Reformation, and it was said that Phillips founded it in expiation of the fact that his family occupied what was rightfully monastic property. They occupy it still. Many monuments to the Phillips family adorn the church of St Botolph at Shepshed, which otherwise is a large, shapeless and unattractive industrial village. Near Shepshed is the village of Belton, where many of those huge shire horses, which Defoe wrote about so admiringly, were bought and sold, for Belton, where a maypole still stands at the village centre, was famous for having the county's largest horse fair.

Just beyond the reach of the gloomy shadows cast by the black umbrella of Loughborough's industry, the pleasanter villages of

Hemington and Lockington stand, close neighbours at the northern extremity of the county in this quarter. Where once only fields and country lanes joined them to each other and to the surrounding villages, they are now perilously hemmed in by the railway, the motorway and the East Midlands Airport, but so far they have managed to survive the poison fangs of these hissing serpents, and provide some pleasant relief from the factory-dominated villages to the south. A walk from one to the other over Dale Acre Hill provides good views of the Trent valley, but, as Professor Hoskins has written, the view "must include the largest concentration of pylons in England and is of inconceivable dreariness".

Hemington's little church has been a ruin for nearly four hundred years, and towards the end of the last century an old woman lived in a hovel she had made for herself in the chancel, until the authorities removed her to the workhouse. No doubt she was better off in the church.

The Church of St Nicholas at Lockington is well known for its splendid Queen Anne coat of arms, dated 1704, above the chancel. There is also a fine alabaster monument to Elizabeth Ferrers, who died in 1501, represented in coronet and long flowing hair and robes. Her husband was Lord Ferrers of Chartley, who was killed at Bosworth Field.

Another interesting thing about Lockington is that traces of a peasant settlement of the Coritani have been found to the north of the village. Aerial photographs in the area revealed clear marks of about twenty circular huts, flanking what was undoubtedly an ancient drove road, near the confluence of the Soar and the Trent. Signs of a villa nearby were also discovered – probably it belonged to the landowner for whom the peasants worked. The village is thought to date from the second century A.D. and is one of the earliest habitation sites of the Coritani so far found.

A squire of Lockington Hall and a rector of Lockington Church, the brothers J. Bainbrigg Story and Rev. Robert Story, shared a passion for cock-fighting with their friend the sporting Marquis of Hastings. It is recorded that the marquis challenged the parson one Sunday morning in the church, and the two produced their birds there and then and held the fight in one of the pews, the parson still wearing his surplice. The squire, of course, was a magistrate, and once when police turned up at Donington Park whilst *his* cock was fighting the marquis's, his friends held the door while he escaped through the window. Next day he fined the lot of them when the police lined them up before the bench.

At Castle Donington we come across one of a number of ancient and important Leicestershire families who had a common interest in this north-western quarter of the county. The Norman castle after which the old market town was named was built by Henry de Lacy, Earl of Lincoln, but during the Wars of the Roses it came into the possession of Lord William Hastings, the Lord Chamberlain of Edward IV. Hastings enlarged the castle at Ashby-de-la-Zouch and built that at Kirby Muxloe, and was undoubtedly the county's wealthiest landowner when Richard of Gloucester had him beheaded for treason. His descendants became the earls of Huntingdon and lived in the more modern Ashby Castle, until the fourth earl demolished the castle at Donington and built Donington Hall. Then after the death of the tenth earl, this too was demolished and a new hall built in the style of the Gothic Revival by his successor Lord Rawdon, the first Marquis of Hastings, who was Governor-General of India after the Battle of Waterloo. But the ascendancy of the Rawdons over Castle Donington was short-lived. They were notorious spendthrifts, and the line ended with the fourth marquis, who died mercifully before reaching his twenty-seventh birthday, after a life of almost unbelievable stupidity in which he gambled away his family's fortune. In 1866, he lost £140,000 on the Derby alone. In the year before his death, he was Master of the Quorn Hunt, and is remembered as by far the worst master in its history. No one ever knew whether he would turn up at a meet or, if he did, whether he would be drunk or sober. "His personal expenditure," said *The Times* on reporting his death, "was as extravagant as his public gambling, and he was as prodigal of his honour as of his wealth."

So Donington Hall declined and almost fell, and for many years it remained empty. In the 1914-18 war, the government took it over as a place of internment for captured German officers, two of whom escaped by tunnelling under the walls. During its subsequent period of desolation, it was taken over for a time as a centre for displaced persons and then it became, almost predictably, an hotel. The park in which it stands, meanwhile, had become well known as a motor-racing circuit.

Opened in 1931 for motor-cycle racing, it was adapted shortly afterwards for car racing, and in 1937 staged a Donington Grand Prix which provided enthusiasts with a spectacle not seen in this country before, with competitors coming from the continent. Car racing has been suspended at Donington Park in recent years, but now promises to return to its former glory, much to the distress of many local residents who consider the airport quite enough to put up with. The place also houses Mr Tom Wheatcroft's Donington Collection of nearly a hundred historic racing cars, which are on permanent exhibition there.

A number of stylish old buildings survive in Castle Donington itself, but the town is now huddled like a circle of covered wagons – with the needle spire of its church like a flag at the centre – surrounded by hostile Indians on the warpath; the airport, the motorway, the race-track and a large power station. On the county boundary between the race-track and the power station, however, is a little beauty spot on the River Trent known as Kings Mills. The earliest mill here was recorded in Domesday Book, and later there were as many as five, occupied in grinding corn, malting, fulling and paper-making. There is a suggestion that banknote paper was made here once, and evidence of a button factory where a row of cottages now stands.

Eventually the mills were superseded by those run on wind-power, and serious fires in 1864 and 1927 finally ended their operations. Now nothing is to be seen of them but their foundations and three surviving mill-wheels – one of which was said to be the biggest in England. Long after Man's works have fallen down, Nature's river still flows fast. The Trent is in Leicestershire at this point, and as it rushes round a small island and tumbles over a weir it makes a splendid scene, with its backdrop of wooded banks. Linking the high banks flanking the road is an unusual chain bridge, made to give access to the residents on either side.

Diseworth, to the south of Castle Donington, gave to the world, for what he was worth, William Lilly, who was born here in 1602. He was educated at Ashby, went to London when he was eighteen, and got employment as a servant to a Leicestershire man who had a house in the Strand. Soon the master's wife died of cancer, and he married again, with unseemly haste, but did not live long enough himself to enjoy his second marriage, and his widow promptly married Lilly. She did not survive much longer, either, and when she died she left her husband the house and a fortune of a thousand pounds. It was then that Lilly turned his hand to astrology, and began to produce almanacs which were as popular as Old Moore and as useless as old rubbish. But one of his pamphlets, 'A Prophecy of the White King and Dreadful Deadman Explained', earned him the notice of Cromwell, who later gave him a pension of a hundred pounds a year.

In December 1648, at Windsor, King Charles I mentioned to his companion, one Allen, that his book spoke well as to the weather.

"What says his antagonist, Mr Lilly?" asked Allen.

"I do not care for Lilly," the king replied. "He hath always been against me."

"Sir," said Allen, "the man is an honest man, and writes but what his art informs him."

"I believe it," the king said, "and that Lilly understands astrology as well as any man in Europe."

The King of Sweden gave Lilly a gold chain and medal "on account of his having mentioned that monarch with great respect in his almanacks of 1657 and 1658". Such credulity on all sides stood Lilly in good stead, and those royalists who saw through his preposterous quackery were yet powerless to harm him with their ridicule, which scornfully derided "Merlinus Anglicus, the Art of discovering all that never was, and all that never shall be." Due to unforeseen circumstances, however, (being "seized with a dead palsy") Lilly died in 1681.

For miles around the north-western corner of Leicestershire one feature dominates the landscape – the church of Breedon-on-the-Hill, perched alone on its rock like a great black eagle, majestic but slightly intimidating. This hill was a fortified settlement in the Iron Age, and the earthworks are still known as the Bulwarks. The first Christian church here was a Saxon priory, and some fascinating and unique frieze sculpture from the eighth century survives in the present church, which was built by the Shirleys. The ancient stones depict fantastic birds and beasts unknown in Noah's Ark, and one feels in looking at them that some magical pre-Christian influence was at work on the craftsmen who carved them. Do I detect a Celtic maze among the geometric patterns carved on the stones, or is imagination getting the better of my judgement? The death-size cadaver on the tomb of Sir George Shirley does nothing to detract from the eeriness of the place, and its only (unintentional) light relief is the plaque to a certain William Shakespear, whose name deserved better for him than oblivion during the Napoleonic Wars, when his frightened horse jumped into the Seine with him still in the saddle.

Some of the villagers do not like the church, and in winter the services are often held in the village below. Although there is a winding road up to it, from the village street where an old conical stone lock-up still stands, it is best to go by the footpath, to understand the villagers' reservations. It is a steep climb, and the wind howls round you, whistling through the church as you open the creaking door into the porch. It is a place that excites awe, more than reverence. Local legend has it that the masons and labourers started to build the church at the foot of the hill, but every morning they found their stones had been moved to the top during the night, perhaps by angels. All one can say to that is, that if angels put the church up there, the devil must be intent on bringing it down again, for the limestone hill has been quarried for centuries, and the church is now precariously situated on a precipice. For those with a love for old churches, Breedon-on-the-Hill is one of the most fascinating and reward-ing places in Leicestershire, and yet, hardly are the words out of my pen before I have to say that just down the road is another, equally fascinating in some respects, and certainly more beautiful.

The Shirley family of Leicestershire, whom we first came across at Ragdale Hall, and who built Breedon-on-the-Hill's church, first entered local history when one of them married Margaret de Staunton in 1423, and thus acquired Staunton Harold, a manor granted by William the Conqueror to Henry de Ferrariis. The estate remained the family home from then onwards for 531 years, and the Shirleys seem to have been related, at one time or another, to half the royal houses of Europe. The village has long since disappeared, and all that remains is the hall and the church, facing each other in a small wooded valley with a lake. Pevsner says the group is "unsur-passed in the country" for its position.

The Palladian hall, begun in 1763 by Washington Shirley, the fifth Earl Ferrers, who was a Fellow of the Royal Society, is fine enough. But it is the church which is unique, and which makes

Staunton Harold one of Leicestershire's most lovable attractions. It was begun during the Commonwealth by the family's most spirited Royalist, Sir Robert Shirley, and his successor had the audacity to place an explicit inscription over the entrance: "When all things sacred were throughout ye nation Either demollisht or profaned Sir Robert Shirley Barronet founded this Church whose singular praise it is to have done ye best things in ye worst times And hoped them in the most callamitous. The righteous shall be had in everlasting remembrance".

The most surprising thing is that both church and inscription have survived intact, and that alone makes this church unique, but Sir Robert soon fell foul of Cromwell, and died in the Tower before he was twenty-nine. The church is Gothic in its architecture and Jacobean in its furniture and fittings. The floor is paved in marble, and the wooden ceiling painted with an eccentric cloud effect, supposed to represent creation out of chaos. The pews, complete with brass candlesticks, are still occupied, traditionally, by men on the right of the nave and women on the left. Colourful old banners hang in the chancel, and the screen – a later addition – is an exquisite piece of wrought-iron work, probably by Bakewell of Derby. Staunton Harold church is the only building in Leicestershire owned by the National Trust, and the hall is now a Cheshire Home for victims of multiple sclerosis.

Among the Shirleys buried in the beautiful little church is the black sheep of the family, Lawrence, the fourth Earl Ferrers. He was a hard drinker with a violent temper, and his long-suffering wife divorced him for cruelty when he kicked her unconscious in front of the servants. One day he called into his presence an old family retainer named Johnson, for whom he had developed a passionate hatred, ordered him down on his knees and shot him dead. After his arrest he was taken first to Ashby, then to Leicester Gaol and finally to the Tower of London, to await trial by the House of Lords in Westminster Hall. He conducted his own defence, using all his eloquence to convince their lordships that he was insane, which he no doubt was, but they did not believe him and, finding him guilty of murder, condemned him to be hanged at Tyburn on 5 May 1760.

Huge crowds gathered to see the execution. Lord Ferrers was dressed in his white satin wedding suit and travelled in his own landau, drawn by six horses, attended by his liveried servants and accompanied by an escort of cavalry and infantry. The march to Tyburn took nearly three hours because of the mass of people lining the route. As the Earl himself observed: "I suppose they never saw a lord hanged, and perhaps they will never see another." He understood the Englishman's weakness for a free show.

Lord Ferrers was indeed the last peer of the realm to be executed as a criminal, and the first person to be hanged (none too successfully, as it turned out) on the more modern type of gallows. Popular myth has it that he was hanged with a silk rope, but there is no truth in this – he had to make do with hemp, like a common criminal. On the scaffold, Ferrers gave five guineas to the executioner's assistant, by mistake, and a scuffle then broke out between the agents of death until the hangman himself, Thomas Turlis, had recovered the money. In due course these grotesque proceedings continued, but when the earl was actually hung, his feet were touching the ground and he was being slowly strangled, so Turlis and his henchman had to grab his legs and pull hard. "He suffered a little by delay," Horace Walpole observed rather nonchalantly, "but was dead in four minutes."

Ashby-de-la-Zouch, so far from being by the seaside, as a popular song had it, is actually by the Leicestershire coalfield – a very different proposition. Yet somehow this little town contrives to remain aloof from the dreariness around it and present to the visitor a face which is, by contrast, quite pleasant. It is generally known in Leicestershire simply as Ashby – "the place by the ash trees" – but there is more than one Ashby in the county, and this most famous of them got its distinguished name from Alain de Parrhoet la Souche, its first Norman overlord. Nor was this the end of the French connection. During the Napoleonic Wars, Ashby-de-la-Zouch housed two hundred French prisoners, mostly officers, for as long as ten years. Some of them married local girls and some of them died here, and Swithland slate headstones engraved with unexpected names such as 'Etienne Lenon' were erected over their graves in the parish churchyard. There is a local tradition that the women of Ashby learned the art of crochet from the French in the town at this time. I do not know if it is true, but crochet work is certainly popular with the older women in the county, and it may be that knowledge of it spread from Ashby.

The town is also familiar to readers of Sir Walter Scott, who knew the district well, and set the famous tournament in *Ivanhoe* in the meadows beyond the town towards Smisby. It was after Ivanhoe that the town's mineral baths were named when the place became a spa early in the nineteenth century. Designed by a local architect, Robert Chaplin, the Ivanhoe Baths with its Doric colonnades was an interesting building which, like so many other fine things in Leicestershire, was given over to demolition experts to exercise their skills on.

Ashby Castle suffered their destructive energy over three hundred years ago, after the Civil War, when William Bain-brigg of Lockington, a general in Cromwell's army, was sent by a Parliamentary Committee in Leicester to "demolish these goodly towers by undermining". The castle had originally been built by the Beaumont earls of Leicester, from whom it soon passed to the Norman la Souche, and eventually to Lord Hastings, Lord Chamberlain, Master of the Mint, Knight of the Garter and Lieutenant of Calais. When Richard, Duke of Gloucester, accused the Lord Chamberlain of treachery, and swore he would not dine until Hastings' head was brought to him, one might have thought the Hastings fortunes were in decline, but they survived both the Plantagenets and the Parliamentarians by many centuries. In his will, Lord Hastings bequeathed ten pounds to the Grey Friars of Leicester, who were very soon to receive the body of the king who had ordered his death. After Bosworth, all the family lands and titles were restored by Henry VII, and Lord Hastings' grandson George was created Earl of Huntingdon.

It would take too much space to relate the history of the Hastings family in detail, but the earls of Huntingdon served many monarchs faithfully (too faithfully, in some cases) and were duly rewarded, although Elizabeth was caused slight discomfiture by the third earl, who was descended from Edward III and therefore had some claim to the throne, though he never pressed it. James I, whose mother Mary, Queen of Scots, was imprisoned in Ashby Castle for a short time, also aimed at keeping the Hastings wealth and power within reasonable bounds. He came to Ashby with his enormous retinue to be entertained in royal style, and left the earl considerably poorer when he left – a fact recorded by Lady Flora Hastings, Countess of Loudoun, in the nineteenth century:

> The bells did ring,
> The gracious King
> Enjoyed his visit much;
> And we've been poor
> Ere since that hour
> At Ashby-de-la-Zouch.

That the king calculated this effect is evidenced by a story that Lord Stanhope, a noted eccentric, was expected at Ashby during the king's visit, but did not turn up. James sent for him and remarked: "I excuse you, for the people say you are mad." "I may be mad, my liege Sovereign," retorted Stanhope, "but I am not half so mad as my Lord Huntingdon here, who suffers himself to be worried by such a pack of bloodhounds."

In 1879 the people of Ashby erected a monument to Lady Flora, the daughter of the first Marquis of Hastings. It was designed by Sir Gilbert Scott in the shape of an Eleanor Cross. Lest anyone should think it a tribute to Lady Flora's achievements as a poet, however, I should hastily add that she was loved in Ashby for more mundane reasons, and Disraeli composed the inscription to this lady who, "sprung from an illustrious ancestry, herself possessed their noblest qualities".

An ancestry equally illustrious produced the wife of the ninth earl. She was Selina Shirley, daughter of the second Earl Ferrers, and when she married Theophilus Hastings at Donington Park, in 1728, she brought to the Hastings household, as part of her dowry, an inherited dose of that Shirley idiosyncrasy it had experienced before, when Sir Henry Shirley had fallen out with the Earl of Huntingdon over his hawking rights. Soon after her marriage, the new countess scandalized her family and friends by declaring that she had been converted to Methodism. (The Hastings were Protestant and the Shirleys Catholic, but to introduce Nonconformism into the affair was going too far!) She supported Whitefield in his controversy with the Wesleys, founded 'The Countess of Huntingdon's Connexion', through which she led the more Calvinistic section of the Methodist Church, and used her fortune to spread religious teaching.

Bigoted and humourless, she had what Edith Sitwell called "the sunken look of piety", but she had lost her two sons to smallpox, and this fact must have influenced her philosophy, and perhaps her looks. When her cousin, Lawrence Ferrers, was awaiting execution, she urged him to repent, and prevented him from seeing his mistress before his death! But among her converts was Lord Chesterfield's former mistress, of whom Horace Walpole said that she had "bestowed the dregs of her beauty on Jesus Christ".

The Hastings Chapel in Ashby's Church of St Helen contains memorials to Selina Hastings and others of the great family, but what attracts visitors here more than the monuments is a curious and probably unique finger-pillory, a contraption by means of which – it is supposed – unruly members of the congregation were uncomfortably humiliated.

Meanwhile, beside the church, the ruins of Lord Hastings' fortified house remain, dominated by the great Hastings Tower. Ashby Castle is impressive even in its ruined state. Its old walls show clearly what a magnificent house it must have been in its days of glory. Its remaining stones look fit to last longer than most of the houses built but yesterday, and are covered with the graffiti of thousands of visitors who, scratching unconsciously at a desperate little share of immortality, fancy the chances of these ancient walls against a soon-forgotten headstone in a cemetery.

After the monuments of the Hastings, the slag-heaps of their successors. Both the Hastings family and the Beaumonts were mining coal here by the end of the sixteenth century, and it is known that there were five pits in operation at Swannington as early as 1520. The towns and villages of the Leicestershire coalfield are avoided by many writers on the county, but the slag-heaps and mine-shafts are among the 'warts' in this portrait of Leicestershire. The area is one of the most densely populated in the county, and it is an active and vital part of Leicestershire's life and economy. Relatively small, it does not have quite the black and horrifying grimness of the coalfields in the north and in South Wales, but that seems to be – in a sense – almost a misfortune, for instead of their awe-inspiring wasteland atmosphere, the Leicestershire coalfield is merely dreary and very depressing.

Villages on the coalfield – Bagworth, Donisthorpe, Ellistown, Ibstock, Measham, Moira, Nailstone (some call it 'Nelson'), Swannington, Thringstone, Whitwick – have names which seem to imply by their very sounds the close red-brick terraces of miners' houses that line their gloomy streets, and signs warning of roads 'liable to subsidence' must add to the nervous tension that characterizes most close communities living in conditions of some stress. One wonders if life expectation is longer on the other side of the M1 motorway, which nowadays rather neatly separates the coalfield from the more rural and attractive half of Charnwood Forest. Statistics on such matters are hard to come by, but when one considers that a primary school had to be closed a few years ago when cracks appeared in the walls, the implications are obvious. The school was at Bagworth, and the children had to be accommodated in temporary mobile school rooms until the county education authorities could build a new school to serve both Bagworth and another nearby primary school which was similarly affected. Modern mining techniques provide less protection against subsidence than they used to. The roofs of tunnels from which machinery has extracted all the coal are not propped or filled in, as they once were. So villages like Moira have many houses which have had to be shored up when tunnels have caved in and caused shifts beneath the streets. Perhaps in the distant future west Leicestershire will have huge craters like the moon, formed when whole mining villages have collapsed into the great chasms below, and mystified historians will wonder what happened to the lost villages of the twentieth century.

Three places here – Ellistown, Moira and Coalville – were creations of the Industrial Revolution. Ellistown and Moira are ignored alike by Mee, Pevsner and Hoskins, but Coalville has thirty thousand inhabitants, so everyone mentions that, if only reluctantly. Coalville did not exist when Nichols published his county history. There was no village on its site until the sinking of mine shafts brought a cluster of houses up on its level ground early in the nineteenth century, and it was christened with a hideous name compounded of Victorian capitalism and American utilitarianism. Now it is the 'Capital' of the Leicestershire coalfield. Its Christ Church was built within fourteen years of the town's foundation, but as it has no long history its memorials are less pretentious and more meaningful to us than most; not to the wealthy lords and knights of ancient times, but to miners who lost their lives underground.

George Stephenson invested in coal mining in the area, whilst he was engaged in building the Leicester and Swannington Railway, and he and his partners built the village of Snibston, where they had sunk four shafts by 1846. The name of Ellistown speaks for itself. The Whitwick, Ibstock and Bagworth collieries were opened in the 1820s, and the important group at Moira when the earl of that name inherited the extensive Hastings properties in the county.

Whitwick is hardly an inviting place now, but it once had a castle owned by the Earl of Leicester, and was on the route by which salt from the Cheshire mines was brought south. Some fine Charnwood scenery is quite near it, such as the rock outcrops at High Sharpley, and one natural monolith nearby is said to be where the local moot was held in medieval times. Perhaps Whitwick's ancient days are hinted at in the curious inn sign in Loughborough Road, The Man Within the Compass. Its meaning is something of a mystery, and suggestions that it is one of the religious signs popular during the Commonwealth, signifying "in the compass of God's mercy", do not seem to me very convincing. There is something more than that, surely, in this strange and unusual name.

It is to Coleorton, however, that special attention is due, for here we are brought to the seat of that family whose name has already appeared frequently in these pages, the Beaumonts, whose heraldic devices are represented in the first quarter of the Leicestershire coat of arms, in company with those of the de Montforts, the Hastings and John of Gaunt. Coleorton is a sprawling village between Ashby and Thringstone, and it was here where the earliest industrial development of coal mining in Leicestershire was made in the sixteenth century, with the Beaumonts well to the fore.

A descendant of those distinguished Beaumont earls of Leicester who came to this country with William the Conqueror, was made a viscount by Henry VI in 1439 – the first Englishman to be given that title. A later Beaumont accompanied Henry VIII's commissioners to Grace Dieu Priory, and when they dissolved it on the trumped-up charge that two of the nuns had given birth to babies, John Beaumont acquired the property. It had been founded as an Augustinian nunnery by Roesia de Verdun in the thirteenth century.

Beaumont built a house out of the priory, and soon afterwards he became Recorder of Leicester and Master of the Rolls. But he forfeited his offices when he admitted to appropriating official funds for his private use, and for a time Grace Dieu passed to the Hastings. After Beaumont's death, the Earl of Huntingdon restored the property to Beaumont's widow, who was a Hastings herself, and it was at Grace Dieu in 1584 that one of John Beaumont's grandsons was born, who was to become Leicestershire's greatest direct native contribution to English literature.

Had he been born in an age short of poets and dramatists, the name of Francis Beaumont would have been among the most illustrious in the language, but he came to life in that time when England was bursting with creative brilliance, and the names of Shakespeare, Marlowe, Jonson and others have taken precedence over his. Nevertheless, Francis Beaumont's collaboration with his friend John Fletcher in producing very successful plays for the Elizabethan theatre earned him immortality. Some of the work they produced was done at Grace Dieu, and although Fletcher, particularly, collaborated with other authors, including Shakespeare, the names of Beaumont and Fletcher are now linked as inseparably as those of Gilbert and Sullivan or Marks and Spencer. Perhaps the best result of their partnership was *The Maid's Tragedy*, but Francis Beaumont's own finest work was 'On the Tombs in Westminster Abbey', among which he himself was at last buried:

> Mortality, behold and fear,
> What a change of flesh is here!
> Think how many royal bones
> Sleep within these heaps of stones;
> Here they lie, had realms and lands,
> Who now want strength to stir their hands,
> Where from their pulpits seal'd with dust
> They preach, "In greatness is no trust."
> Here's an acre sown indeed
> With the richest royallest seed
> That the earth did e'er suck in
> Since the first man died for sin:
> Here the bones of birth have cried
> "Though gods they were, as men they died!"
> Here are sands, ignoble things,
> Dropt from the ruin'd sides of kings:
> Here's a world of pomp and state
> Buried in dust, once dead by fate.

The Beaumonts left Grace Dieu for Coleorton when their mining interests made them a fortune, and the converted priory eventually passed to Sir Ambrose Phillips of Garendon, whose successors pulled down parts of the building and built a new manor house in the grounds, before they too deserted the estate and left the old house to fall into further ruin, and the new one to become a school.

At Coleorton, meanwhile, the Beaumont line had produced another great name in English cultural history, and it was this Sir George Beaumont who rebuilt Coleorton Hall in 1808. Sir George was a connoisseur of painting and literature, and a gifted painter himself. He was a generous friend and patron of Wordsworth, Byron, Constable, Wilkie, Scott, Southey and others, and he had a very fine collection of paintings by such masters as Rembrandt and Claude Lorrain. Wordsworth and his petticoat retinue – wife, sister, sister-in-law – spent a few winter months at Coleorton Hall Farm, at Sir George's invitation, during the time when the hall was being rebuilt, and Wordsworth wrote some not very inspired lines on the Grace Dieu ruins and other local curiosities, and gave Sir George some not very inspired advice about the layout of his gardens.

Benjamin Haydon visited Coleorton with Wilkie, and left us an account of how they "dined with Claude and Rembrandt before us, and breakfasted with the Rubens landscape", and talked of nothing but painting, and how Sir George lamented that when they left him "he should be compelled to attend to his coal mines". His veneration for Sir Joshua Reynolds led him to remark once that "a good picture, like a good fiddle, should be brown", an opinion which Constable later ridiculed by placing a violin on the lawn and pointing out the difference in colour. But the demonstration failed to win Sir George over to Turner, whose brilliant colours and high key he regarded as "vicious".

Sir George erected a monument to Reynolds in the grounds at Coleorton, with some lines by Wordsworth, and Constable's painting of it is in the National Gallery, although he added busts of Michelangelo and Raphael in the picture which in fact were not there. Constable spent six weeks at Coleorton in the autumn of 1823, and found it so enjoyable that he did not want to leave. His wife wrote to him "it was complimentary in Sir George to ask you to remain the Xmas, but he forgot at the time that you had a wife". Sir George Beaumont contributed enormously to the foundation of the National Gallery, and left his own superb pictures to the nation in his will, for which we should be eternally grateful. They included Claudes and Rembrandts, and that Rubens landscape, *The Château de Steen,* which once graced the breakfast room at Coleorton. Coleorton Hall was in the possession of the Beaumonts until 1934, and it still stands, but perhaps only because, ironically, it was taken over by the National Coal Board, which now has its South Midlands Area headquarters there.

The hamlet of Griffydam, north of Coleorton, embraces in its name a legend which was no doubt, like the giant Bel, the invention of a medieval jester. The story goes that one morning the villagers found an obstinate griffin blocking their way to the well - their only water supply. After three days, who should pass by but a knight, asking the gasping villagers for a drink. When they told him the story he slew the griffin with a bow and arrow, and saved the community from drought.

The coalfield area is not all unrelieved gloom, as we have seen, and the village of Donington-le-Heath, near Coalville, is of interest because it possesses the oldest house in Leicestershire. It was built about 1280, and it was around that time that coal was first mined there. The house was inhabited until quite recently, and now the County Council has restored it and opened it as a museum.

Before we leave the coalfield, we should take a look at Thornton, a village near the motorway, with a reservoir named after it in the valley on its eastern side. At first sight, one might wonder what possible interest this place can have. It is an ordinary village stretched out along its main road. But the Church of St Peter has a maze in the floor of its fourteenth-century nave. It is not mentioned by Nichols, oddly enough, and I have to admit that I have never yet succeeded in getting into this permanently locked church to see it for myself, but photographs show it to be an elementary spiral design made of large stones. If only they could speak and tell us their secret! One of the vicars of Thornton was John Kendall, who married Abigail Erick's sister, Jane, and it was to this uncle that Swift communicated his low opinion of Leicester folk. The church-yard slopes down towards the reservoir, and the church porch is shaded by a yew tree which was planted in 1723, not long after Abigail Erick's death.

Now here is a curious coincidence worth pondering for a moment. It is not only the epicentres of earth tremors in Leicestershire which follow a roughly north-west/south-east axis, but also the points where we have noticed mysterious hints of Celtic influence. Draw a line on the map through Breedon-on-the-Hill and the Dane Hills, for example, and you find that it passes through Copt Oak, and close to Thornton, Whitwick, the Roman town of Ratae, and further south-east, Hallaton, following the line of the Gartree Road, sometimes called Via Devana. I wonder if that road really *did* go to Chester, after all?

The twin villages of Appleby Magna and Parva, near the western border of the county, also have interesting buildings to show. Magna has the surviving gatehouse of a medieval moated manor house. Parva has what was originally a grammar school, built by Sir John Moore, a Lord Mayor of London, in 1697. It seems a trifle overwhelming for such a tiny place, but is an imposing building with a cupola on the roof.

A little to the east of Coalville, Bardon Hill, which is Leicestershire's highest point, 912 feet above sea level, is the surviving summit of that primeval volcanic activity that gave us the mining and quarrying industries. It is also the highest point in a wide area of the Midlands, and there are many old accounts of the distant views to be obtained at its peak, from Lincoln Cathedral to the Sugarloaf in Monmouthshire, and from the hills of Shropshire to the Dunstable Downs. I suspect these assertions are rather fanciful, but as I have never been up Bardon Hill, on a clear day or any other, the curious reader must test them for himself. One side of Bardon Hill has been quarried for its porphyroid rock for many years, and its proximity to the coalfield renders it uninviting. An old Leicestershire saying has it that "When Bardon Hill has a cap, hay and grass will suffer for that," but as precious little hay and grass is grown in its immediate vicinity, I doubt if the observation is very scientific. It is remarkable how these rather daft country sayings survive in spite of all the evidence against them. How often have I heard a hard winter confidently predicted because of the heavy crop of berries on the hawthorn, and how often have I seen the saying disproved, only to be trotted out again the next autumn with a knowing wag of the head, as if Nature is bound to obey rules that Man has dreamed up for her: "Mark moi words, we're gooin' to 'ev 'ard winter, wi' all them berries on the 'edges."

Just across the motorway at its nearest point to Bardon Hill is a tiny hamlet called Copt Oak, where, as its name implies, a pollard oak used to stand near one of the important crossroads in

Charnwood Forest. The tree was reputed to be two thousand years old, and sacred to the Druids, but it was blown down by a gale in 1855. Copt Oak was one of the three meeting places of the old forest 'swanimotes' or governing bodies, and its church was built in 1837 to serve the forest community.

We are in the more rural and attractive part of Charnwood Forest now, and though it has not been a forest in the strict sense of the word for many centuries, it is still a wild unspoilt area of hills, woods, streams and ancient tracks, with houses built of local stone and Swithland slate, and outcrops of rock which make it unique in England. It is a romantic area, wild and still close to nature, but its beauties need to be discerned at length, like a shy friend. They do not force themselves on the attention and inspire visitors like Wordsworth, whose Leicestershire poetry is dreadful, or Leland, who dismissed Charnwood as a barren waste, and added: "In this forest is no good toune nor scant a village." Rather they gently seduce the local man, who knows their every mood and feeling. It was Michael Drayton, the contemporary of Shakespeare, born, like him, in Warwickshire, who captured their atmosphere best:

O Charnwood, be thou called the choicest of thy kind,
The like in any place what Flood hath hapt to find?
No tract in all this isle, the proudest let her be,
Can shew a sylvan Nymph, for beauty like to thee.
The satyrs and the fauns, by Dion set to keep,
Rough hills and forest-holts, were sadly seen to weep,
When thy high-palmèd harts the sport of bows and hounds
By gripple borderers' hands, were banishèd thy grounds.
The Dryads that were wont about thy lawns to rove,
To trip from wood to wood, and scud from grove to grove,
On Sharpley that were seen and Cadman's aged rocks,
Against the rising sun to braid their silver locks;
And with the harmless elves, on heathy Bardon's height,
By Cynthia's colder beams to play there night by night,
Exiled their sweet abode, to poor bare commons fled,
They with the oaks that lived, now with the oaks are dead.

Although Drayton was born at Hartshill, Leicestershire may claim him as one of its notable contributions to literature, for he came of an old Leicestershire family which took its name from Drayton-in-the-Clay (now Fenny Drayton).

Near Copt Oak, on the other side of Poultney Wood, are the

remains of Ulverscroft Priory, founded by the Earl of Leicester in 1134 for the Black Friars of the Augustinian Order. When the priory was suppressed, the Earl of Rutland acquired the property, but did nothing with the ruins, and now they stand isolated in a farmland valley. The prior's lodging has been converted into a farmhouse and where once the weary traveller could be sure of a night's lodging and a modest meal, the inhospitable stone walls support only ivy. It is to be hoped that one day the National Trust might acquire these ruins before the walls crumble beyond recognition, for they are among the most attractive remains in the county, but at present they are private property.

Markfield and Groby (pronounced Grooby) have been concerned, like so many of the villages of Charnwood, with quarrying, but Groby is known nowadays chiefly for its pool, which is the largest natural lake in Leicestershire, not that that is saying much. But it was once twice as large as now, and an old local saying was: "I'll thatch Groby Pool with pancakes." It signified what was impossible, and Sir Walter Scott used it in one of his novels. That malicious parson whom Squire Boothby pushed into Groby Pool was a fat man named Pike, so it soon became a local joke that an eighteen-stone pike had been caught in the pool. On summer days, when it is a popular place for an outing, flotillas of waterfowl eagerly join the picnic parties round its circumference. Some writers have said that Swithland Reservoir is the most beautiful stretch of water in Leicestershire, but I find both Groby Pool and the Eyebrook Reservoir more attractive, and only time will tell whether the new Empingham Reservoir will outshine all these smaller lakes.

Another popular natural spot is Beacon Hill, near Woodhouse Eaves. This is the county's second highest hill, and is a much more attractive place than Bardon. It is probable that it was a hill fort, or a Bronze Age habitation site, though the evidence is not conclusive. It commands extensive views, at any rate, and its rock outcrops remind us once again of the fiery origins of this soil whose turf and bracken now help to make it such an inviting place. Woodhouse Eaves itself is a pleasant enough forest village, where a group of cottages in Maplewell Road, built entirely of rough stone and slates from the Swithland quarries, is well worth seeing.

From Woodhouse, the parent village of the two, there is an

approach to Beaumanor Park. The Beaumonts owned this at one time, but in 1595 it was bought by Sir William Herrick, a London goldsmith, and Beaumanor remained the family seat of the Herricks for over three hundred years, until the thirties of the present century. Sir William Herrick, naturally enough, became Mayor of Leicester, and he lived to a great age, as did his wife, to whom he was married for fifty-two years. In the nineteenth century the Herricks were among the county's richest land-owners, and their monuments are in Woodhouse Church and Leicester Cathedral, but there is no evidence to suggest that either of their famous literary relations, Robert Herrick and Jonathan Swift, ever saw the inside of the mansion the family built at Beaumanor. After the Second World War, the place was acquired by the War Office, and it remained government property until quite recently – somewhat forbidding and secretive, its name removed from the Ordnance Survey maps. Now it has been bought by the County Council, for use as a residential in-service training centre for teachers, though the army still retains some of the land.

Perhaps the most attractive of all the forest villages is Newtown Linford, and here is one of the entrances to Bradgate Park, an estate of nearly a thousand acres which was given by the industrialist Charles Bennion in 1928 to the people of Leicester-shire, "to be preserved in its natural state for their quiet enjoyment". If my advocacy of the county's attractions had to rest on one piece of evidence, I would unhesitatingly direct judge and jury to Bradgate Park. I swear on my honour that there is not a more romantic and unspoiled place in England, and for that we have to thank, partly, the good taste of another great Leicestershire family, the Greys.

In this beautiful park, with its rock outcrops and ancient oak trees, herds of deer, and its stream meandering towards Cropston Reservoir, Thomas Grey, the first Marquis of Dorset, built a mansion of red brick at the end of the fifteenth century. It was the first country house in Leicestershire and one of the first in England, and the bricks with which it was built were made on the site. The marquis was the eldest son of Sir John Grey, Lord Ferrers of Groby, and his wife Elizabeth Woodville. After her husband's death at St Albans whilst fighting for the Lancastrians, Elizabeth Woodville married the Yorkist king, Edward IV, and became the mother of Edward V and his brother, the princes murdered in the Tower. The Hastings were not the only Leicestershire family to suffer at the hands of Richard III.

The second marquis, also Thomas, was a familiar figure at the jousting tournaments of his day, being a noted exponent of the sport, and he was a friend of Henry VIII in the king's more youthful days. This Thomas Grey's son Henry, the third marquis, after divorcing his first wife, married Lady Frances Brandon, daughter of the Duke of Suffolk and granddaughter of Henry VII, and at Bradgate in October 1537, Lady Frances gave birth to a daughter Jane, the first of three, whose father became Duke of Suffolk himself when his father-in-law's heirs all died.

Lady Jane Grey grew up to be a beautiful and very accomplished girl. Her parents secured for her the most learned tutors of the day, Roger Ascham and John Aylmer, and she soon mastered Greek, Latin, French and Italian. When the rest of her family were out in the park hunting, she would be found in the house reading Greek – a circumstance which led Ascham to ask her why she did not share in her parents' pleasures:

Smiling she answered me, "I wisse all their sport in the parke is but a shadow to that pleasure I find in Plato. Alas, good folke, they never felt what true pleasure meant."

"And how came you, madame," quoth I, "to this deeper knowledge of pleasure, and what did chiefly allure you to it, seeing not many women, but very fewe men, have atteynd thereunto?"

"I will tell you," quoth she, "and tell you a troth, which perchance ye will marvel at. One of the greatest benefites that ever God gave me is that he sent me so sharp and severe parents and so gentle a schoolmaster, for when I am in the presence of either father or mother, whether I speak, keep silence, sit, stand or go, eat, drinke, be merye or sad, be sewing, playing, dancing or doing anything else, I must do it as it were in such weight, measure and number, even so perfectly as God made the world – or else I am so sharply taunted, so cruelly threatened, yea presently sometimes with pinches, nippes and other ways which I will not name, for the honour I beare them, so without measure misordered, that I think myself in hell, till tyme come that I must go to Mr. Elmer, who teaches me so gently, so pleasantly, with such fair allurements to learning that I think all the time I am with him as nothing. And when I am called from him, I fall on weeping, because whatsoever I do else but learning is full of greifs, trouble, fear and whole misliking unto me, and thus my book hath been so much my pleasure and bringeth daily to me more pleasure and more, that in respect of it, all other pleasures, in very deed, be but trifles and troubles unto me."

But this rare being soon became a helpless pawn in the political ambitions of her scheming relatives. When she was sixteen, she was married to Lord Guildford Dudley, son of the regent, the Duke of Northumberland. At the same ceremony, Northumberland's daughter married Lord Hastings of Ashby. Jane had intended to marry the Earl of Hertford, but was prevented by her ambitious father, and she hated the Dudley household so much that she soon suffered a nervous breakdown. Northumberland, meanwhile, had induced the weak young king Edward VI to bequeath the throne to Lady Jane. When the king died, the unsuspecting Leicestershire girl was proclaimed Queen of England. She had no aspirations to power, and fainted on being told the news.

Northumberland and Suffolk, however, had reckoned without the possibility of the people rallying to Mary Tudor's side, and when they did so, Jane was thrown into the Tower, her nine days' reign over, and at length she was, with her husband and her father, executed for treason – soon to be followed to Bloody Mary's scaffold by that other Leicestershire Protestant, Hugh Latimer. There was some suggestion that Jane was pregnant, a circumstance that might have saved any other woman from execution, but in her case it could only have served to make her death the more urgent. The milk of human kindness curdled in Mary Tudor's breast, and if there were no truth in the rumour of Jane's pregnancy, her fate was sealed, nevertheless, by the actions of her father, who supported Wyatt's rebellion against Mary.

As Jane went to her execution, she met the headless body of her husband being brought from the block for burial. Lady Jane Grey had a handkerchief tied over her eyes as she stood on the straw scattered round the block to soak up her blood. Asking the executioner to dispatch her quickly, she reached out saying: "What shall I do? Where is it?" And having been guided to the spot, she laid her head on the block and said: "Lord, into Thy hands I commend my spirit."

She was seventeen years old when they chopped off her head within the Tower precincts. The recently rediscovered painting of the scene by Delaroche in the National Gallery is taken to be a fairly accurate representation of the execution, except that the painter has set the scene indoors for greater dramatic effect. In fact, Jane Grey was beheaded on the green beside the White Tower. They were afraid of executing her in public on Tower Hill, in case of yet another switch of the fickle loyalties of the populace. The head and body were buried in the chapel of St Peter-ad-Vincula, and when the coffin was opened, many years later, the remains crumbled to dust as soon as they were exposed to the air. Legend has it that the oaks at Bradgate were pollarded as a mark of mourning for Lady Jane.

Jane's mother and sisters fared little better. The Greys, representing the Suffolk line of succession, were almost as much an embarrassment to Elizabeth as they had been to Bloody Mary. Jane's sister Katherine, "the lady of lamentations", died at twenty-seven after years of enforced separation from successive husbands, the second of whom was the Earl of Hertford, who had intended to marry Jane. Mary Grey married beneath her, to a husband who was imprisoned and then forbidden to see his wife when he was released. Lady Mary had once gaily described the May Day celebrations of her childhood at Bradgate:

> when the merrie May Pole and alle the painted Morris dancers with Tabor and Pipe beganne their spritelie anticks on oure butiful grene laune, afore that we idel leetel Bodyes had left owre warme Bedds, woulde goode Mistress Bridget the Tire-woman who our Lady Mother alwaies commanded to do owre Biddinge, com and telle us of the merrie men a-dancing on the Grene.

The girls' mother, the Duchess of Suffolk, no less, subsequently married her 'horsekeeper', Adrian Stokes, fifteen years her junior, and went to live at Beaumanor, which the Greys owned between the Beaumonts and the Herricks. "Has the woman so far forgotten herself as to marry a common groom?" Queen Elizabeth gasped. She had, and the Greys' fortunes continued to decline until Henry Grey was created Baron of Groby by James I. He died in 1614, and there is a fine alabaster monument to him and his wife in the surviving chapel at Bradgate. Beneath the chapel there is a sealed vault, unseen for centuries, in which earlier members of the Grey family still lie.

The first Marquis of Dorset had been a bitter rival of Lord Hastings, not only because of their clashing political ambitions, but also because they both sought the favours of Jane Shore, the upper-class prostitute who was Edward IV's 'merriest' concubine.

The family rivalry continued for centuries, and during the Civil War, the Hastings were for the king and the Greys for Cromwell. Colonel Hastings, son of the Earl of Huntingdon, stormed Bradgate and terrorized the household, but this time the Greys were on the winning side, and Thomas Grey was one of the chief signatories to the death warrant for Charles I, who had made his father Earl of Stamford.

The origins, intermarriages, financial interests and political activities of the great Leicestershire families provide more possible permutations than a football pools coupon, but let us be content to observe here that, in the Civil War period, the Hastings, Greys and Manners were Protestant, and the Beaumonts and Shirleys Catholic. All were Royalists, however, except the Greys, who had good cause to be sick of the monarchy. In their Leicestershire interests, the Hastings had been the wealthiest, the Beaumonts the most powerful from the days of the Conquest, and the Greys had put one of their number on the English throne, but in the long run the Manners came off best, for they are still there, looking down from Belvoir Castle on the ruins of the others.

Bradgate was brought to ruin, reputedly, by the Countess of Stamford (wife of the second earl) who, unable to tolerate the place, set fire to it in 1694 and ran away by the light of the blaze. This story is a romantic fiction, however. If the countess *did* set fire to the house, comparatively little damage was done. The family did desert the house after the earl's death, as his successor lived in Staffordshire, and the building began to decay. Although the Greys owned Bradgate until the early years of the present century, and continued to use the park for hunting, the house was never restored. Perhaps they all felt the same about this place which had seen so much tragedy. George-Harry Grey, the seventh earl, was a master of the Quorn Hunt, but as he had married a former bareback rider in a circus, his image with the aristocrats at Melton was not especially good, they evidently believing that there is only one way to make a fool of oneself on horseback, and soon after this earl's death the Greys' connection with Leicestershire came to an end, the niece who inherited Bradgate having decided to sell.

So the home of the most beautiful and cultured, but shortest-lived queen of England, is now a favourite weekend spot for people in Leicestershire and beyond. The landscape has hardly changed since her family hunted deer in the park, and that is Bradgate's greatest virtue. Its beauty is entirely natural because it has never been cultivated or landscaped. I shudder to think what capabilities Lancelot Brown would have perceived here. As it is, the deer roam freely among the bracken and trees whose gnarled and exposed roots fasten on boulders of granite as if to squeeze water from them, whilst peacocks strut and scream round the old brick walls, and overlooking all is Old John, a tower and arch where a windmill once stood on top of a hill – a memorial to the miller who was killed by a falling pole burned through by a bonfire.

At Anstey, a mile or so down the road, there is an ancient packhorse bridge which was probably built by the Greys to facilitate their journeys into Leicester, and it is a convenient route by which to leave Charnwood Forest and make for the final quarter of our exploration of the county.

IX

STOCKINGOPOLIS

IN THE south-western quarter of Leicestershire, where the miner's helmet gives way to the cloth cap, all those villages which are not in the clutches of Leicester itself can be regarded as satellites of Hinckley, which has been at the forefront of the hosiery industry since the seventeenth century. This is the quarter which has least to offer in terms of sightseeing, and the one which gives travellers on the M1, the A5 and now the M69, the wrong impression that all of Leicestershire is a dreary flat land of brick-built manufacturing villages. I hope I have adequately dispelled that idea, but it has to be admitted that the south-west *is* dominated by the footwear and hosiery industries, and that the houses and factories are not much to look at.

On the other hand, there is a good deal of historical and human interest in the area, and as this book is a portrait, and not merely a guide to tourist spots, we shall find many things to pause over, not least of which is Bosworth Field, one of the most important battlegrounds in English history. There is little to see there, except King Dick's Well, where Richard is assumed to have taken his last drink, but it is not difficult to conjure up a vision of the brief, decisive and significant encounter that took place there in 1485.

We noted King Richard III and his troops leaving Leicester by the Bow Bridge on the morning of Sunday 21 August. He was heading to intercept Henry Tudor, who had landed in Wales with two thousand men and was marching on London. By that morning Henry's army had increased to about five thousand and he had reached Atherstone. The armies of the Stanleys were situated at Stoke Golding and Shenton.

Richard, the last English king to lead his army into battle, marched his men via Kirkby Mallory to Sutton Cheney, and then to the southern edge of Redmoor Plain where, in consultation with his officers, he decided to occupy Ambion Hill at first light next morning. His scouts brought him news that Henry had left Watling Street and was approaching on the Roman road from Mancetter. As it grew dark, the king could see the flickering of his enemy's camp fires about a mile away.

Our chief source for the details of the ensuing battle is Polydore Vergil, that Italian rector of Church Langton, who said that Richard's army consisted of "twice so many and more" as Henry's five thousand, but when the Stanleys joined the rebels, the royal troops were outnumbered. The August morning was sunny and warm. Henry attacked first with arrows and cannon, and then the soldiers joined in hand-to-hand combat with swords and battleaxes. After half an hour's fighting, Richard braced himself for an all-or-nothing charge on the person of Henry Tudor himself. If the rebel leader were slain, the issue would be decided. Richard, mounted on his white charger, in full armour and with his crown over his helmet, galloped forward with his bodyguard, slashing right and left with his battleaxe in his determination to get through to Henry. But his bodyguard was slaughtered around him, and before he could reach his quarry he was brought down in a flurry of blows. "King Richard, alone", Vergil records, "was killed fighting manfully in the thickest press of his enemies." He was thirty-two. The battle had lasted scarcely an hour and hardly more than a hundred men had been killed.

Richard's naked and bloody corpse was slung on the back of a horse and carried into Leicester where, according to tradition, his head struck the parapet of Bow Bridge, as the old woman had foretold. The body lay exposed in the priory of the Grey Friars for two days, and was then buried without ceremony. At the dissolution of the monasteries, half a century later, the body of Richard Plantagenet, King Richard the Third of England, was taken from its grave and thrown into the River Soar, never to be seen again.

Perhaps the ghost of Lord Hastings smiled from the battlements of his fortified house at Kirby Muxloe when the dead king passed by on the road not far distant. This 'castle', like Ashby, was still in process of building when Hastings was executed. It was designed round a central quadrangle, with a square tower at each corner, and surrounded by a moat. The ruins are not so impressive as Ashby's, but the chief interest of Kirby Muxloe Castle is that it was built of brick, not stone. It was the first medieval brick-built building in Leicestershire and, as at Brad-gate, the bricks were made on the site.

The village of Kirby Muxloe, with its strange name which Hoskins says is a refinement of 'muckless', is now within an ace of being gripped in the crab-like claws of Leicester's built-up area – a fate also destined to overtake places such as Enderby, Blaby and Whetstone. Other strange names abound in the district: Newtown Unthank, Dunton Bassett, Broughton Astley, Newbold Verdon. Villages like these often took their names from the medieval lords who owned them, but Newtown Unthank is supposed by Nichols to refer to the hard and unyielding soil of the area. It is at once noticeable when you glance at the map that there are fewer villages of Danish origin in this quarter. No doubt they were not keen on establishing new communities too near the frontier of the Danelaw, but it is also true to say that the area had little to offer until the growth of industry. There are no prehistoric remains in this part of the county, and when Domesday Book was compiled, it was still the most sparsely populated area of Leicestershire apart from Charnwood Forest. True, the Romans had driven their Watling Street and Fosse Way through what they calculated to be the centre of England here, and had at least three camps on the fringes of what is now Leicestershire – Tripontium, Venonae and Manduessedum. And the Latin influence survives in the names of various twin villages having Magna and Parva attached to them – Appleby, Ashby, Claybrooke, Sheepy and Wigston. But the good relations between the Romans and the Coritani meant that the older scattered inhabitants were left in peace here, and perhaps ensured that longer-lasting Celtic influence which shows itself in the high incidence of blood group O in the Hinckley area, and perhaps in the survival of the village-name Leire. It is no surprise to learn that Hinckley has a Druid Street.

No one but the farmers wanted this relatively unproductive land until the introduction of industry, and even some of the villages which had existed for a long time were deserted, a few of them disappearing for ever. Then, in the course of two hundred years, it was transformed from an empty rural area into one of the most densely populated parts of the county. The centre of all this activity was Hinckley, which has for a long time run neck and neck with Loughborough as the county's second largest town.

Hinckley has been done scant justice by most writers on Leicestershire. Even Nichols, who might have allowed the discovery of his second wife there to excuse him a little sentimental affection for the place, devoted only a few pages of his enormous survey to it, though he spares room to give us the entire pedigree of the Green family. Perhaps readers will be indulgent, therefore, if I choose to linger in Hinckley rather more than is customary. It was, after all, the cradle of Leicestershire's modern prosperity. The county's first stocking frame was set up here when Charles I was on the throne.

Everyone says that Hinckley is a dreary place, and so it is, but it has had its moments. Did William Shakespeare walk its streets once, I wonder, when the annual fair was held? Why, unless he had seen it himself, should he mention this place rather than any other town in his *Henry IV*, in which Davy enquires of Justice Shallow whether he means to stop any of William's wages, "about the sack he lost the other day at Hinckley Fair."?

Half a century after this reference John Cleveland, the Royalist poet, lived in the town. He was born in Loughborough, but his father was appointed vicar of Hinckley, and was here at the beginning of the framework-knitting industry. Though Cleveland has been called an "exquisite orator, and eminent poet", his work is unread now. Charlotte M. Brame, the romantic novelist, also lived here, and before anyone protests that Hinckley's literary associations deteriorate rapidly in quality the more I go on, I will only add that Lawrence of Arabia's Chapman ancestors were Hinckley people.

A bit of social history was made here in 1834, when Joseph Hansom, the architect of Leicester's New Walk Museum and the 'Pork Pie Chapel', built the first hansom cab in Regent Street, and drove it at full gallop along Coventry Road and Watling Street to demonstrate that it could not be over-turned. The diameter of the wheels on the original model was eight feet. Hansom received only three hundred pounds for his invention. It was twenty years before it became popular, and then only because of a rumour that smallpox patients were being taken to hospital in the four-wheeled carriages.

Regent Street was once known as Duck Paddle, and where this meets Coventry Road, the town used to hold its annual horse fair. I recall the last of these, when gypsies and farmers trotted their ponies (inferior-looking animals, as I remember) up and down the streets for inspection by prospective buyers. An event like that today would cause traffic chaos throughout the Midlands, I expect, but there were still one or two blacksmiths and saddlers in the town then, and you might even see a horse pulling a barge along the Ashby Canal. This had been opened in 1804 to bring coal from the Leicestershire coalfield to the Bosworth and Hinckley areas, but what little trade it took away from the Warwickshire mines was soon killed off by the opening of the Leicester and Swannington Railway, and the canal is now left for fishermen, towpath walkers and boys who bounce flat stones off the surface of the water, as I did.

Another link with Ashby was Hinckley's nineteenth-century aspiration to become a spa and health resort. It was a short-lived dream, and not surprisingly. Apart from the proximity of the mineral baths to the Ashby Road cemetery, which must have put the efficacy of the curative waters in some doubt, anything less like a health resort than Hinckley can scarcely be imagined.

A pageant used to take place in the town called 'The Riding of the Millers'. This, like Leicester's 'Riding of the George', was organized by one of the trade guilds. The 'Baron of Hinckley' and his wife were represented, and the procession was led by the 'King of the Millers', elected for the occasion like a May Queen, and followed by representatives of other trades in the town. Hinckley had an annual cheese fair, too, held on the first Monday following 28 October.

In those days, the assizes for the whole county were held at Hinckley, having been moved here in 1610 from Leicester, because an epidemic of the plague was raging there (over 140 Hinckley people died from it in 1626). The gallows where condemned criminals were executed stood on the road to Derby (now Ashby Road), near the gravel pits, and there is still a Hangman's Lane there.

Hinckley has long been known locally as 'Tin Hat'. The nickname began, it seems, when some Victorian merrymakers at the Crown Hotel saw an inverted bucket on the old pump outside, and one of them remarked: "I see they put tin hats on the pumps at Hinckley." The joke stuck, and subsequent publicans exploited the name by displaying outsize tin hats on their premises. Hinckley was well known for the quality of its ale, and it still has an enormous number of public houses.

The Tin Hat story might have appealed to a man buried in Hinckley churchyard beneath a Swithland slate headstone: William Burton, who died in 1774, is described as a 'comedian'. Such was the reputation of the theatrical profession in those days that Nichols felt it necessary to say that he was a "well-behaved, intelligent man". His daughter acted in Garrick's company at Drury Lane. It was only four years after Burton was buried there that the spire of St Mary's Church was rebuilt, in the very year when Nichols married Martha Green, the original steeple having been damaged by lightning and high winds. It is a tall recessed spire, and I have always thought it elegant in its proportions, though neither Pevsner nor Hoskins has much to say for it.

An even earlier gravestone in Hinckley churchyard attracted some curiosity and not a little morbid veneration at one time. A young saddler named Richard Smith had been killed by a recruiting sergeant in 1727, and locals began to notice with some alarm that 'tears of blood' appeared on the tombstone which tells of his end in rhyming couplets. Friable sandstone actually accounted for the phenomenon, which only appeared in wet weather!

Looking out of my study window as I write reminds me of the fields of Hinckley where I used to walk. Most of them are covered with housing estates now, but the lanes which led out to them from the town survive – Butt Lane, from which one could cross the fields, keeping a wary eye open for a bull, and get to Burbage Common, sometimes stopping to listen to frogs croaking in one of the ponds; Rogues Lane, a good walk that took one round the area called Hinckley Fields in the open-field days, into which Middlefield Lane naturally led, from the end of the graphically named Factory Road; Barwell Lane, where my mother and I were once chased by an angry gaggle of geese asserting their territorial rights; Dark Lane, where one could always see yellowhammers and blackcaps; Doctor Nutt's Lane, named after a noted local apothecary of obvious Scandinavian ancestry. Many of these lanes are heavily built up now, but those that are not are even more silent than they were then, since nobody walks anywhere today. Even the old 'lovers' lanes' are deserted nowadays, unless you can get a car along them. An alternative route to Burbage Common was via Brick Kiln Hill, which shows that bricks were made at Hinckley a long time ago, and the familiar Midland shortening of the name to 'Brickle' is still common in the town.

Hinckley has suffered in recent years from the difficulties of the hosiery and knitwear industries, but it does not appear, on the face of it, to be much the worse for its experience, having built a new shopping centre and council offices. Every so often there is talk of combining Hinckley and Nuneaton as a new county borough, but so far the old Watling Street remains what it has been since the tenth century, a boundary line rather than a town thoroughfare.

Hinckley even has a new theatre, called Concordia, where local amateur productions are staged. Its name was the idea of a Welsh Baptist minister, long since dead, whose fiery sermons gave me some of my earliest lessons in the use of words. The Rev. T. Tudor Rhys, Bachelor of Arts and of Divinity, spoke a multitude of languages and seemed to me then the wisest man I knew. While the headmaster of the grammar school was caning wayward boys and – even worse – sending them to Borstal institutions from the bench where he sat as a local magistrate, Mr Rhys was explaining in his fascinating way, why Shakespeare's *The Tempest* is the greatest of his plays because it is concerned with forgiveness. I remember his impassioned denunciation, one Sunday evening, of H. G. Wells's *Mind at the End of its Tether.* His eloquent Welsh voice boomed out his electrifying sermon on despair, punctuated every so often by his fist crashing down on the pulpit, making all the old ladies jump with fright. But he was a kindly man when out of his pulpit, and although I have since abandoned most of the beliefs he held, I still remember him as a teacher more valuable to me than most of the schoolmasters I encountered, with one notable exception, to whom this book is dedicated.

In this town, in my years of innocence, I fed the swans in the castle moat (it is doubtful if there ever was a castle) and rolled down the grass banks in Hollycroft Park, and believed in Rupert and Nigger, and God and Father Christmas, and played ball in the street against the wall of a hosiery factory, when a passing vehicle was only a rare interruption. I recently heard a girl shout: "Let 'im be, yo, yer gret bully!" at two boys fighting in a school playground, and realized that many things have not changed all that much. But I also saw front-room curtains drawn when a neighbour had died, and watched working men take off their cloth caps as a funeral procession passed by, and eavesdropped on the gossip of old women on buses. Then I saw the flames of the Coventry blitz leaping into the sky, fourteen or more miles away, and on my way home from school each day I passed a huge poster with a skull on it publicizing 'VD' – that mysterious abbreviation like a military honour – whilst Hinckley Grammar School (now the John Cleveland College) prepared me for adult life by teaching me all the stations on the Canadian Pacific Railway route from Vancouver to Winnipeg.

My memory still unwillingly retains the names of far-distant places I never had the remotest interest in – Moose Jaw, Medicine Hat – but a ritual itinerary of more immediate concern was current in 'Tin Hat' before the Canadian Pacific Railway was even thought of:

> Higham-on-the-Hill,
> Stoke in the dale,
> Wykin for buttermilk,
> Hinckley for ale.

Wykin was a depopulated village on the north-west side of Hinckley, with only the old gabled brick hall left to show for its one-time independence. Its chapel was "long since decayed and gone" even in 1622, so the rhyme is an ancient one. In this century, however, Wykin has grown up again, though only as an appendage of Hinckley, and it has recently opened its own comprehensive school, called Redmoor.

The Stoke of the rhyme is Stoke Golding. It is an unattractive village, but it possesses what Hoskins has called "one of the most beautiful and dignified village churches in England", and Pevsner, more cautiously, "one of the most beautiful churches in Leicestershire". It is a finely proportioned small unrestored church with a recessed spire, lavish detail in its carving, and windows with flowing tracery. But as with most of the churches worth preserving as works of art, it is usually kept locked these days.

Close by is Dadlington, where the lane from Stoke meets the Ashby Canal at a corner where the water is carried higher than the road level. Further along the canal, another road out of Dadlington crosses it with a humpback bridge to end all hump back bridges – I warn visiting motorists to approach it cautiously. Dadlington's chief curiosity is the unusual name of its village inn, the Dog and Hedgehog. More examples of those old roads with exceptionally wide verges can be seen between Dadlington and Shenton, and especially the attractive gated road leading from Market Bosworth to Sutton Cheney. The latter village has an impressive brick house at Hall Farm dating from the seventeenth century.

Higham-on-the-Hill is noted for its line of rectors named Fisher. Three members of the family ministered to the spiritual needs of this parish from the Napoleonic Wars to the Great War, and then a later Fisher, Geoffrey, became Archbishop of Canterbury and subsequently Lord Fisher of Lambeth. He did much to modernize the Church of England and – a leading light of the Ecumenical Movement – became the first Archbishop of Canterbury to visit the Pope since the Reformation. His sometimes reckless unorthodoxy and his impish humour made him a true son of Leicestershire, though I have never been certain which of the two characteristics led him to subscribe to the notion that ignorance is bliss.

Near Higham is Lindley, where the Motor Industry Research Association has its proving ground. The original village disappeared soon after the Battle of Bosworth, but there remained a few houses, and at the grandest of them, Lindley Hall, two brothers named Burton were born four hundred years ago. The elder, William, became the county's first historian with his *The Description of Leicestershire* published in 1622. But his younger brother, Robert, born on 8 February 1577, published a work which was not merely of local interest but became famous throughout the world and remains so today – *The Anatomy of Melancholy*.

This fantastic book purports to be a medical treatise, but it is in fact a mine of classical learning, philosophy, politics and every conceivable subject touching on the life of man, from which many a famous writer since has dug for information and inspiration, from Milton and Sterne to Oscar Wilde and H. G. Wells, doing exactly what Burton truly said all writers do, what he had done himself, and what I am doing at this precise moment: "They lard their lean books with the fat of others' works." Among the causes of melancholy Burton cites are poverty, bad air, excessive smoking, anger and bad diet. Beef, he says, breeds "gross melancholy blood", and as for hare, he declares that it "causeth fearful dreams".

The Rev. Burton was awarded the living of Seagrave, in the Wolds, later in his life, but he spent nearly all his time at Oxford University and, having forecast that he would die in 1640, did so – a more accurate prophet than his contemporary, William Lilly. His birthplace was demolished in 1926. Perhaps if the Americans had known about Lindley Hall, they might have bought it and shipped it to the States. They did this with a cottage in Fenny Drayton, a little further along Watling Street. I am surprised they have not made an offer for Bosworth Field – but give them time.

The Fenny Drayton cottage was the birthplace of another influential Leicestershire man, George Fox. In the course of this portrait of Leicestershire we have encountered a curious mixture of native figures – the charlatan William Lilly, the scientific Robert Bakewell, the psychopathic Titus Oates, the unscrupulous George Villiers, the notorious Lawrence Shirley, the beautiful and tragic Lady Jane Grey, the brilliant Lord Macaulay, the colossal Daniel Lambert, the diminutive Jeffery Hudson. But to my mind, the most extraordinary character ever born on Leicestershire soil was George Fox, the founder of the Society of Friends, or as they soon became known, the Quakers.

Fox first saw the light of day in 1624, three years after the publication of Burton's *Anatomy*. His father was a weaver in the village, which was called Drayton-in-the-Clay then. Christopher and Mary Fox apprenticed their son to a local shoemaker, but when he was nineteen he left home and began to wander about the country preaching his own peculiar brand of divine truth, having concluded from his discussions with priests and professors that no one was competent to teach him.

Early in his new career, he came within sight of the three spires of Lichfield Cathedral, and heard the voice of the Lord commanding him to take off his shoes and walk through the town crying "Woe to the bloody city of Lichfield", which – needless to say – he promptly did. The extent of the curiosity aroused by this peculiar behaviour seems to have been limited to the enquiry of some friends: "Alack, George, where are thy shoes?" He had left them in a field with some startled shepherds. Fox was opposed to the established church, whose buildings he called 'steeple-houses', to paid clergy, military service and capital punishment. So far, so good. But he began to interrupt people at their worship, wore unorthodox clothes which got him known as 'The Man in Leather Breeches' and shook with the fervour of his own preaching, thus giving rise to the popular nickname for his sect. He was persecuted in Leicestershire as elsewhere – arrested at Whetstone and at Swannington (by Lord Beaumont); imprisoned in Leicester; stoned in Bosworth. He was a fascinating mixture of ignorance and madness, simple faith, great courage, and a callous indifference to the suffering of others.

The stupefying thought processes by which Fox arrived at his singular notions confounded his critics and nonplussed his judges, and his grasp of the English language was even more fragile than his understanding of logic. He expounded his doctrines in epistles with unfathomable titles like: "A Warning to the World that are Groping in the Dark". Or even worse: "Concerning Good morrow and Good even, the World's customs, but by the Light which into the World is come by it made manifest to all who be in the Darkness".

His writings were subsequently translated into the King's English by his disciples William Penn and William Barclay, but his incomprehensible manner ensured that he went down in history as a mystic, though not in the history of Macaulay, who said that Fox was "too much disordered for liberty, and not sufficiently disordered for Bedlam". I have quoted, however briefly, from most of the important writers connected with Leicestershire, but perhaps I may quote Macaulay on George Fox at a little more length, for the passage in his *History of England* reveals Macaulay at his most engaging and Fox at his most obscure:

One of the precious truths which were divinely revealed to this new apostle was, that it was falsehood and adulation to use the second person plural instead of the second person singular. Another was, that to talk of the month of March was to worship the bloodthirsty god Mars, and that to talk of Monday was to pay idolatrous homage to the moon. To say Good morning or Good evening was highly reprehensible; for those phrases evidently imported that God had made bad days and bad nights. A Christian was bound to face death itself rather than touch his hat to the greatest of mankind. When Fox was challenged to produce any Scriptural authority for this dogma, he cited the passage in which it is written that Shadrach, Meshach, and Abednego were thrown into the fiery furnace with their hats on; and, if his own narrative may be trusted, the Chief Justice of England was altogether unable to answer this argument except by crying out, "Take him away, gaoler." Fox insisted much on the not less weighty argument that the Turks never show their bare heads to their superiors; and he asked, with great animation, whether those who bore the noble name of Christians ought not to surpass Turks in virtue. Bowing he strictly prohibited, and, indeed, seemed to consider it as the effect of Satanical influence; for, as he observed, the woman in the Gospel, while she had a spirit of infirmity, was bowed together, and ceased to bow as soon as Divine power had liberated her from the tyranny of the Evil One. His expositions of the sacred writings were of a very peculiar kind. Passages, which had been, in the apprehension of all the readers of the Gospels during sixteen centuries, figurative, he construed literally. Passages, which no human being before him had ever understood in any other than a literal sense, he construed figuratively. Thus, from those rhetorical expressions in which the duty of patience under injuries is enjoined he deduced the doctrine that self defence against pirates and assassins is unlawful.

On such slippery foundations are the mighty edifices of religious dogma built.

Sheepy Magna and Parva lie on opposite sides of the River Sence, a tributary of the Anker. The largely rebuilt steeple-house of All Saints at Sheepy Magna, though not otherwise attractive, has stained-glass windows by Burne-Jones and Kempe, while Parva has an old mill – one of a number surviving along the course of the Sence – though its broken windows and derelict appearance now foretell its doom. There are two rivers named Sence in the county. This one rises at Bardon Hill and flows fifteen miles to join the Anker at Atherstone. The other, shorter, flows into the Soar from near Billesdon. The name is an old English word for a draught or cup, and presumably signifies an abundance of clear water.

At New House Grange, near Sheepy, there is a medieval timbered tithe barn, nearly 150 feet long. Another tithe barn, built in 1250, was later rebuilt as an inn, and is well known as The Cock at Sibson. Dick Turpin is reputed to have used it on occasions when he was working Watling Street, and as its name implies, it was a venue for cock-fighting. It seems the local vicar used to announce forthcoming contests from the church pulpit.

Running parallel with the course of the Sence is a lane leading to Bilstone. It is called Gibbet Lane, and there beside the road, just before you reach the village, stands the hideous 'monument' after which the lane is named, as if it were a source of local pride. And as if to confirm this impression, the rotting old post is protected by a fence and celebrated by an official notice which gives the year of its erection, although this, like the dates on Leicester's Clock Tower, is wrong. It is stated that the body of John Massey was hung here after he had been executed for murdering a woman in the spinney half a mile away, in February 1800. In fact, the woman was his wife, and the date of the murder was not February 1800 but March 1801. Massey was a heavily built man of fifty-four, who had been a wrestler in his time, and had been nicknamed Topsy Turvey for his customary feats of strength in tossing his opponents over his head. The *Leicester Journal* of the time recorded that he was "much addicted to passion", and when he killed his wife, his ten-year-old daughter, who was the chief witness against him, narrowly escaped death herself when Massey threw her into the mill-dam. The judge ordered Massey's body to be handed over for dissection after his execution, in those days when anatomical study could only be made on the bodies of executed criminals, but Massey had petitioned to be buried between his two wives, so he was ordered to be hung in chains instead, having been hanged at Birstall on 23 March.

Worms, having no flesh to live on nowadays, are slowly consuming this loathsome timber, which is allowed to remain here defiling the English countryside when many a less offensive relic has been removed. I am happy to add that I have done my bit toward rotting it when passing this way. Not that Bilstone's gibbet was the last one used in the county. As late as 1832 a man named Cook, who had committed a murder in Leicester, was hanged before a crowd of twenty to thirty thousand people in front of the Welford Road gaol, and then suspended from a gibbet set up in Aylestone Road. It is probable that this was the last gibbet in England, for the Home Office ordered the removal of the body shortly after it had been hung there.

Bilstone is a pleasant enough agricultural village, and it is a pity that its only claim to mention in the books is its rotting monument to barbarism. Perhaps that is why Nichols, with his insatiable appetite for facts, felt bound to tell us that on 16 May 1737 a Bilstone woman named Rebecca Yates spent a quarter of an hour under water without drowning. Now I should like to know more about Miss or Mrs Yates, and no doubt you would too. How did she come to be under the water in the first place? Was she having a swim? Did she fall unconscious in her bath? Was she ducked as a witch? Alas, Nichols, having provoked our curiosity, tells us nothing more, except to admit that Rebecca's experience was not a record. Nichols himself must have been a sort of record-holder, for recounting useless information.

Across the fields to the west of Bilstone is Twycross, where the East Midland Zoological Society has its zoo, opened in 1963 from modest beginnings, and now having quite a collection. Twycross is the residence of that troupe of tea-drinking chimpanzees well known on television. You can see pink flamingoes from the roadside as you pass by – one of the more unexpected sights of Leicestershire. It is Twycross Church, however, which holds the biggest surprise here. It is an ordinary enough village church at first glance, but its east window contains some of the finest old stained glass in Europe. Naturally enough, it got here by devious means from France, where it once graced an assortment of medieval churches, including Le Mans Cathedral and Sainte-Chapelle in Paris. Concern for its safety during the French Revolution led to its removal from the original windows, and then it came across the Channel and into the hands of William IV, who presented it to Earl Howe of Gopsall, and he in turn gave the precious glass to his parish church. It was removed again for safety during the Second World War. When it had been replaced the French government offered to buy it back, but this time it stayed put, and the light coming into the little church of St James passes through one of Leicestershire's most splendid works of art.

Gopsall Park, lying north of the road between Twycross and Bilstone, was originally the home of Charles Jennens, who built a mansion there around 1750, with a family fortune made in the iron industry in Birmingham. It had Corinthian columns at its south front and its wings were formed by a library and a chapel with an interior built of cedar. The house was designed by John Westley, of Leicester, and cost the equivalent of more than a million pounds in today's terms. Jennens was an eccentric patron of the arts, and was nicknamed 'Solyman the Magnificent' because of his vulgar ostentation. He never walked anywhere without a flunkey going before him to clear his path of obstacles, and his more usual mode of travel was in a coach drawn by four horses. But he was known as a benevolent gentleman, and was a friend and patron of Handel, who composed parts of his oratorios *Messiah* and *Israel in Egypt* at Gopsall, though that was in the previous house on the site.

Jennens' niece Esther married Viscount Curzon, and their son Penn Assheton Curzon, who was a Leicestershire Member of Parliament in 1792, married the daughter of Earl Howe. Jennens left the estate to Curzon on his death, and thence it became the property of Earl Howe. Eventually the Howe family sold the estate to Sir Samuel Waring, the furniture manufacturer, and by that time it had a deer park of over a thousand acres. Edward VII had been an occasional visitor there, armed with his usual weapons, with which he no doubt laid low a few birds in the mansion as well as out in the park. Then during the Second World War Gopsall Hall was taken over by the War Office, and when the army ceased to occupy it, the house was in such a bad state that it was only fit for demolition, so in 1951 it was pulled down.

I have already mentioned Barton-on-the-Beans, where the luxuriant crops in its fields once gave Leicestershire a nickname it did not care for, but beans were not the only fruit of this village's labours. Although it had never had its own church, Barton had the first local chapel of the General Baptists, founded in 1745, and missionaries of this persuasion went as far as India (somewhat presumptuously, as it seems to me) to convert the natives whose own religion had been serving them long before the birth of Christ. Prominent among these Baptists were the Deacon family, who were clockmakers, and in Leicester the workshop of Samuel Deacon can be seen in Castle View, where it was reconstructed after being acquired by the museum in 1951.

It is a little over two miles (or as we should say now, three and a half kilometres) from Barton-in-the-Beans to Market Bosworth, whose name has passed the lips of every schoolboy in Britain for nearly five hundred years. It is a village of no great size or distinction, save for its former grammar school, which had a high reputation in the Midlands. Yet Bosworth also gave its name to the local parliamentary constituency. The explanation is that it was an ancient market town of some importance before the rise of hosiery manufacturing. But the all-consuming grasp of industry did not take hold of Bosworth as it did Hinckley and many other villages around, so Market Bosworth remained small and keeps some of its old character about its centre.

The Dixies were the prominent family here for centuries, and it was they who built the hall and founded the grammar school. Both buildings survive, though the old family home is now the Bosworth Park Infirmary, and the school has become comprehensive and moved to Desford. One of the Dixies married the daughter of a Beaumont, which did a lot for the family finances. The old Dixie Grammar School numbered Robert Burton among its pupils and Samuel Johnson among its teachers. The young Johnson got his first job here after leaving university, and hated it so much that even Boswell failed to induce him to talk much about his time there. He found the overbearing manner of Sir Wolstan Dixie intolerable, and after a few months "relinquished a situation which all his life afterwards he recollected with the strongest aversion and even a degree of horror". Well, I have to say that I, in company with Squire Cradock's wife, recoil from the pompous and overbearing side of Dr Johnson's own character, so however much Johnson hated his employer, he evidently learned something from him which he would have done better without. The extensive grounds of Bosworth Park have been acquired in the present decade by the County Council, and an arboretum is in process of development here. It is being devoted to oaks, maples and other trees of striking foliage colour – an important and worthy addition to Leicestershire's amenities.

Newbold Verdon gets its curious name from Bertram de Verdon, who was lord of the manor in the time of King Stephen, and took his own name from the fortress town of Verdun in France. The hall and estate came into the possession of Edward Montagu in the eighteenth century, and so for a time the village became the residence of his more famous wife, Lady Mary Wortley Montagu, the one-time friend of Swift and Pope. As she was one of the original 'blue-stockings', perhaps it is apt that she lived here, in a way. The popular expression for a woman of literary tastes derived from a certain Benjamin Stillingfleet, who was a member of her intellectual society, and habitually wore blue worsted stockings instead of the formal black silk. Ironically, Lady Mary was the woman who introduced inoculation against smallpox into western Europe, following a stay in Turkey when her husband was ambassador there. She liked the

Leicestershire estate, having described it in one of her letters as "one of the most charming and pleasant places I ever saw".

Desford always means aeroplanes to me, because during the war pilots used to be trained in Tiger Moths at the aerodrome there, and they were always to be seen flying over Hinckley and putting those versatile little bi-planes through their paces, and sometimes causing alarm to local people with their 'hedge-hopping' exercises. Now the former airfield is occupied by the huge Caterpillar Tractor Company, a big employer here, which has its own sports and social club on the site.

The noise made in the vicinity by those aircraft was nothing compared with the dreadful roar of the motor-cycles which invade this corner of Leicestershire on their way to Mallory Park. The racing circuit here was started on a modest scale by an Earl Shilton builder, but soon expanded into big business, and at weekends when meetings are held, the roads of the county seem to become race-courses themselves, with the crash-helmeted youth of half of England making screaming tracks for this altar where the monstrous noise of machinery is worshipped as if it were the sound of holy music in their ears.

In the churchyard of All Saints at Kirkby Mallory is a monument to Augusta Ada, Countess of Lovelace, the daughter of Lord Byron. In the year of Waterloo, Byron, then the darling of society, had married Anne Isabella Milbanke, heiress to the Noel family, many of whose tombs are in this church, the Noels having been here since Elizabethan times. But the prim Lady Byron and her husband were temperamentally incompatible, and after the birth of their daughter she accused Byron, amid dark and unsubstantiated hints of incest and sodomy, of cruelty and insanity, and left him. Lady Byron came to the estate of her father, Sir Ralph, at Kirkby Mallory, wrote to Byron that she would never return to him, and feared that the poet would come to Kirkby during the night and steal the child from her; her mother, the Hon. Judith Noel, armed herself with two pistols to protect them. Byron was distantly related to Elizabeth Howard, the Duchess of Rutland, whose father the Earl of Carlisle had been Byron's guardian. Lady Byron was a friend of the duchess, and at Kirkby was disturbed by the news of the fire at Belvoir Castle, and anxious for the safety of the duchess's children who were asleep there when the conflagration occurred. Byron, meanwhile, was ruined socially by all the scandal surrounding his name, and he left England, returning only when he was in his coffin, six years later.

During an illness at Kirkby, Lady Byron was attended by Sir Henry Halford, whom she considered a "cold-blooded animal". Peckleton Church, on the other hand, has a memorial to another distinguished surgeon, Doctor Robert Chessher, who was born in the village and practised at Hinckley. He was celebrated for his special knowledge of spinal diseases. Among his patients were William Wilberforce, Mary Christiana Bonaparte (Napoleon's niece), and George Canning, the statesman who was one of England's greatest foreign secretaries, and became Prime Minister in 1827, but died a few months later, not long after Byron. Canning lived at Castle Hill House in Hinckley for four years, and then at Burbage for a time. From here he used to take a regular walk to Stoke Golding via the road now known as Hollycroft, and it was thus called 'Canning's Walk' at one period. Canning's son Charles married Charlotte Stuart, whose younger sister Louisa became the wife of the 'mad' Marquis of Waterford, and was a friend of John Ruskin – a more unlikely combination of personalities than could be dreamed up by any writer of fiction.

Barwell and Earl Shilton are villages of red-brick factories and houses in which it would be forgivable to think that man had created them out of nothing in the nineteenth century; but a few years ago, Nature, as if to remind the villagers of her constant presence, dropped a small meteorite on Barwell, and gave the people and the *Hinckley Times* something to think about as a change from local politics and Women's Institute meetings. It was the most sensational thing to have happened to Barwell since George Geary took ten wickets in an innings in 1929.

Two hundred years ago, the villagers of Earl Shilton nearly drowned a supposed witch. The village was then named Earl's Shilton, and being long held by the Earl of Leicester, was so called to distinguish it from the Shilton not far away in Warwickshire. Its churchyard has a memorial to one Samuel Marvin, who died in 1787. He was a wrestler, and I doubt that a more ludicrous tribute was ever laboriously carved on a headstone than the lines to Marvin's memory –

At length he falls; the long, long contest o'er,
And Time has thrown whom none e'er threw before. . .

And so on, *ad nauseam.*

It is hard to believe that these two villages, totally dominated by the hosiery and footwear industries, have any ancient history (even Earl Shilton's church is a modern rebuild, though Barwell's is fourteenth century and attractive). But Barwell produced some startling evidence of a past when a portrait bust of Romano-British origin was found there. It is in Leicester Museum now, and is one of the earliest surviving pieces of British sculpture. It is made of Ketton stone, and how it came to be at Barwell is anybody's guess.

We should also glance at Elmesthorpe, nearby. Its Danish name-ending is scarce in this part of the county, and it was a deserted village as long ago as the fifteenth century, when some of Richard III's officers slept in the church before the Battle of Bosworth. Then the church itself fell into ruin, and was once used as a cattle pen. To this day its nave lies open to the sky, though the chancel was rebuilt when the village began to grow again. Elmesthorpe even had a railway station until the Beeching axe fell heavily on the line between Hinckley and Leicester, leaving only one station *en route* out of the original four.

The Constitutional Club in Earl Shilton's Station Road (the station was Elmesthorpe's) was familiar territory to me when I was a boy, and I used to wonder at the strange mystique of this adult and largely male world with its strict rules for members and its barrel-filled cellar, and the smell of beer outside as well as inside, rising into the air from the crates of empties stacked up at the back. When Surrey were playing Leicestershire at Grace Road, the Bedser twins might drop in for a drink with Sammy Coe, and on Saturday nights the ballroom upstairs was alive with music and dancing, but every night of the week the real drinkers – some with bulbous noses – sat playing dominoes or watching games of billiards and snooker from their chairs on the raised platform near the tables.

These villages stand on a low plateau, and the ascent from the main road from Leicester to Earl Shilton's High Street used to be the terror of lorry and bus drivers. It has been levelled out in recent years, and a road from the top leads across country to Croft, crossing another conglomeration of pylons, one or two streams, and the new Leicester–Coventry motorway. The village of Croft stands at the foot of a granite hill which is a prominent landmark for miles around, and is skirted by the River Soar on its way to Leicester. The King of Mercia is said to have held a council on the hill in 836, and Professor Hoskins has convincingly deduced that the hill was the scene of the court of the Sparkenhoe Hundred, where the elders met under the presidency of the king's reeve to administer the law in local matters. The *Anglo-Saxon Chronicle* report a gruesome judgement there in 1124, when the court "hanged more thieves than ever were known before; that is, in a little while, four and forty men altogether; and despoiled six men of their eyes and of their testicles". The president of that barbarous court was Ralph Bassett, of that family who were lords of the manor at Sapcote. One of his descendants followed his neighbouring landlord, Simon de Montfort, in the Barons' Revolt. Since those times Croft Hill has been defaced by quarrying, and the neighbouring villages of Stoney Stanton and Sapcote also have quarries which have been worked for a long time, and from which the former castle in which the Bassetts lived was probably built.

I do not know whose ghost it was that was supposed to haunt 'Scholar's Bridge' which crossed one of the streams near Stoney Stanton; perhaps one of those hanged men. Leicestershire has few ghost stories to tell, compared with most counties of England – probably because of its dogged materialism! But Arthur Mee's description of the Turville monuments in Thurlaston's church always makes me think that one of them was a homicidal maniac. "The altar tomb of Hugo Turville," he says, "who died in 1347, shows him in a tunic and hood, holding his heart in his hands, and beside him is the battered figure of his wife."

Narborough and Enderby were once quiet little country villages which now find themselves surrounded and traversed by motorways and railways, and may soon be engulfed in the outward spread of Leicester. The Roman Fosse Way, which still follows its straight course from near Sapcote into Leicester as the A46, goes awry only through Narborough, where the twin towers of the Carlton Hayes mental hospital form another well-known local landmark. The church at Narborough was struck by lightning in 1786 and has been much rebuilt, but there is a good collection of Swithland slate headstones in the churchyard.

Only the River Sence separates Blaby and Whetstone from Leicester. As with nearly all the villages in this quarter of the county, they are bluntly industrial, but Blaby's face is saved by its rose gardens, well known to gardeners throughout the Midlands. No such saving grace presents itself to the visitor at Broughton Astley, but here George Fox testifies in his *Journal* that the Lord opened his mouth, and he preached one of his first sermons to a gathering of Baptists and others: "For in that day the Lord's power began to spring, and I had great openings in the Scriptures."

A distance of three miles separates Ashby Magna from Ashby Parva, but the two Wigstons are ten miles apart, and do not appear to have the slightest connection with each other. Wigston Parva is a pleasant hamlet with a tiny church, tucked between Watling Street and the A46 like a nut in a pair of crackers. As for the Ashbys, they have nothing to recommend them to the visitor, their names having been eclipsed by that more famous town in the north of the county.

Ullesthorpe is in the parish of Claybrooke, and these villages, too, had many homes devoted to framework knitting in the nineteenth century. Claybrooke, indeed, was called "large and populous" in 1793, and "where the worsted trade whirls away". It consists of Magna and Parva and it is the latter, oddly enough, which has the only church and has a fine chancel with beautiful windows.

One of the rectors of Claybrooke was the Rev. Auley Macaulay, M.A., brother of Lord Macaulay, and in 1791 the rector published *The History and Antiquities of Claybrook*, dedicating it to John Nichols, who printed it for him. The reverend gentleman had none of his brother's literary genius, but what he lacked in style he more than made up for in an unbelievable combination of bigotry and naïvety that would have got him lynched by today's 'Women's Lib' champions:

> Between six and seven years ago, a man and a woman in this parish were presented by the churchwardens in the spiritual court for fornication, and they both did public penance by standing in the middle aisle, during the time of divine service, invested with white sheets. If the discipline of the Church in this and other matters were strictly enforced, it might tend to give some check to that unbridled licentiousness of manners which has of late pervaded our villages. . . Modesty and Chastity are no longer the characteristics of the lower class of females . . . Hence it is that we frequently see the bridegroom reluctantly dragged to the altar, guarded like a felon by the parish

officers, and compelled to give his hand to a licentious and abandoned woman.

Claybrooke is only just over a mile from High Cross, or Venonae, where the Romans made the junction of their two greatest British roads at the country's centre. In the back garden of a house here there is a stone pillar which is the remaining part of a monument set up early in the eighteenth century by the Earl of Denbigh to celebrate the end of the war with France. But Nature shattered with lightning what Art had devised in tribute. Roman coins, spearheads and the remains of building foundations have been found at High Cross, over the passing centuries, and there is a tradition that a Roman city called Cleycester stood here, and that Claybrooke is a corruption of that name. But the hard evidence for such a belief is totally lacking, and Dr Stukeley's observation that the line of the Watling Street points direct to Rome is hardly more than an attribution of fanciful significance to imperial geometry.

A hamlet called Smockington, near Wigston Parva, was said by Rev. Macaulay to be the scene of a break-in which led to the growing of turnips as food for livestock in this neighbourhood. It seems that some sheep raided the garden of the Red Lion Inn there and ate the turnips greedily, whereupon the farmer took the hint and grew acres of turnips which were readily consumed by sheep and cattle alike. Cheese was the locality's contribution to human diet, however, and it is strange to stand in industrial villages like Sapcote and Aston Flamville and think that they were once as renowned in the Midland cheese markets as Edam and Gouda are in the Netherlands.

Burbage – always perilously close to Hinckley – is now flanked on its other side by the M69, but this village, though red brick and factory-bound today, has one or two unspoiled corners with some decent Georgian and neo-Gothic building (including much of its church). Its name was originally Burbach, and evidently came from the bur thistle, another name for spear thistle, which grew abundantly in its fields, 'bach' being a small stream. It was a stylish and prosperous village at one time, and one of its earlier incumbents was the ninth Earl of Kent, rector here for fifty years. One of the monuments in the church is to Richard Wightman and his two wives and eight children, and though he died in 1568, his family name is still prominent in the district.

Cotes is another name of significance in Burbage. In 1682 Roger Cotes was born here, the son of the rector. He took holy orders himself, but not before he had become a professor of astronomy and experimental philosophy. The intellectual promise of Cotes was such that Isaac Newton had remarked of him: "Now the world will know something." But Cotes died when he was only thirty-three, and Burbage and the world lost a mathematician of genius.

Burbage has a fine large common and a wood which are the most magnetic bits of countryside for people in both Burbage and Hinckley, quite apart from the golfers who have a course there, and that part remains relatively untouched by building development. But many of the fields between the town and the village, where I used to walk, are now covered by housing estates, and it is difficult to tell where Burbage ends and Hinckley begins, for Hinckley, like Leicester and Loughborough, has reached out with grasping arms to take all it can to its heaving industrial bosom. Sketchley, on the Burbage side of Hinckley, has long been a suburb of the town, but it was once a separate village in the parish of Aston Flamville. It had eight houses in 1790.

Here, in Stockingopolis, with nothing much to look at but the effects of manufacturing industry, we are in the fittest place to set off on an excursion into Leicestershire's past and present working life, which is not nearly so dull and uninteresting as the reader might suspect. Stand in Hinckley's Bond Street, between a group of timber-framed cottages on one side of the road and a large modern hosiery factory on the other, and you are at the centre of a story of hardship and prosperity; ignorance and eloquence; crime and punishment; triumph and tragedy; the despoliation of the countryside and the beautification of women; all of which have been contributors to that evolution of Leicestershire which we have been observing in previous chapters.

X

LEICESTERSHIRE AT WORK

If ALL the sporting parsons of Leicestershire were laid end to end, they would not reach as far in distance or in value as the effects of one simple idea that occurred to a Nottinghamshire curate in 1589. The Rev. William Lee's imagination was set in motion by watching his wife knitting stockings by hand, and he thereupon invented the stocking frame, on which there was a separate needle for each loop, making a whole row of stitches at one operation, instead of casting all the loops on to one needle. True, the thread had to be placed over the needle by hand, and it was over two hundred years before this operation was successfully mechanized, but all the same, Lee's machine created an industry, and Leicestershire was much in need of it.

The county's first stocking frame was set up at Hinckley in 1640 by William Iliffe, and within twenty years fifty frames were at work in Leicestershire, compared with Nottinghamshire's hundred. Leicester itself did not have its first frame until about 1680, but early in the following century, the number of frames in Leicester had overtaken the number in Nottingham, providing the earliest large-scale answer to the problem of 'setting the poor to work', and beginning that slow but steady flow of people into the towns from the outlying villages and hamlets.

When there was plenty of work, the clatter of the stocking frames could be heard in well over a hundred towns and villages of Leicestershire, and Defoe could easily believe that the whole county seemed to be employed in the hosiery trade. There was a huge demand then for stockings to adorn the legs of men, as well as women, and the knitters enjoyed independence and plenty of leisure time, which accounts in part for the early popularity of cricket in the county.

Capitalism and exploitation were the early masters in the stocking trade, however, and the climb to the general prosperity of the twentieth century was over the starving bodies, workhouse inhabitants and wrecked machinery of the earlier framework-knitting industry. The stocking frames were owned by the manufacturers and hired out to 'masters' or middlemen, who employed the labourers. These workers – often illiterate – operated the machines in their homes, earning their wages at piece-work rates for the number of stockings they produced. But they were completely at the mercy of the masters. There was no agreed minimum rate, and the knitters had to pay weekly frame-rent, the cost of lights during the winter, a wage to a woman 'seamer', oil for the machine; and all this out of the mere pittance they earned in the first place, by sitting at their frames for perhaps thirteen hours a day. They might be lucky, in hard times, to have four and sixpence a week left after stoppages.

The growing iniquities of the masters put intolerable pressures on the knitters. The practices of 'truck' and 'stinting' became widespread, and then price-cutting appeared, and the situation of the labourers gradually got worse. 'Truck' was the system whereby the middlemen, who frequently had other business interests, often in the form of retail trade, used their profits to acquire stocking frames and become owners themselves. They paid the knitters their wages with goods instead of money, and as the knitters relied on the middlemen for their work, they were in no position to refuse. 'Stinting' meant that, when work was short, the middlemen spread it out over a large number of frames, instead of just enough to produce the work at full capacity. But the knitters still had to pay their full week's frame-rent. Thus they were contributing to the masters' profits from both retail trade and frame-rents. If the machines broke down, they were expected to be their own mechanics, so that every hour spent on repairs was an hour's less production towards their scanty wages. Growing desperation led them to adopt the only apparent solution to their problems – they rented extra frames and trained their children to operate them.

By the end of the eighteenth century, stocking frames had been adapted to make such things as shirts and gloves as well as socks and stockings, and specialization had become apparent in the three main hosiery-producing counties, worsted hosiery being the chief concern in Leicestershire, silk in Derbyshire and cotton in Nottinghamshire, although the Hinckley manufacturers also specialized in cotton products. New inventions and technical improvements were laying the foundations of a giant industry, but they were doing so largely at the expense of the poor framework-knitters, and in 1773 came the first signs of the revolt that was to trouble the Midland counties for almost a hundred years, when a mob in Leicester destroyed a newly invented machine which they believed – rightly – would take work away from them.

More violence followed in Nottinghamshire, and in 1787 another riot occurred in Leicester, when an angry mob broke up a new worsted spinning machine, attacked the houses of its owners, Coltman and Whetstone, and stoned the Mayor when he tried to pacify them by shouting: "Come, my lads, give over – you've done enough – quite enough: come, give over, there's good lads, and go away." He died later from the injuries he received.

This resort to violence had the desired effect. The masters agreed to standard price lists which kept the framework-knitters reasonably happy for a few years. Then in 1795 a disastrous harvest rocketed the price of wheat to eight pounds a quarter, and there were bread riots during which, in Leicester, a mob tried to seize a wagon of wheat. The Lord Lieutenant of the County (the Duke of Rutland) called out the Leicester Troop of Cavalry, and some rioters were killed or seriously wounded in the resulting affray, which became known as the 'Barrow Butchery'.

Meanwhile, the wearing of trousers by men had drastically reduced the demand for stockings, and the hosiery trade seemed to be crumbling under the burdens of this change in fashion and the opposition to advanced techniques. It was then that the manufacture of 'cut-ups' was introduced. This was the method by which unfashioned stockings were cut from the fabric and sewn together, being shaped afterwards by heating and steaming. This system led to the introduction of wide frames, which could make several stockings at once, and the knitters saw this machinery taking out of their mouths even what little bread they could afford. The stage was all set for more drama, and the curtain went up at the end of the first decade of the new century when a half-witted youth at Anstey, named Ned Ludd, smashed the stocking frame at which he was working, as revenge for a punishment he had received.

The so-called Luddite Rebellion took its name from this incident. The retarded apprentice who thus unwittingly wrote his name in the pages of history could scarcely comprehend the wider issue which motivated the violence following his mindless private action. Nor was Leicestershire the main centre of Luddite activity, which was much more serious in Nottinghamshire, and soon spread to Derbyshire and Yorkshire. Nevertheless, in two years Luddite mobs broke a thousand machines. On 11 April 1811, stocking-makers at Hinckley went on a rampage through the town, breaking windows and plundering and burning houses. The startled government, with minds full of the consequences of revolution in France, appointed Secret Committees to enquire into the riots.

For those able to divert part of their minds from the suffering and hardship of the period, it is easy to see reaction to the Luddite movement as one of the more hilarious episodes in the history of English government. As early as 1793 a Leicestershire journalist and bookseller, Sir Richard Phillips, had been imprisoned for selling Tom Paine's *The Rights of Man*, though the real cause of complaint against him was that he edited the radical *Leicester Herald*. Now, in 1812, the 'Secret Committee of the House of Lords on the Disturbed State of Certain Counties' reported that the source of all the trouble was – a secret committee! There was much talk of sedition, political insurrection, and subversive elements, and little recognition of the simple economic fact of life – that the Midland population was trying to save itself from starving to death. One observer reported that "it became a long and widely spread practice to still the cravings of hunger in the adults by opium taken in a solid form ..."

It was all very well for sensible men like Cobbett to urge the framework-knitters to refrain from violence, but Pitt's Combination Act of 1800 prevented them from forming any kind of legal common voice, and Mr Cobbett, after all, was not starving to death. Besides, all political attempts to ease their appalling condition had failed. It is true that the Luddite movement took on all the ridiculous appurtenances of a secret society, with a mythical 'General Ludd' who was supposed to issue his orders from Sherwood Forest, and an idiotic password which compounded nonsense with tautology:

> Q. What are you?
> A. Determined.
> Q. What for?
> A. Free liberty.

But what were they to do? In 1816, at Hinckley, out of a total population of six thousand, nearly four thousand people received parish relief. The Rev. Robert Hall saw the plight of the Leicestershire knitters clearly:

> Some provinces, it is confessed, abounded with more splendid objects, with more curious specimens of art, and grander scenes of nature; but it was surpassed by none in the general diffusion of prosperity. But what a contrast is now presented in the languid and emaciated forms and dejected looks of the industrious mechanic who with difficulty drags his trembling limbs over scenes where his fellows gazed with rapture . . . A rapid depression of wages preys upon their vitals like a gangrene and exhausts their strength.

Nevertheless, the government made machine-breaking a capital offence, and it was against this measure that Byron, who had seen the pitiful state of the knitters in Nottinghamshire, made his impressive maiden speech in the House of Lords, referring to the knitters as "men, liable to conviction, on the clearest evidence, of the capital crime of poverty."

> "Suppose one of these men, as I have seen them," Byron said, "meagre with famine, sullen with despair, careless of a life which your Lordships are perhaps about to value at something less than the price of a stocking-frame; – suppose this man surrounded by the children for whom he is unable to procure bread at the hazard of his existence, about to be torn for ever from a family which he lately supported in peaceful industry, and which it is not his fault that he can no longer so support; – suppose this man . . . dragged into court, to be tried for this new offence, by this new law; still there are two things wanting to convict and condemn him; and these are, in my opinion, twelve butchers for a jury, and a Jeffreys for a judge!"

Byron's eloquence was lost on the majority of their Lordships, however. They still seemed to be suffering under the delusion that the stocking-makers were anarchists and revolutionaries plotting to bring down the government and emulate the French. Perhaps 'General Ludd' was the English Robespierre, or even worse, the English Napoleon! Byron's only support came from those who had seen the situation of the hosiery workers for themselves, such as Sir Francis Burdett, a fox-hunting man who lived at Kirby Bellars during the season, and was himself imprisoned for his advocacy of parliamentary reform.

In 1816 the worst incident in Leicestershire's troubles occurred, at the factory of Heathcoat, Lacy and Boden in
Loughborough. Mr Heathcoat, who came from Hathern, was
the inventor of various technical improvements to the bobbin-net
machines with which the Loughborough firm manufactured
lace. His rivals infringed his patent rights, and he cut the wages of
his workers in order to reduce his prices. On the night of 28 June
of that year, a number of men with blackened faces broke into
the factory and smashed fifty-three machines, valued at six
thousand pounds, and during the raid they shot and wounded
one of the factory watchmen, John Asher. Six men were hanged
in front of Leicester gaol for this crime, at noon on 17 April 1817,
and three others were transported. Mr Heathcoat removed his
business to Devon, and Leicestershire lost its connection with
Nottingham's lace trade.

In Leicestershire, at least, physical violence on a large scale
subsided after this event, although hardship was to continue for
many years yet, and there were serious disturbances in Hinckley
and Loughborough in 1830. Sick clubs were being formed, but
most of them had to close down because their members could
not afford to pay their subscriptions. Even so, when the Poor
Law Act of 1834 reduced outdoor relief to a minimum, the
hosiery workers, still proud of their independence, preferred to
survive as best they could on low wages rather than enter the
workhouse, "abhorred", as Laurie Lee has written, "more than
debt, or prison, or beggary, or even the stain of madness".

At this time Leicester had over four thousand stocking frames,
followed by Hinckley with one and a half thousand, Shepshed
with nine hundred, Earl Shilton with over seven hundred, and
Loughborough almost as many. Wigston Magna, which had
been the second largest town in the county in medieval times,
also ranked high, with Burbage, Barwell and Sileby, and then a
great many other villages possessing smaller numbers of frames.

Meanwhile, the older industries which nature had provided –
farming, mining and quarrying – had been developing slowly for
centuries. Agriculture had always been the predominant industry in the eastern half of the county, but it had to wait for
men like Bakewell and Thomas Paget to revolutionize its
methods, whilst mining and quarrying had been taking advantage of nature's resources since the Roman occupation, but
only in a modest and primitive sense until the Industrial

Revolution. Man being one of nature's less perfect creations, it took him a long time to realize the full potential of the earth he stood on.

Among the early mine-owners who put the Leicestershire coalfield on the map, the Beaumonts and the Hastings were prominent. The Beaumonts were active at Coleorton and Measham in the sixteenth century, and at Swannington also in the seventeenth, by which time the Hastings were extracting coal at Heather. Their operations were chiefly in the exposed field at that time, and it has been estimated that about fifteen thousand tons were being produced annually at the end of the sixteenth century.

The problem of transport was to tax the minds of the coal-owners for 150 years. Coal which sold at Measham for one shilling and sevenpence a ton, in 1611, cost ten shillings a ton by the time it reached Leicester, coming in by cart or packhorse via Coal Pit Lane (now Braunstone Lane). But improvements in the mines themselves were rapid. There was a steam engine at work in a pit at Swannington before 1720, and an increasing number of collieries were being opened, with shafts sunk to deeper levels.

Operations were small but profitable. There were fifteen pits near Coleorton by 1779, and collieries were opened at Whitwick, Ibstock and Bagworth in succeeding years from 1824, yet there were hardly more than three hundred miners employed in the whole Leicestershire coalfield at that time. Children were employed in the pit until Lord Shaftesbury's Bill was passed in 1842, but not women, and there was a good record for safety in the Leicestershire mines, one of which was working at a depth of 600 feet by that time. In the 1870s when the coalfield produced over a million tons in a year for the first time, a hewer earned five shillings a day, and a boy employed to lead ponies would get half that amount.

The mine-owners' transport problems were solved, to some extent, by the construction of canals. There had been a sudden flurry of activity among canal engineers and the coal magnates, who were anxious to take advantage of any method of moving coal in bulk, and within a few years the canal companies were paying out huge dividends to their delighted shareholders.

The first of the canal operations in Leicestershire was the Loughborough Navigation, which made the River Soar navigable from the Trent to Loughborough, and allowed coal from the Derbyshire collieries to be brought to Leicester by barge and road to compete with the Leicestershire coal, which had to be brought in by road via Desford. The Loughborough Navigation was opened in 1778, and soon afterwards, after opposition from some landowners, the Wreake was also made navigable to Melton Mowbray. Among the shareholders in this project were the Duke of Rutland, the Earl of Harborough, and Earl Ferrers.

Meanwhile, plans were in hand for extending the Soar Navigation to Leicester itself, and for constructing a canal directly across Charnwood Forest from the Leicestershire coal-field to the city. It was also proposed to connect Oakham with the Melton Mowbray Navigation, and to link the Leicestershire pits to the Coventry Canal, to take coal to south-west Leicester-shire and Warwickshire.

The first of these schemes to be realized were the Leicester Navigation, opened early in 1794, and the Charnwood Forest Canal, opened later in the same year. Their total cost was about eighty thousand pounds. The Leicester Navigation consisted partly of making the Soar navigable from Loughborough, and partly of creating diversions through artificial canals. It was prosperous at once, although it helped the Derbyshire coal-owners in their competition with the local pits.

The Charnwood Forest line was a disaster almost from the start. Intended to give the Leicestershire coalfield fair competi-tion against Derbyshire coal, it failed to do so, and ceased to be used commercially within five years of its completion. It was a combined tramroad and canal linking Loughborough with the pits at Thringstone, Coleorton and Swannington. The Black-brook Reservoir, between Whitwick and Shepshed, had been constructed at the same time to supply water to the canal, but in the winter of 1799, after a thaw of heavy snow, the reservoir burst, doing great damage to surrounding farmland and to the embankments and an aqueduct. Although the reservoir was repaired and the line reopened, the coal-owners had lost what little faith they ever had in it, and the canal was gradually abandoned and the land sold.

By this time, work was in progress on the Oakham and Ashby Canals, and on a more ambitious project, the Leicestershire and Northamptonshire Union Canal. The Act authorizing the latter was passed in 1793, and allowed for making the Soar navigable

from Leicester's West Bridge to Aylestone, and then continuing
by canal to join the Grand Junction Canal at Northampton,
with a short branch line to Market Harborough. There would
then be navigable waterways from the Trent to the Thames, and
the canal's promoters, who included Lord Moira, Earl Ferrers
and Joseph Cradock, foresaw huge benefits to Leicestershire
trade.

Operations on this line soon ran into labour troubles,
however. Three hundred navvies marched into Leicester after a
wage dispute, and a mob caused disturbances at Kibworth. Faced
with these problems, as well as with mounting costs, construction errors in the Saddington Tunnel which had to be put right,
and squabbles about the means of joining the canal to the Grand
Junction, the company completed the project as far as Gumley
and then stopped. It was ten years before the canal got under way
again, on Telford's route via the locks at Foxton and the line to
Market Harborough. The canal thus far had cost over two
hundred thousand pounds, but its receipts soon rocketed to over
ten thousand a year. No wonder the businessmen concerned
gathered at the Angel in Market Harborough for a "sumptuous
entertainment".

On the horizon, however, dark clouds were looming for the
canal companies. The projected Leicester and Swannington
Railway had already caused much shaking of heads among the
canal shareholders reaping fat dividends. "Someone," declared
one of them, ought to "expose the fallacy of the proposed
advantages to the public" of the coming age of rail. What these
fallacies were, no one made clear, and when the railway opened
in 1832 it had an immediate beneficial effect for the Leicestershire coalfield, but an equally depressing one for the canals.

Sir George Beaumont built himself a private extension of the
railway to Coleorton, but Lord Moira (Hastings) continued to
rely on the waterways to a large extent, having been one of the
promoters of the Ashby Canal, with the Earl of Stamford
(Grey), who owned the limeworks at Breedon, Earl Ferrers
(Shirley) of Staunton Harold, and the Hon. Penn Assheton
Curzon of Gopsall Hall. The Ashby Canal was the longest of the
waterway projects in Leicestershire, being over 30 miles in length
from the coalfield terminus to its junction via Market Bosworth
and Hinckley with the Coventry Canal at Griff.

In 1815, *The Times* carried the following announcement:

"Those who are curious in the truly English blessing of Coals, and give some attention to domestic comfort and economy, would do well at this season to attend to a new quality of Coal found in Leicestershire at Ashby de la Zouch and called Moira Coal." The piece went on to say that this coal was brought to Paddington by canal at about forty-seven shillings per ton, which was a little more expensive than the coal brought by sea from Newcastle, "but on the trial of its economy in use, burning very slow, clear and bright, without the aid of a Poker, without smoke or smell, and having no cinders, it will be found a most agreeable and desirable fuel for the Public Office, the study, bedroom, apartment of the sick, hospital, parlour, and drawing room . . . " It was in 1826 that salt water was found in one of the Moira pits, and its supposed medicinal properties were responsible for the building of the Bath Hotel at Moira and subsequently for the brief glory of Ashby-de-la-Zouch as a spa.

Although the Grand Union (which had taken over the Leicestershire and Northamptonshire Union Canal) prospered for a while by carrying to Market Harborough the Leicestershire coal delivered to Leicester by rail, instead of the Derbyshire coal which came all the way by barge, the rapid advance of the railways spelt the doom of the waterways, and the euphoria of the great canal age lasted no more than half a century. The canals had transported coal from the Midland pits; granite from Mountsorrel; limestone from Breedon; iron ore from Asfordby; but the volume of traffic rapidly declined, the wharves became silent and neglected, and some of the channels were even dewatered, the rest being given over largely to pleasure vessels.

There is some reason to believe that a Leicestershire man was the original pioneer in English railway history. Before the end of the sixteenth century, Huntingdon Beaumont, the younger brother of Sir Henry, used a primitive form of wooden railway at his mines in Nottinghamshire and Northumberland, to convey coal from the pits to the rivers. It was a long haul from this experiment to the Leicester and Swannington Railway, but the strong interdependence of coalmines and railways remained until the time when the Stephensons and the Ellis's would think it natural to have an interest in both industries. John Ellis succeeded the formidable George Hudson as Chairman of the Midland Railway Company, and was buried near Thomas Cook in Leicester Cemetery, where their bones are still rattled by the trains that made both their fortunes.

> Here they lie, had realms and lands,
> Who now want strength to stir their hands...

The building of the railways caused as much alarm to the populace as the digging of the canals had done. Anxious fathers locked up their daughters when the railway navvies came into town for their drunken revelries. But the railways into Leicester involved demolition of much slum property, so they brought benefits for the poorer people in other ways, as well as in the lower price of coal.

Expansion of the railways was accompanied by expansion in the mining industry. At the end of the nineteenth century nearly ten thousand Leicestershire men were employed in the mines, and new towns had been created to accommodate them. By the beginning of the Great War they were producing over three million tons of coal a year. Production, wages and the degree of mechanization were all above the national average. Since nationalization, it has been difficult to obtain statistics for the Leicestershire pits alone. In 1948 the Leicestershire and South Derbyshire coalfields were merged as Area 7 of the East Midlands Division, and then in 1967 this was joined with the Warwickshire coalfield to become the South Midlands Area. Practically all East Midlands coal was cut mechanically by 1959, and mechanically cleaned, loaded and transported too. The Leicestershire miners are well known for their moderation in industrial disputes, and I have already remarked on the Leicestershire man's aptitude for hard work. Productivity remains high in Leicestershire, and the mines here have been profitable at times when others have not. The Leicestershire coalfield now produces coal of lowish grade which is supplied mainly to the power stations of the nearby Trent, which seem to offer mining in Leicestershire a secure future.

Leicestershire's farmers were affected relatively little by the activities of the mine-owners, canal and railway companies. Of course, there were constant negotiations for the purchase of land, the provision of access bridges for livestock across canals and railway cuttings, and occasionally compensation for damage caused to farmland by such accidents as the bursting of the Blackbrook Reservoir. But these were inconveniences which the farmer had to get used to in an age of growing industry, and generally speaking, he was left to get on with his own important business without interference.

What *did* affect the farmer directly was the growth of the boot and shoe industry. It seems ironic that Leicestershire, which had long been famous for the quality of its sheep and the quantity of its wool, should never have become a centre for the manufacture of woollen goods, and that its farmers were eventually called on to supply the materials for the footwear industry. The explanation lies partly in the type of long-staple wool the county produced, and partly in the lack of adequate water-power for the 'fulling' of wool.

There was little sign of a footwear *industry*, as such, until the mid-nineteenth century in Leicestershire, but Leicester itself had possessed a high proportion of butchers and tanners as early as the sixteenth century, and the discovery of a considerable number of ox-heads beneath the remains of a house in Blue Boar Lane has been taken as evidence of a tanning industry in much earlier times. It was around the mid-nineteenth century when the number of sheep reached its peak in the county, as well as in Northamptonshire, and then began to decline rapidly, whilst the number of cattle increased at a similar rate.

By this time, Leicester had two hundred shoemakers, Hinckley thirteen, Market Harborough nine and Earl Shilton seven. The first Leicestershire employer described as a "boot and shoe manufacturer" appeared at Anstey in 1863, but most of the employers at that time were still using labour from the depressed hosiery villages – particularly Earl Shilton – and these people were 'out-workers' who made and finished the footwear in their own homes.

Northamptonshire had been well in advance of Leicestershire in footwear manufacture, in both time and scale, but in 1860 Leicester introduced mechanical riveting of soles, and this enabled the county to increase its production enormously. Before the end of the century Leicester had considerably more workers in the footwear industry than Northampton, although the latter's satellite towns and villages made the trade more significant there, compared with other industries. In 1901 Leicester had twenty-six thousand men and women making footwear, with heavy concentrations also in Anstey, Hinckley, Earl Shilton and Barwell, and that specialization had begun to appear which still exists – Leicestershire concentrating on women's and children's footwear, and Northamptonshire on men's. In the 1960s, Leicestershire was producing about a quarter of the nation's output of footwear, and the huge British Shoe Corporation had built, on the western outskirts of Leicester, what was believed to be the biggest warehouse in Europe.

The growth of the footwear industry, the progress of the older hosiery trade, mining, quarrying and the coming of the railways, all contributed to the importance of that great variety of light engineering which has, since the Second World War, been Leicester's leading industry. The Britannia Iron Works of the Cort Brothers was in operation by 1804, making the city's first gas-lamp standards, and metal parts for stocking frames. One of Cort's apprentices was that Josiah Gimson who helped to found the Secular Society, and his son Sidney was a pioneer in creating the engineering school in the Leicester College of Technology. When Josiah Gimson opened his Vulcan Works in 1842, construction of the light machinery needed by the footwear manufacturers was the making of his firm.

Great diversity followed these beginnings born of local necessity, and Loughborough followed Leicester into the engineering field. The pumping equipment needed by the coal mines, castings for railway bridges, machines for the footwear, hosiery and knitting manufacturers, were soon but a part of the operations carried out in Leicester and Loughborough firms. Wadkins became the country's largest manufacturers of wood working machinery, and the late lamented Imperial Typewriter Company was an important innovator in bringing women into the hitherto exclusively male domain of engineering.

Another notable company was Taylor, Taylor and Hobson. Founded in 1886 by William Taylor, it soon became famous in the field of precision engineering, particularly for its photographic lenses, used by camera manufacturers throughout the world, including Germany. It was Taylor, Taylor and Hobson who solved the problem of how to produce sharp images in the three primary colours, which led to the production of Technicolor films in Hollywood; and it was the same firm which developed the special instruments required for mass radiography after the war. Then – shortly after the Managing Director had made an impressive statement about the virtues of specialists working in small units – the company became part of the Rank Organisation. It continued to make optical and metrology instruments, working to unimaginably precise measurements like millionths of an inch, under two separate divisions of that unimaginably vast industrial empire, until it became expendable.

Meanwhile, Charles Bennion and his partner Pearson had, with American support, formed the huge British United Shoe Machinery Company, and Mellor Bromley had fought stiff competition from the United States and Germany to take the lead in the British market for hosiery machinery, whilst at Sketchley, Alfred Hawley had founded Sketchley Dye Works to serve the hosiery and knitwear manufacturers, and this has since grown to become even more famous as the nationwide Sketchley Cleaners.

Leicester also became important in printing, and has been regarded as second only to Watford in that industry. One of the more curious aspects of this development has been the sprouting of a number of private presses on which amateur printers, not dependent on commercial success, produce small editions of short works on which they can lavish a care for the craft of printing which has disappeared from the industrial scene. This unusual preoccupation owes its existence in Leicestershire largely to the enthusiasm of John Mason, a papermaker who became head of the bookbinding department at the Leicester College of Art.

One of the productions of Leicestershire's private presses was an edition of John Clare's 'Lines Written in Northampton County Asylum', of which Rigby Graham – one of the leading spirits in local private printing – has said that "scores were offered for next to nothing in pubs, used as beer mats, and eventually hurled at sneering crowds in the Market Place one Sunday evening". There you have Leicester in a nutshell. But it is not only in the city where private printing goes on. Beautiful books have been produced at such unlikely places as Huncote and Wymondham, and by the monks at Mount Saint Bernard Abbey, and among the original literary works of value in this local enterprise has been an impressive history of the Oakham Canal.

Throughout all these developments, the hosiery trade progressed, if only slowly. There was a growing inclination on the part of the frame-owners to build 'shops' at the backs of their houses, where knitters were employed on the premises, so cutting out the middlemen. Some of these early factories can still be seen in the county, with their high windows running along the whole length of the buildings. And as the trade picked up, so the owners made hosiery their chief interest, instead of a mere sideline. The founder of the Leicester firm, Corah's, for instance, was the son of a farmer who had also owned a few stocking frames. Allotments were among other provisions intended to relieve the stocking-makers' hardships, by providing occupation when there was a shortage of knitting work, and producing food for their families at the same time.

At Hinckley in 1861, the first members of the local Co-operative Society included well-known names in the district like Jephcote, Flude, Hood and Bolesworth. They each paid threepence to set up the Society in an attempt to improve the social condition of the working classes, taking their hint from Robert Owen, whose bust looks down from Leicester's Secular Hall, and who was also the chief spirit behind the 1819 Factory Act which put some control on the use of child labour. The gradual improvements in conditions brought about by these and other measures rendered the Chartist movement more or less stillborn in Leicestershire, although Leicester had given birth to one of the leading exponents of its extremist philosophy, Thomas Cooper.

The most far-reaching changes in the old order commenced in 1864, when William Cotton introduced power-operated frames at the firm of Warner and Cartwright at Loughborough. The hosiery trade was already well on the way to conversion to a factory industry, employing an increasingly large number of women, while the men were finding jobs in the expanding footwear and engineering industries. The growth of the factories was accelerated by the Education Act of 1870, which deprived the knitters of their child labour, and four years later frame-renting was abolished by law. By 1894 there were more than twenty factories in Hinckley, and throughout the county increasing confidence between management and workers. The circular machine, invented by Brunel as long ago as 1816, had come into use to make a seamless knitted tube, and technical improvement in the trade went on apace.

The last hand-frames had become museum property by the end of the First World War, and in the late 1920s Leicestershire hosiery companies were producing twenty-five million dozen pairs of stockings a year, worth forty million pounds. The options open to girls leaving school in the hosiery villages were not between office, shop or telephone exchange, but between seaming, linking or mending in the local factories for fourteen shillings a week. The depression of the 1930s left Leicestershire relatively unscathed, and by 1939 some forty-six thousand people were working in the hosiery trade, the majority of them women and girls.

With rapidly rising hemlines, the demand for fine fully-fashioned stockings became even greater throughout the western world. Legs were in fashion, and Leicestershire produced both the stockings and the high-heeled shoes which emphasized their length and shapeliness. Although the manufacturers would scarcely have seen it that way, the county was cashing in on a vast new twentieth-century market for sex appeal. And the women who made the stockings were among the most eager to wear them - never was there an industry in which, to such an extent, the social level of the workers allowed them to benefit from the merchandise they were paid to produce.

Meanwhile, synthetic fibres were coming in to replace the silks and cottons and wools on which the industry had been built, and the 15-denier seamless nylon stocking became all the rage, followed by the unveiling of more leg with the advent of the mini-skirt, creating a universal demand for tights. And the knitting process was producing every kind of outerwear and underwear garment which had previously been made only by weaving.

Storm clouds had been appearing on the horizon for Leicestershire, however, since the manufacturers themselves - ironically - had started to import cheap stockings from Italy. The situation snowballed, and many small firms were forced to close down by their failure to compete with foreign goods, especially when cheap nylon tights began to come in from the Far East, Portugal and Eastern Europe. At the same time, foreign competition was hitting the footwear industry, in Leicestershire more than Northamptonshire.

After anxious discussions about the hosiery and knitting industry between the Trade Minister and Leicester Members of Parliament, Prime Minister Wilson said in April 1975 that there would be no import restrictions, and few notes of optimism were being sounded in Leicestershire throughout that year. Some restriction of imports of knitted outerwear and underwear was announced, nevertheless, towards the end of 1975, in the form of "redistribution of the low-cost import burden among EEC countries".

For a hundred years Leicester has been fortunate in its ability to counter depression in one of its trades with the prosperity and employment capacity of the others, but in March 1975 the *Leicester Mercury* cried "Leicester's Jobless is All-Time Record". Seventy per cent of the county's hosiery firms were working below full capacity, and a Hinckley manufacturer said: "1974 was certainly the worst [year] in my business experience. Times are indeed hard." Many of the towns and villages have suffered from a too narrow specialization. Practically all the shoe factories have disappeared from Hinckley, and a lot of the people now work outside the town, travelling - for example - to Coventry, to work in the motor industry.

Local hosiery manufacturers did not exactly jump for joy at the news that an Austrian firm had produced the first totally ladder-proof tights. What would this do to the demand for about twenty-eight pairs a year from the average British woman? But the Austrian product was expensive, and Leicestershire respond- ed by introducing 'stocking tights', in which separate legs are supplied, each with its own waistband, so that if one leg has a run, the cost of replacement is lower. Machinery has also been developed which can make a pair of one-piece panti-hose in three minutes, and which has been called "the ultimate in producing a complete garment from a knitting machine".

Did I say that materialism does not breed imagination? Let me qualify that slightly. Exploiting the market for stockings and tights led the imagination of the manufacturers to take flight through dreamy geographical and alliterative alphabets in inventing the most alluring shades of brown, from Bengal Bronze to Vienna Vogue. The simple one-time choice between light brown and dark brown has become a mind-boggling decision between Burnt Sugar, Persian Delight, Quietly Cara- mel, and hundreds of other exotically named variations in shade, although when girls took to wearing coalminers' boots in the mid-70s their legs might as well have been encased in concrete for all the feminine charm they displayed.

The hitherto familiar scene through the factory windows of west Leicestershire - multi-coloured bobbins of yarn in circular motion about their vertical axes – is one which may or may not change, according to how successful manufacturers are in coping with problems of foreign competition and changes in fashions. But the future of Leicestershire's landscape is in the hands of the farmers, and signs of change are already apparent.

Recently I watched a sparrowhawk hovering high over a small triangular field bounded by hawthorn hedges, with a few ash trees along each side. The bird swooped down, perhaps to take a vole or a mouse, and I wondered if that sight would soon be a thing of the past. Human evolution will dictate that the small, irregularly shaped grazing fields, each known to the farmer by name, like Trefoil Close (signifying a clover field) at Hinckley, will be absorbed into huge square prairies fenced in by wire, in which crops of protein value are grown to feed the ever-increasing population with substitutes for meat, and since neither leather nor wool will be needed, sheep and cattle will be obsolete. The fox coverts will all be ploughed up, as fox-hunting will have ended, and the foxes will have been exterminated deliberately by poisoning and the sparrowhawks and owls accidentally by absorption of insecticides. Mice will thrive in the absence of their natural enemies, and will reduce the numbers of bumblebees, but that will not matter because there will be no small clover fields left which the bees were once needed to fertilize.

Will it be a better Leicestershire? Not to those of us who have grown to love it as it is. But our descendants will take it all for granted, and read books about the strange landscape that presented itself to the visitor in the twentieth century, when they used to keep tame animals in fields, to eat and make clothes from. Liberated women in Leicester will stand at the monorail stopping point near the new Snow Monument, or the crumbling Clock Tower (showing different times of day on each of its clock faces), and shake their heads over the primitive ways of the past: "It's obvious they was a backward lot in them days, i'n't it, duck!"

Former county boundary
of Rutland   — · — · —

0   Miles   10

SOURCES

1. Books about Leicestershire

The following list is by no means exhaustive, but gives those works on which I have chiefly relied in writing the present book.

William Andrews (ed.), *Bygone Leicestershire* (J. & T. Spencer, 1892)

B. J. Bailey, *A Prospect of Leicestershire* (Inglenook Press, 1973)

Alice Dryden (ed.) *Memorials of Old Leicestershire* (George Allen & Sons, 1911)

Rev. I. Eller, *The History of Belvoir Castle* (Tyas & Groombridge, 1841)

Colin D. B. Ellis, *Leicestershire and the Quorn Hunt* (Edgar Backus, 1951)

—— *History in Leicester* (Leicester Publicity Dept., 1969)

A. B. Evans, *Leicestershire Words, Phrases and Proverbs* (Trübner & Co., 1881)

Pearl Finch, *History of Burley-on-the Hill, Rutland* (John Bale, Sons & Danielsson Ltd., 1901)

J. B. Firth, *Highways and Byways in Leicestershire* (Macmillan & Co., 1926)

H. J. Francis, *A History of Hinckley* (Pickering & Sons, 1930)

W. G. Hoskins, *Leicestershire: The History of the Landscape* (Hodder & Stoughton, 1957)

—— *Rutland: A Shell Guide* (Faber & Faber, 1963)

—— *Leicestershire: A Shell Guide* (Faber & Faber, 1970)

—— *The Heritage of Leicestershire* (Leicester Publicity Dept., 1972)

Rev. A. Macauley, *The History and Antiquities of Claybrook* (London, 1791)

Arthur Mee, *The King's England – Leicestershire and Rutland* (Hodder & Stoughton, 1937)

Bernard Newman, *Portrait of the Shires* (Robert Hale, 1968)

John Nichols, *History and Antiquities of the County of Leicester* 8 vols (London, 1795-1815)

Guy Paget & Lionel Irvine, *Leicestershire* (The County Books) (Robert Hale, 1950)

A. Temple Patterson, *Radical Leicester* (University College, Leicester, 1954)

Nikolaus Pevsner, *The Buildings of England – Leicestershire and Rutland* (Penguin Books, 1960)

N. Pye (ed.), *Leicester and its Region* (Leicester University Press, 1972)

Jack Simmons, *Life in Victorian Leicester* (Leicester Museums, 1971)

——— *Leicester, Past and Present*, 2 vols (Eyre Methuen, 1974)

Cyril A. Smith, *Frisby Before 1914* (Frisby-on-the-Wreake Historical Society, 1975)

Joan Stevenson, *The Greys of Bradgate* (Bradgate Park Trust, 1974)

J. & A. E. Stokes, *Just Rutland* (John Hawthorn, 1953)

Eric Swift, *Inns of Leicestershire* (Chamberlain Music & Books, N.D.)

J. E. O. Wilshere, *Leicester Clock Tower* (Leicester Research Services, 1975)

James Wright, *History and Antiquities of the County of Rutland* (London, 1684)

Historical Account of the Ancient Kings Mills (Castle Donington W.E.A. Group, 1960)

Victoria County History of Leicestershire, 5 vols (1907–64)

Victoria County History of Rutland, 2 vols (1908–35)

Leicestershire & Rutland Notes & Queries (1891–95)

Transactions of the Leicestershire Archaeological Society

Files of the *Leicester Journal, Leicester Mercury* and other local newspapers

2. Other Works

D. Elliston Allen, *British Tastes* (Hutchinson, 1968)

Horace Bleackley, *The Hangmen of England* (Chapman and Hall, 1929)

William Cobbett, *Rural Rides* (Peter Davies edition, 1930)

C. Davison, *A History of British Earthquakes* (Cambridge University Press, 1924)

Daniel Defoe, *A Tour through the Whole Island of Great Britain* (Penguin Books edition, 1971)

G. H. Dury, *Regions of the British Isles: The East Midlands* (Thomas Nelson, 1963)

Malcolm Elwin, *Lord Byron's Family* (John Murray, 1975)

Irvin Ehrenpreis, *Swift*, 2 vols (Methuen, 1962, 1967)

George Fox, *Journal* (Everyman's Library edition, 1949)

Robert Graves, *The White Goddess* (Faber & Faber, 1961)

Charles Hadfield, *The Canals of the East Midlands* (David & Charles, 1966)

B. A. Hains & A. Horton, *British Regional Geology: Central England* (H.M.S.O., 1969)

W. G. Hoskins, *Midland England* (Batsford, 1949)
—— *Provincial England* (Macmillan, 1963)

Paul Murray Kendall, *Richard the Third* (Allen & Unwin, 1955)

Ada C. Kopeć, *The Distribution of the Blood Groups in the United Kingdom* (Oxford University Press, 1970)

Margaret Wade Labarge, *Simon de Montfort* (Eyre & Spottiswoode, 1962)

Lord Macaulay, *A History of England*, 5 vols (London, 1848–55)

K. B. McFarlane, *The Origins of Religious Dissent in England* (Collier Books (New York), 1966)

J. B. Priestley, *English Journey* (Heinemann and Gollancz, 1934)

Edmund Swinglehurst, *The Romantic Journey* (Pica Editions, 1974)

Malcolm Todd, *The Coritani* (Duckworth, 1973)

G. M. Trevelyan, *English Social History* (Longmans Green, 1944)

Brian Vesey-Fitzgerald, *Town Fox, Country Fox* (André Deutsch, 1965)

R. J. White, *Waterloo to Peterloo* (Heinemann, 1957)

Neville Williams, *Elizabeth I: Queen of England* (Weidenfeld & Nicolson, 1967)

Files of *Knitting International* (formerly *The Hosiery Trade Journal*)

INDEX